AF522386

**CAREER IN MEDIA**

# CAREER IN MEDIA

**N. Afaque Shamsi**

**ANMOL PUBLICATIONS PVT. LTD.**
**NEW DELHI - 110 002 (INDIA)**

**ANMOL PUBLICATIONS PVT. LTD.**
*H.O.:* 4374/4B, Ansari Road, Darya Ganj,
New Delhi-110 002 (India)
Ph.: 23261597, 23278000

*B.O.:* No. 1015, Ist Main Road, BSK IIIrd Stage
IIIrd Phase, IIIrd Block,
Bangalore - 560 085 (India)
Visit us at: www.anmolpublications.com

*Career in Media*



First Published, 2006

ISBN 81-261-2663-9



PRINTED IN INDIA

Published by J.L. Kumar for Anmol Publications Pvt. Ltd., New Delhi - 110 002 and Printed at Mehra Offset Press, Delhi.

# Contents

*Preface* ix

1. **The Profession** 1
   - Content and Nature
   - Real Picture
   - Different Facets
   - Different Avenues
   - Influence Area
   - Basic Theory
   - Guiding Theory
   - Global Norms

2. **Media, as Career** 99
   - Historical Knowledge
   - New Method
   - Growth in Number
   - The Press
   - Value of Publicity
   - Forces of Opposition
   - Existence of Dissent
   - The Trouble
   - Ne Suggestions

3. **Media in Practice** 149
   - Freedom of Press

- Critical Problems
- Setting of Format
- Global Agencies
- Different Agencies
- Factors at Work
- Work Nature

**4. News Selection** **209**

- Process of Selection
- How to Present News?
- Taking a Start
- Audience of News
- Technology and its Role
- Proper Order
- Some Compulsions
- Fulfilment of the Task
- Working Bodies
- Abroad-oriented News
- Disputing Points
- Distinguishing Strata
- Crime and Reporting
- Formation of News
- News Procurement

**5. Team at Work** **263**

- Editorial Desk
- Work Skill
- Computers' Use
- Heads of Sections
- Authority in Charge
- Social Awakening Effort
- The Communication
- Mass Taste
- Editor's Job

**6. System at Work** **305**
- Fundamentals and Guidelines
- Problems of Crucial Nature
- Reorganising Process
- Course of Action
- Political Angle

*Bibliography* 359

*Index* 365

# Preface

Media is the plural of 'Medium' and 'mass' means a large number. Thus, by mass-media, what is meant is 'the main means of communication at a large number' i.e., all those means, which are used to communicate with people on a vast level or at a great number, as, newspapers, magazines, radio and television, etc.

Though communication has always been an important need of life, it assumed the status of the most essential and one of the basics of life in the later half of the 20th century. As a result, a number of different and diverse forms of media emerged and institutions imparting their thorough knowledge mushroomed throughout the width and length of the country and world.

In this battle of survival and cut-throat comptetion, the one which won the greatest appreciation and applaud of the masses is the Electronic Media by virtue of its being capable of communicating to people, live and pulsating coverage of news and events occurring in every nook and corner of the world and in all the strata of the society ranging from the laymen to the top brass of Government, Semi-Government and non-Government administrations.

Given the above-discussed situation, there was an urgent demand for such an Encyclopaedia, which may cater to the maximum requirements of the seekers of knowledge in this regard. This series has been prepared with a view to encapsulating most of the stuff required by a media-lover.

Should we succeed in our attempt and get a favouring feedback excluding unnecessary brickbats, we would put a more enlightening, informative and comprehensive ocean of knowledge in the hold of your hands.

**Editor**

# The Profession

## Content and Nature

Communication is an integral part of one's life. We constantly exchange our ideas, thoughts and emotions with others, in our everyday life, to satisfy our physical, emotional or other needs. Infact, it is impossible for the society to survive in the absence of communication. There are various meanings to the word 'communication', like "sharing of experience on the basis of commonness" (Wilbur Schramm); "one mind affecting another" (Claud Shannon); "the transfer or conveying of meaning" (Oxford Dictionary).

Communication is a dynamic process of action and interaction towards a desired goal. Thus, it is "a process of sharing or exchange of ideas, information, knowledge, attitude or feeling among two or more persons through certain signs and symbols."

## Real Picture

Communication needs a sender, a receiver and a channel, be it language, paint, song or anything. Being at the heart of all social action and interaction, communication is a relating tool that creates understanding, facilitates work, and strengthens collective living among people.

The primary function of communication is to inform, educate, entertain and influence people to make them function smoothly. It also has a secondary function to perform as well through debates and discussion, cultural promotion and integration; it fosters creativity and understanding among people, groups, and societies so that they live in peace and harmony. These functions have been discussed below:

Information is regarded as power. The more informed you are, the more powerful you become. Communication provides us enormous information about the environment in which we live. Information such as news of war, danger, crisis, famine etc., is important for that helps us in taking appropriate steps to safeguard our interests.

Instructing, educating and socializing the members of the society is one of the major functions of communication. Communication creates awareness, provides a fund of knowledge, expertise and skills, gives direction and opportunity to people so that they can become an active member of the society.

With the passage of time this has become one of the major functions of communication. Persuasion helps in reaching decision on public policy in order to make possible to control and govern.

Entertainment is the need of every individual in order to break the monotonous routine of daily life and to divert their attention from the troubles and tensions. It not only revitalise our personality but also educate us. Communication provides entertainment through films, music, drama, art, literature, comedy, sports etc.

Debate and discussion are the two ways in media through which public can clarify different viewpoints on issues of public interest and come to a general agreement on matters that concern all.

Communication is a great integrating tool. It enables different individuals, groups or cultures to come to know each other, and appreciate others, way of life. It also provides opportunity for culture to be preserved and promoted.

**Different Facets**

All of us are engaged in a variety of communication acts. There are:

> It is talking to oneself, listening to oneself and relating one to oneself. This helps us contemplating, conceptualizing and formulating our thoughts or ideas before we actually indulge in overt communication.

This is the universal form of communication that takes place between two individuals. It is person-to-person contact, which includes everyday exchanges that may be formal or informal by means of words, sounds, facial expressions, gestures, postures etc.

There is face-to-face interaction between two persons in interpersonal communication and so it becomes very effective because one gets immediate feedback. It is also possible to influence the other person and persuade him or her to accept your point of view. It also has an emotional appeal and can motivate, encourage and coordinate work in a much effective manner than any other form of communication.

This is an extension of interpersonal communication, where more than two individuals are involved in exchange of ideas, thoughts, skills and interests. This kind of communication provides an opportunity for people to come together and discuss topics of common interest.

Communication in a group serves many goals like collective decision making, self expression, increasing one's effect, elevating one's status, relaxation etc. On the other hand it also has many limitations, as it is time consuming and often inefficient. In addition imbalances in status, skills and goals may distort the process and the outcome sharply.

Another form of communication which involves communication with mass audience in Mass communication and the channels through which this kind of communication takes place are referred to as mass media. But both mass media and mass communication are generally considered synonyms for the sake of convenience. Any mechanical device that multiplies messages and takes it to a large number of people simultaneously is called Mass Communication.

Thus, it is clear from the above definition that mass communication is a special kind of communication in which the nature of the audience and the feedback is different from that of interpersonal communication.

The two main components of mass communication are thus audience and feedback.

Whosoever is the recipient of mass media content constitutes its audience. Here the audience is large, heterogenous and anonymous in character. Heterogenous in the sense that messages are sent to people in all walks of life, each person with unique, characteristics. By anonymous, we mean that the receivers of the messages tend to be strangers to one another and to the source of those messages.

Feedback in mass media is slow and weak. It is not direct as in face to face exchange and is invariably delayed. Considerable time and money are required to process the feedback received from the audience.

**Different Avenues**

Mass media is broadly divided into print media and electronic media. Print media has a history of about 500 years. Whereas the electronic media are products of the 20th century.

It includes newspapers, magazine, books and other printed matter. Their growth was slow in the beginning but as the demand for education and information increased, they evolved quickly and flourished greatly.

It includes radio, television, satellite TV, cinema etc. They provide instantaneous communication and their impact is greater. This differentiate it from print media. Electronic media are quicker than print media as the latter takes more time for mass production and delivery to a widely dispersed population.

Time of its inception is in 1920s. And since then its network has expanded a great deal. One of the best advantages that radio has over other media is that it can serve and entertain an audience which is otherwise occupied. However, the radio has suffered a setback in the recent times because of TV, which has attracted especially the urban population.

With a modest beginning in the 1930s, it has become a powerful media of mass communication. It has grown into a massive network of mass information and mass entertainment.

The newer development in network technologies is that of satellite-Cable television. Audiences now have multiple choices ranging from news and information to entertainment of wide variety.

Films are considered a major mass medium because of their mass appeal and influence on society. They set trends in styles and tastes, dominate the popular radio and television entertainment programmes.

There has been rapid expansion of mass media all over the world in recent times. People now have more access to mass media whose reach is getting wider due to technological advancement. The mass media are now not limited to urban population but have made inroads into small towns and villages. People now have more access to information and thus have become better and more informed and educated. However, despite the growth of media, its reach is largely limited to urban areas in India.

The Print Media, although a powerful means of communication cater only to audiences that are literate. There are about 20,000 newspapers and other printed matter produced in major metropolitan and big cities in the country but only a small fraction of reaches the rural masses.

The television network has also increased tremendously covering 80 percent of the, population. But again TV is out of reach of the majority of the rural masses. Only the few in the village have access to it. The new development in this direction have been the linking of satellites via cable to the TV at home. Again even if audiences in small towns and villages have access to these sophisticated media, the messages are lost on them because they are not area specific and lack local cultural flavour and relevance, which is very necessary for audience to identify with and understand.

Radio is one of the significant media of mass communication. Government owned All India Radio covers 80% of the area and 90% of the country's population. But again the broadcast receiving facilities are limited. There is also a vast imbalance between the availability of radio sets in rural and urban areas. Inspite of the imbalance, radio is the only medium which is said to be truly a mass medium in India because it is a low cost mobile means of communication.

Films has become a major medium of popular entertainment. But again film exhibition facilities in the country are limited. Most of the cinema houses are in the metropolitan cities and towns.

**Influence Area**

Our age is the age of mass communication and mass communication performs certain functions that are useful to us. Millions are exposed to a variety of messages each day. But the question is what is the extent and nature of its impact?

By and large mass communication messages are positive i.e., Pro-communal harmony, anti-drugs, anti-AIDS, anti-war, anti-terrorism, pro-national and so on. Infact, it has helped in promoting national integration and has created awareness among people about the socio-economic and political development of the country.

But the adverse effects of mass communication have also been felt and that to not so much from print media as from television and cable TV and overdose of TV is bad and gives ideas about a materialistic culture that doesn't exist.

A model is an abstracted representation of a reality. It only represents the reality of communication for better understanding of the communication process and is not a reality. Models are based on assumption that theorists make as to how communication functions and what effect it has upon individual and society.

The earlier models of communication were simple but inadequate. Aristotle constructed a model which had only-speaker-speech-audience-these three were elements, and the basic function of communication was to 'persuade the other party'.

By 1950s models became more elaborate and adequate. The universally applicable models of communication are those of Shannon and Weaver's.

Lasswell presented a strictly verbal model which takes the form of a question-

Who

Says what

In which channel

To Whom

With what effect?

Identification of source, analysis of message content, choice of channel, characteristics of audience and evaluation of effects are the 5 components of communication process. It is the 'effect' that the model emphasizes the most change in one of these elements will lead to a change in the effect.

They were the first to develop an engineering model of human communication based on telephone communication. In this model communication begins with an information source who creates the message, he transmits it by means of his vocal apparatus which acts as a transmitter, through the air as the channel with noise interference to the hearing mechanism of the person he is communicating with acting as the receiver which recreates the message so that another person, a receiver, can receive it.

Their model is important as it introduces the concept of 'Noise'. Noise refers to channel that may interfere with the signals transmitted and produce different signals.

His model is different from the earlier attempts in the sense that it doesn't follow the conventional pattern of communication from source to channel to receiver.

He emphasized the point that each participant in the communication process sends as well as receives messages and as such encodes, decodes and interprets messages. This is particularly true in interpersonal communication.

He adopted Shannon and Weaver's model and introduced two concepts of encoder, decoder, redundancy, feeback and noise into his model. He stressed the importance of feedback and noise, where feedback refers to response that a receiver makes to a source's communication.

According to him in a conversation between two people, one is constantly communication back to the other. The feedback obtained in such situation plays a very important role in the communication process as it tells the source how his messages are being received and interpreted. The 'Noise' may contaminate the message and make communication ineffective. In many instances a message is likely to suffer deterioration before it is decoded and interpreted by a receiver.

Wilbur further viewed the communication process as a complex one in the context of personal, social and cultural factors. Communication, according to him is a process of sharing of experience. The source can encode and the destination can decode only in terms of experience each has had; for e.g., if we have never learned German, we can neither encode nor decode in that language.

He further elaborated this model by bringing into focus the frames of reference of persons participating in the communication process. A (source) and B (destination) have the same kind of situation, have the same social resources and face similar constraints. If the destination decides that the message is interesting and promising enough, he selects some of it or all of it, interprets it according to his frame of reference and disposes it according to his needs, values, social imperatives and constraints.

In his model communication is seen as a transmission of messages. There are three stages in his model. The first stage is horizontal. It starts with an event E as perceived by M (Human being directly or through a Machin). M selects E according to his perception of the event. Thus, the process involves interaction and negotiation.

In the 2nd stage, which is vertical dimension, converts whatever we have perceived into a signal. This is called message. Here, it is also important to select the appropriate 'means'-the medium channel of communication.

The 3rd stage is again horizontal. Here the meaning of the message is not 'contained' in the message itself, but is the result of an interaction or negotiation between the receiver and the message.

This model tries to explain the role of communication in a society or a social relationship. According to it, communication maintains equilibrium within the social system. This model assumes significance in the light of people's increasing need for information. Infact, in a democracy people need adequate information about their social environment so that they can identify their problems and share with their group, and know how to react.

This model is an extension of Newcomb's model and specifically adapted for the mass media. It is based on the assumption that messages in mass communication pass through check points called 'gatekeeper' before they are actually received by audience. They decide on which messages are to be transmitted and how their content are to be modified. Thus, the audience's exposure to an event's reality is in the gatekeeper's hands.

But this model also has a drawback and that is that it applies only to mass media and fails to take account of the relationship between the mass media and the other systems through which we fit into society like family, work, friendships, school, trade unions etc.

Every communication order is ultimately conditioned or influenced by the political system and cultural milieu and the ends and purposes for which it is to be used. What could India's freedom mean to the concept of mass communication? What could be the type of new orientation for individual media, their functional roles and dimensions, their goals and priorities?

With the dawn of freedom, the Indian media were delinked from the apron-strings of British political and cultural imperialism. As part of the sovereign national system, they could now be used to serve the people and the nation according to new visions and national goals, policies and targets set by the new architects of the nation, the media managers and experts.

However, when the Britishers left, India was emaciated by the Partition and was left at the lowest level, politically, economically, socially and communication wise. There were yawning gaps in the communication infrastructure. India's tryst with its new density was therefore very uncertain.

Politically, the Constitution of India, enforced on 26 January 1950, the first Republic Day, had granted to every citizen and media the freedom of speech and expression and to every adult the right to vote and elect legislators. The establishment of a representative system of government, gave the right to every citizen to be informed, that is to have reasonable access to social, political, aesthetic, normal and other ideas and information vital for the grooming of enlightened voters and inculcation of democratic citizenship.

It also implied the right to reasonable access to competitive sources of information and media. These rights which flowed out of democratic citizenship enjoined new obligations on the communication media and government to inform and educate the citizens and children of the country and at the same time stimulate awareness about fundamental and other civic and social duties. It was generally agreed that mass media of communication would have a key role in the building of our democratic polity and illumination of our social fabric.

With the beginning of the era of planned development since 1950-51, another role of the media of mass communication came to the forefront. It would provide communication support to the plans and inform people about the philosophy and objectives of plans, about the targets and benefits accruing to them as also about their responsibilities involved in the planned efforts. The other demand on communicators was to enthuse and involve people by removing ignorance and superstitions, by changing their negative attitudes and motivating them into purposeful action, all through persuasive and two-way communication.

The dimension of their task was underlined by the Study Team on Mass communication sponsored by Ford Foundation, which observed that "India's development task is so great and her population so large that only by the most efficient possible programme of public information necessarily emphasising mass communication can communicators hope to reach people often enough and effectively enough to activate, on the needed scale, discussion process and subsequent action in the cities, towns and villages." In this context, the Vidyalankar Committee stated that the principal aim of publicity or communication was to prepare the minds of the people to meet the challenges of these new problems.

On the basis of studies on development and communication done in India, UNESCO and various developing countries, as also on the basis of field-based experience and communication and promotional research studies and surveys, a new professional thinking on the concept, role and process of relevant communication gradually emerged.

Broadly speaking, the purpose of communication came to be understood as (1) politically to create, inform and enlighten public opinion, the basis of a democratic developing society to create awareness among individuals as also about their fundamental duties and obligations to promote scientific temper and national cohesion in society and inculcate the spirit of cooperative partnership among all sections of people, and to foster the establishment of feedback loops and research methodologies to assess public opinion and interpret it; (2) economically, to act as an activist in the extension of technology transfer among various sections of farmers, workers and other members of the working force, to provide a supporting pad to efforts at modernization and economic growth, afford market and tourist information and to stimulate advertising and promotional campaigns; and (3) culturally to foster individual and community expression, discovery, enrichment, creativity and enlightened reaction.

This type of purposeful and dynamic communication system couldn't grow out of the mass media-oriented Western concepts, models and theories, which were not very relevant to rural areas in India or any other developing country. It had to be evolved out of a process of trial and error, experimentation and deliberation. Conceptually it had to be envisaged and shaped by professional committees or bodies especially to be set up for the purpose and reinforced by the directions and guidelines of intentional, regional, national and local seminars, conferences or memorial lectures. Such a system could not grow it was sustained and nurtured by the committee, trained and socially and professionally oriented practitioners and their managers as also by a competent research base. But above all, none of these things would happen unless the efforts in this direction get the policy backing and financial and administrative support of the government and proper appreciation and cooperation of the media and their organisations and the people.

***General Criteria :*** After Independence, challenges and experimental opportunities came in quick succession. Rehabilitation of refugees, the problem of integrating the recognised states, the Kashmir issue, green revolution, communal disturbances, strikes, inflation, abject poverty, colossal unemployment, malpractices in the public distribution system, corruption, shortage of essential commodities and housing facilities, wars, local and general elections, student unrest, gheraos, walkouts and many more problems constituted serious challenges. Fortunately, policy support and communication aid sanctions flowed from the dynamic and supporting leadership of the various Indian Prime Minister's and their governments. New dimensions of importance were given by these personalities.

As a supporting measure professional introspection, trend setting and guidelines came from the various mass communication and professional bodies and media commissions and committees set up by the government from time to time. Eminent among the bodies which left their impress on the communication scene of India included the first Press commission, UNESCO sponsored Evaluation Study Team on TV, the Study Team on Mass Communication sponsored by the Ford Foundation, the Vidyalankar Committee for the Study of Five Year Plan Publicity, the Chanda Committee on Broadcasting and Information Media. All these bodies were set up or functioned in the sixties and seventies.

The Verghese Committee on Autonomy for Akashvani and Doordarshan, the Kuldip Nayar Committee on News Agencies, the second Press Commission, Satellite Instructional Television Experiment evaluation teams and the Joshi Panel on TV Software deliberated and submitted professional guidance emerged from the numerous UNESCO or international, regional and national communication and media seminars, conferences and evaluation and promotional surveys and reports undertaken by various research teams.

*View of Political Arena* : A look into the visions and dynamic and supporting leadership of the various Indian Prime Ministers and their governments would reveal that without them many Indian communication systems and patterns or strategies of mass communication would have remained still-born. In fact, the individual trend and directional setting in the communication process by each Prime Minister has been pronouncedly significant. For instance, Pandit Jawaharlal Nehru, India's first Prime Minister, sought to make mass communication a process of dialogue more than a merely to and fro communication, and certainly more than downward communication.

A builder of modern India, he was also a builder of the communication system and media in our country. His package contribution was the laying of the foundation, securing extension a modernization of media, introducing professionalism, tempering of media freedom with social responsibility and giving a rural and research orientation.

The second Prime Minister, Lal Bahadur Shastri, reinforced Pandit Nehru's directional and managerial model by adding a focus on professional integrity and dedicated service. The third Prime Minister, Indira Gandhi and her government have provided a thrust for sophisticated multi-media technology. Blending and balancing with the resurgent indigenous technology, it aimed to ultimately strengthen and streamline the entire communication network to make it more rural service worthy, elastic and effective enough to offer services of international standard to prestigious international meets in India as also to provide communication support to the implementation of the 20-point programme.

The new technology helped in rearing the confidence building-role of the electronic media which operate in the public sector. Smt. Gandhi's government also recognised the importance of a free press but insisted on its responsible functioning and observance of a code of ethics in the discharge of its professional and social responsibilities. There was a focus on the need of the Indian media and practitioners to play a leading role in the New World Information and Communication Order to seek a balanced and two-way flow of information in the world, so as to contribute to the maximum extent possible to the South to South cooperative communication efforts and programmes.

There was an emphasis on using media for national unity and integration. Liberalisation of the import policy for facilitating media machinery and material for faster mechanisation of the media units, ensued while offering encouragement to communication research and training and media development programmes. The fourth Prime Minister, Morarji Desai and his government sought to emphasise on autonomy of media, including that of Akashvani and Doordarshan, austerity and professional integrity.

The fifth Prime Minister, Choudhary Charan Singh and his government, during his short tenure, endeavoured to bend the functioning of the media primarily for the benefit of rural areas and agriculturists. The seventh and the present Prime Minister and his government are additionally focusing on the application of computer and other modern technologies and are emphasising on open university educational aspect of mass media and better professionalism and programming.

There is a consensus of media experts, however, that the real architects of India's present modernised, multimedia, integrated, development oriented system of communication were Pandit Nehru and Indira Gandhi—as a matter of coincidence father and daughter. If India has entered the satellite, electronic and modern visual communication age, it is primarily for the vision and dynamic leadership of these two Prime Ministers. If our country has developed and revitalized traditional and other indigenous media, and made them in conjunction with modern mass media as instruments of innovative and development communication, specially in the areas of family welfare, health, agricultural extension and eradication of illiteracy, the credit for this too goes primarily to the incisiveness and initiative of these two leaders and their governments.

Apart from bequests of national leaders, there are existent visible and invisible contributions of several other professional and individual entrepreneurs, exponents, trainers and researchers who have helped individually and co-operatively in making our communication system what it is.

***Recent Trend :*** Since Independence, the concept of mass communication in India has been transformed. From the Western theories-based hypotheses it has now become most flexible, relevant and development-oriented. Now, a participatory type has been envisaged by the 7th Plan for a decentralised form of planning system at the district level. Four stages have marked this transition in our country:

(1) communication considered as a process of transmitting information, ideas, thoughts, feelings and attitudes to large anonymous audiences with an accompanying hypodermic model of who says what in which channel to whom with what effect;

(2) a distinction being made between informational communication and persuasive communication seeking to influence the behaviour or attitudes of the respondents;

(3) focus in media strategies shifting from mass media to media mix or relevant communication technologies. Experience and research revealing that with literacy,

financial and technical problems rampant in a country, there could be very little success by adopting only big media strategies. Attention thus started being fixed on low cost small media such as low powered radios and indigenous or folk form of channels as well;

(4) communication being accepted as a multi-disciplinary science or a distinct discipline supported by its own hypotheses, systematic knowledge, research methodologies and trend and case studies.

This nebulous concept of positive, multi-lateral promotional communication of participatory type came to be known by different names, such as development communication, development support; communication, integrated rural communication, participatory communication and the like. The philosophy behind these themes was to provide a meaningful system in developing countries to harmonise development and communication efforts aimed at giving the rural and urban people a better deal. While the relationship between the two was accepted by all, the issue of cause and effect has remained still unresolved.

In other words, which is the mover and which is the moved, remains a chicken and egg question. Whatever the perception, both development and communication are now considered engaged in a reactory system, one helping the other, complementing and supplementing each other in the process of fostering balanced growth and progress. If people have access to mass media, and the messages are segmented and relevant, even rural people with low literacy rates and per capita incomes can be sensitised, motivated and changed.

Being considered different from terms like advertising, public relations, propaganda, agriculture extension, rural communication, promotion, marketing communication and even the Western concept of mass media-oriented communication, the term 'development communication', in the Third World countries has acquired a more positive and pragmatic role and result-oriented connotation. As explained by Nora Quebral of Indonesia, this brand of communication implies "the art and science of human communication applied to the speedy transformation of a country and the mass of its people from poverty to a dynamic state of economic growth that makes possible greater social equality and the larger fulfilment of human potential." This development support concept of mass communication is thus dynamic, purposive, practical and promotional in approach and nature.

It is a new hope for development and social change in the Third World. Though not a panacea for all ills, it is one of the vital components in any development planning and implementation. This science and art of communication views an individual, a society or a nation in its totality, transcending thereby from a piecemeal or a segmented view of rural or urban society, economic and human development. In our country development communication combines in it the philosophy of humanism of Pandit Nehru, intending to achieve a better, richer and fuller way of life, along with the growth and development of the country as a whole. Another strand of the concept which is typically Indian is that development communication should grow mostly out of people's participation and people's satisfaction, the essential ingredients of which are:

(a) a sense of feeling to have actively participated;
(b) a sense of pride in evolving co-operative solutions to the problem in hand;
(c) a sense of achievement, reflected in the concrete betterment of poorer sections of the people and of backward areas.

Research studies based on Western models ascribe to mass communication different roles in development, varying from nil to the enthusiastic, from a cautious to a pragmatic position. Lloyd Sommerlad a UNESCO expert projected a balanced and pragmatic picture about the role which communication can play in national development. In his view "communication is an important element in the matrix of influences which lead to innovation and modernisation of a society. If used constructively, the media can help create an environment favourable for change and development. They can enlarge horizons, bring information about the experience of others, raise aspirations and help to provide the motivation for improved practices and social conditions. They are part of the process of teaching new and better ways of working and living.

The extent to which communication, both interpersonal and mediated, contributes to development depends on the policies and strategies adopted and the skill with which the tools are used. Essential will be the planned use of extension services and the media, co-ordination of the parallel channels of communications, co-operation between various government and private agencies involved in the development; a programme appropriate to the cultural background and provision of participation, feedback and a multilateral flow of information."

The communication revolution in India is experiencing the confluence of three stages of technological growth: wire, wireless and integrated. True to its tradition of assimilation of foreign and indigenous elements, India is pressing into service the earlier and modern media and using high cost and low cost communication technologies. Her Song and Drama Division, Field Publicity units and extension agencies, padyatras, folk media and human activist system on the one hand and satellite, colour TV, video, cassette, computer, electronic and digital technologies used in press communications and telecommunications on the other indicate the balance the country holds so as to meet the needs of her mammoth, multi-media mass communication exercises, movements and campaigns.

Some of the innovative multi-media programmes involved in the green and white revolutions in the northern states, TV coverage during the course of SITE, Kheda, on-going SITE and INSAT—IB experiments and the 9th Asiad, 7th Non-aligned and recent Commonwealth Summit and Namedia meets are pointers to the evolution of the spirit and urge for innovation and experimentation. Similar trends were visible in the video technology based experiment for intercommunity communication near Delhi, the Farms School programme of All India Radio and the newspaper communication support for Chattera Village initiated by the Hindustan Times, a Delhi English daily.

Apart from these illustrations, the government sector publicity media units provide more robust and wider display of media mix. For instance, outside publicity done through Field Publicity units undertake a variety of publicity programmes like film shows, group discussions, talks, seminars, song and drama programmes and photo displays. These pertain to major national themes like national integration adult education, child welfare, family welfare, agriculture and agro-based small-scale industries. Similar programmes are also organised to make people aware of social evils like untouchability and drinking.

The Song and Drama units utilise live entertainment media to make the masses aware of the various national programmes and objectives. It has a wide range of stage forms like puppet shows, plays, dances, dramas, ballads, harikathas and sound and light shows.

The mix used by the Directorate of Advertising and Visual Publicity is a visual package. It comprises press advertisements, illustrated printed material like posters, folders, leaflets, cinema slides, metallic tablets, radio and television spots and photographic exhibitions.

Another set of print medium mix for mass circulation is brought out by the Publications Division of the Ministry of Information and Broadcasting comprising books, pamphlets and journals in Hindi, English and other Indian languages on a wide range of subjects including art and culture, history and tradition, political evolution, democratic process, economic development and social resurgence.

Thus we see that whether it is the sphere of agriculture, family planning or government publicity India has been pursuing the policy of appropriate mix of media and technologies. This has entailed the use of face to face, group, written, printed, visual, folk, computerized electronic, outdoor or even a mix of them. The approach has been multi-media and cross-disciplinary, goal and result oriented. Centralisation in core programmes have been successful in so far as it has sought to stimulate unity in basic plan programmes or achieving integration in national cultural programmes, but it has equally underlined the importance that at grassroots level the development programmes should be localised and area specific and implemented as far as possible by the involvement of local people, but you need to support decentralisation which has inherent value, by an integrating system.

Here the challenge to media practitioners and managers is in finding ways of making satellite and other big media an integrating force, at the same time making them help to knit together several decentralised activities at the grassroots level.

The family planning communication package is an example. It envisages an all out effort at dovetailing of population education in the formal educational system as also in the non-formal training programmes of functionaries of development departments. It has centralised programmes integrated with decentralised activities. Its media package is wide complexioned and involves a still more dynamic package comprising radio, TV, colour films in 16 mm film strips, cinema slides, exhibitions, tape recorders, newspapers, magazines, posters, folders, brochures, leaflets, hoardings, wall paintings, bus boards, match box labels, dramas, puppet shows and other local folk art media.

Its symbols and slogans are splashed all over, from mud

walls in villages to telephone and telegraph poles in cities, reminding people that family planning is an intrinsic part of the environmental scene and an aid to family welfare.

Alongwith discovering new media mixes, strategy of field publicity or extension is also changing. The necessity of people's involvement and obtaining their feedback is calling for modification in the strategies known by various names as area approach, pooling plans or district-level decentralised plans.

India has made use of another multi-dimensional, multimedia and demonstrational audio-visual aid called exhibition. In size, stature and character it varies from stationary to mobile or even exhibition on wheels; from simple village exhibitions, trade fairs and a seasonal market to very big, modernly designed multi-levelled complexes, known as national and international exhibitions or world trade fairs. These exhibitions use a package of communication media ranging from spoken word, exhibits or visuals to video, TV, films, radio, projectile aids, traditional media, promotional literature, outdoor publicity aids, balloons, neon light and sky splashed advertisements. Cumulatively these exhibitions draw large crowds and their impact differ from creating awareness and publicity to more dramatic results in terms of transfer of technology and sale of goods and machinery. Policies and programmes of government are also publicised through photographic exhibitions. Art exhibitions and gallaries promote education about art forms of various kinds.

Whatever form that these innovatory types of communication strategies may take-person-to-person or group, written, printed, visual, folk or electronic, indoor or outdoor, hot or cold, or even a mix of them-the basic feature is that these programmes are goal oriented, research fed, professionally planned and executed and assessed. They are pragmatic and multi-media and disciplinary in approach. They are fairly sensitive and alive to criticism and suggestions and in a sense quite responsive and flexible.

The dimensions of integrated communication system which are found relevant to rural India warrant closer relationship between the administrative and communication agencies; credible and knowledgeable sources; segmentation of messages for different audiences; linkage of information to the felt needs of the people; and projection of timely usable, solution-oriented and people-beneficiary messages. The other requisite preconditions of a successful system of communication are management decentralisation for effective participation of people and the inculcation of the philosophy of empathy among the media practitioners and managers and policy makers.

Despite a large measure of success in mass communication, one big lesson that emerges out of the Indian scene of communication is that we must continuously rediscover the goals and dimensions of mass communication and its media. To this end, our communication system, our postulates, our media's role and their functions need to be periodically or as a part of inbuilt research, assessed, modified or revamped. This would help us realise our cherished dreams of a sunny future without being swept off our feet or alienating us from our fundamental values. Here the application of feedback research is significant.

So is the contribution of a professionally and media-oriented and socially activising training system, which can strengthen the country's capacity for attracting to the communication, advertising and public relations professions, man of vision, integrity, independent judgement and professional aptitude. This would help equip them with media climated and field based knowledge and skill to serve our society.

Long before the mass media were invented, Plato may have provided the opening round in the controversy over the social costs and benefits of mass culture. In his commentary on the training of the children who were to become the leaders of his ideal Republic, he saw the mass culture of his day as posing a threat to the minds of the young:

Then shall we simply allow our children to listen to any stories that anyone happens to make up, and so receive into their minds ideas often the very opposite of those we shall think they ought to have when they are grown up?

No, certainly not [replies, Glaucon].

It seems, then, our first business will be to supervise the making of fables and legends, rejecting all which are unsatisfactory; and we shall induce nurses and mothers to tell their children only those which we have approved... Most of the stories now in use must be discarded.

This theme-popular entertainment is harmful to the minds of the young has been a consistent one from the beginnings of mass communication. It has been claimed from time to time that such charges can be validated by scientific evidence, but repeatedly this evidence has turned out to be difficult to interpret and therefore controversial. Social sciences insist that any important conclusions about the effects of the media be supported by solid evidence. Because of such insistence upon data rather than emotion, they sometimes find themselves in the awkward position of seeming to defend the media when actually they are simply refusing to accept the inadequately supported claims of critics.

Nevertheless, the insistence that conclusions be based on adequate evidence has never deterred the literacy critic from charging the media with a deep responsibility for society's problems. Most nineteenth-century American writers at some point in their careers took time to criticize and condemn the newspaper for superficiality and distortion. The following excerpts from the pens of well-known and influential literacy figures are samples of the climate of opinion prevailing among the literary during the time when the mass newspaper was diffusing through the American society:

The penny-post is, commonly, an institution through which you seriously offer a man that penny for his thoughts which is so safely offered in jest. And I am sure that I have never read any memorable news in a newspaper. If we read of one man robbed, or murdered, or killed by accident, or one house burned, or one vessel wrecked, or one steamboat blown up, or one cow run over on the Western Railroad, or one mad dog killed, or one lot of grasshoppers in the winter we never need read of another. If you are acquainted with the principle, what do you care for a myriad instances and applications? To a philosopher all news, as it is called, is gossip, and they who read it and edit it are old women over their tea.

That awful power, the public opinion of this nation is formed and modelled by a horde of ignorant self-complacent simpletons who failed at ditching and shoemaking and fetched up in journalism on their way to the poorhouse.

A newspaper is a collection of half-injustices which bawled by boys from mile to mile, Spreads its curious opinion to a million merciful and sneering men, while families cuddle the joys of the fireside when spurred by tale of lone agony. A newspaper is a court where everyone is kindly and unfairly tried by a squalor of honest men. A newspaper is a market where wisdom sells it freedom and melons are crowned by the crowd.

A newspaper is a game where his error scores the player victory, while another's skill wins death.

A newspaper is a symbol; it is a feckless life's chronicle, a collection of loud tales concentrating eternal stupidities, that in remote ages lived unhaltered, roaming through a fenceless world.

One remarkable aspect of these statements is that you could simply substitute the word "television" for "newspaper" and obtain a rather parallel version of the hostility and attacks primarily directed at television by critics today.

The tenacity and stability of the mass media generally in the face of such a long history of criticism by powerful voices needs explanation. The problem at first seems deceptively simple: the media appeal to the masses and the masses want the kind of content they get and so the media continue to give it to them.

Many social scientists, such as Skornia, have exposed the inadequacy of this explanation by nothing the old chicken-and-egg problem. It is difficult at best to know if the public taste determines the media fare or if the media fare determines public taste. The answer probably lies somewhere in between with public taste being both a cause and effect of media fare. The relationship between public taste and media fare thus becomes a circular one which, in terms of the chicken-egg analogy, is an ongoing process of chickens producing eggs and eggs producing chickens.

The structural functional analysis of social systems (or "functional analysis" for short) concerns itself with the patterns of action exhibited by individuals or subgroups who relate themselves to one another within such systems. A social system is, for this reason, an abstraction—but one not too far removed from the observable and empirically verifiable behaviours of the persons who are doing the acting. The social system, then, is a complex of stable, repetitive, and patterned action that is in part a manifestation of the culture shared by the actors, and in part a manifestation of the psychological orientations of the actors (which are in turn derived from that culture).

The cultural system, the social system, and the personality systems (of the individual actors), therefore, are different kinds of abstractions made from the same basic data, namely, the overt and symbolic behaviours of individual human beings. They are equally legitimate abstractions, each providing in its own right a basis for various kinds of explanations and predictions. Generally speaking, it may be difficult or nearly impossible to analyse or understand fully one such abstraction without some reference to the others.

But, granted that the term "social system" is a legitimate scientific abstraction, how does this general conceptual strategy help in understanding the mass media of communication? To answer this question, we need to set forth in greater detail exactly what is meant by the term social system, and what type of analysis it provides. To aid in providing such an explanation we turn briefly to several ideas that are important aspects of the study of social systems. One of the most important of these ideas is the concept of the "function" of some particular repetitive phenomenon (set of actions) within such a system. The fact that such content has long survived the jibes of influential critics was said to require explanation. One form of explanation will be provided by noting the function of such a repetitive phenomenon within some stable system of action.

The term "function" in the present context means little more than "consequence." To illustrate briefly, we might hypothesize that the repetitive practice of wearing wedding rings on the part of a given married couple has the function (consequence) of reminding, them as well as others that the two are bound together by the obligations and ties that matrimony implies. This practice thereby contributes indirectly to maintaining the permanence of the marriage, the stability of that particular social system. The practice is in a sense "explained" by noting its contribution to the context within which it occurs. A comparison of a number of such systems with and without this particular item (but in other respects matched) would test the assertion.

In the above example, the social system is a relatively simple one. There are only two "components," and each of these happen to be the behaviour pattern of an individual. Their patterns are derived both from the individual psychological makeup of the partners and from the cultural norms concerning marriage prevailing in their community, social class, and society. It is a miniature system whose stability is dependent upon satisfaction of its "needs." For example, such a system requires that the partners perform roles that meet the expectations each has of the other and the expectations the community has of married couples. This can be thought of as a "need" for adequate role performance, without which the stability of the system would be endangered. Other "needs," related to economic matters and emotional satisfactions, could be cited.

More complex illustrations of social systems can easily be pointed to, where the "components" of the system are not the actions of individual persons but subsystems. A department store, for example, is a complex social system consisting of the actions of managerial personnel, buyers, salespersons, the clerical staff, customers, transportation workers, a janitorial team, and security employees. Each of these components is a smaller system of action within the broader system of the store itself, and it in turn is a complex system of action carried out within the context of the external social conditions of the community. In spite of the complexity, any given set of repetitive actions might be analysed in terms of their contribution to maintaining or undermining the system's stability. Granting to employees the right to buy merchandise at cost could have the function (consequence) of maintaining their morale and loyalty, and thus would contribute fairly directly to the maintenance of the system.

Rigid insistence on the observance of petty rules, such as docking the pay of an employee who on rare occasions was late for work, might be disruptive of morale and loyalty, and by contributing to labour turnover it could be dysfunctional. Instead of contributing to the maintenance of the system, it could cause disruptions and instability. Such inductively derived conclusions would be subject to testing for validity, of course, but the functional analysis would have generated the hypothesis to be tested (an important role of theory).

A "functional analysis," then, focuses on some specific phenomenon occurring within a social system. It then attempts to show how this phenomenon has consequences that contribute to the stability and permanence of the system as a whole. The phenomenon may, of course, have a negative influence, and if so, it would be said to have "dysfunctions" rather than "functions." The analysis is a strategy for inducing or locating hypotheses that can be tested empirically by comparative studies or other appropriate research methods.

The analysis of social system is extremely difficult, No infallible rules specify precisely how to locate and define the exact boundaries of a given social system, particularly if it is relatively complex. As yet, no completely agreed upon criteria exist for establishing linkages between the components of a system, and no standard formulas can uncover the precise contribution that a given repetitive form of action makes to the stability of a system. A functional analysis of the contribution of some item to the stability of a system, then, is a procedure that is somewhat less than rigorous. But in spite of this source of potential criticism, this strategy has proved useful in our attempts to understand complex social phenomena, such as the mass media.

How can this type of analysis be applied to the mass media? First, we can identify that portion of the content of the mass media that is in "low" cultural taste or provides gratifications to the mass audience in such a manner that it is widely held to be potentially debasing as the "relatively persistent trait or disposition" of the mass media we seek to explain. It would be difficult in practice to construct a set of categories under which to analyse the content of the media so that material of "low" cultural taste can be identified readily. It would be difficult, but actually it would not be impossible. Excessive violence, the portrayal of criminal techniques, horror and monster themes, open pornography, suggestive music, and dreary formula melodramas are typical categories of content that arouse the ire of critics.

Considerable disagreement would probably occur as to the exact content that should be included in any given category. There would also be debates over the number of categories used. There would also be debates over the number of categories used. Nevertheless, it is theoretically possible to identify the content of any given medium that is most objected to by the largest number of critics. We will assume that given sufficient time and resources, and using survey techniques, preference scales, attitude measuring instruments, and other research procedures now available that the content of any given medium could be divided roughly into something like the following three categories:

This would be media content widely distributed and attended to by the mass audience, but which has consistently aroused the ire of critics. Examples would be crime dramas on television that emphasize violence, openly pornographic motion pictures, day time, confession magazines, crime comics, suggestive music, or other content that has been widely held to contribute to a lowering of taste, disruption of morals, or stimulation toward socially unacceptable conduct. Whether or not such charges are true.

This would be media content, widely distributed and attended to, about which media critics have said very little. It is not an issue in the debate over the impact of the media on the masses. Examples would be television weather reports, some news content, music that is neither symphonic nor popular, magazines devoted to specialized interests, motion pictures using "wholesome" themes, and many others. Such content is not believed either to elevate or lower taste, and it is not seen as a threat to moral standards.

This would be media content sometimes widely distributed but not necessarily widely attended to. It is content that media critics feel is in better taste, morally uplifting, educational, or in some way inspiring. Examples would be serious music, sophisticated drama, political discussions, art films, or magazines devoted to political commentary. Such content is championed by critics as the opposite of the low-taste material, which they see as distinctly objectionable.

Of course, the first of the above categories is the one to which we wish to direct most of our attention. It is the repetitive phenomenon whose contribution to the media (as a social system) needs analysis. Nevertheless, it would also be possible to study the other two categories with somewhat parallel perspectives, but this will receive relatively little attention in the present discussion.

We need now to begin to identify the components and boundaries of the social system within which low-taste content occurs so that eventually the contribution it makes to the system can be inductively hypothesized.

Rather than develop a purely descriptively scheme that will apply only to a single medium, it will be more fruitful to attempt to develop a general conceptual scheme into which any or all media could be placed, with suitable minor modifications in details. Such a general scheme will emphasize the similarities between media, particularly in terms of relationships between the components in the system.

The first major component of the social system of mass communication is the audience. This is an exceedingly complex component. The audience is stratified, differentiated, and interrelated in the many ways that social scientists have studied for years. Some of the major variables that play a part in determining how this component will operate within the system are the major needs and interests of audience members, the various social categories represented in an audience, and the nature of the social relationships between audience members. These variables point to behavioural mechanisms that determine the patterns of attention, interpretation, and response of an audience with respect to content of a given type.

The rough typology of content suggested is in some degree related to the characteristics of the audience. Organizations devoted to research, to measuring the performances of media audiences, or to various forms of market research provide information to those responsible for selecting the categories of content that will be distributed to the audience. There is a link, then, between the audience as a component in the system and the market research-rating service organizations as a second component. In purely theoretical terms, both components are role system themselves and are thus actually subsystems. This is in a sense a one-way link. For very minor (or usually no) personal reward, audience members selected for study provide data about themselves to such an agency, but very little flows back. This linkage between components is by comparison relatively simple.

The content itself, of whatever type, flows from some distributor to the audience. The role system of the distributor component varies in detail from one medium to another. In addition, several somewhat distinct subsystems exist within this general component. First, there are local outlets, which are likely to be in the most immediate contact with the audience. The local newspaper, the local theatre, the local broadcasting station play the most immediate part in placing messages before their respective audiences. But inseparably tied to them are other subsystems of this general component. Newspaper syndicates, broadcasting networks, or chains of movie theatres pass content on to their local outlets. The link between these two subsystems is a two-way one. The local outlet provides money, and the larger distributor supplies content. Or the link age may be that the local outlet provides a service, and the distributor (who is paid elsewhere) provides money.

The relationship between audience and distributor seems at first to be mostly a one-way link. The distributor provides entertainment content (and often advertising), but the audience provides little back in a direct sense. However, it does provide its attention. In fact, it is precisely the attention of the audience that distributors are attempting to solicit. They sell this "commodity" directly to their financial backer or sponsor. In addition, the audience supplies information to the research component and this is indirectly supplied to distributors in the form of feedback so that they may gauge the amount of attention they are eliciting. The linkages between components grow more complex as we seek the boundaries of the system.

To the audience, the research, and the distributing component, we may add the role system of the producer of content. This component's primary link is with the financial backer (or sponsor) component and with the distributor, from whom money is obtained and for whom various forms of entertainment content are manufactured. A host of subsystems are included in this producer component, depending upon the particular medium. Examples are actors, directors, television producers, technicians, foreign correspondents, wire-service editors, film producers, labour union leaders, publishers, copyeditors, clerical staff, and many, many more.

Linking the sponsor, distributor, producer, and research organization are the advertising agencies. Paid primarily by the sponsor, this component provides (in return) certain ideas and services. For the most part, it provides the distributor with advertising messages. It may have links with the research component as well.

Over.this complex set of interrelated components, there are other subsystems that exert control. The legislative bodies, at both the state and national level, which enact regulative statutes concerning the media, constitute an important part of such a control component. Another important part of this role subsystem is the official regulative agencies, which implement the policies that have been legislated. The link between the legislative body (control component) and the audience is, course, one of votes and public opinion, to which the component is presumably sensitive and dependent. Information lines between audience, legislative bodies, and regulatory agencies are more or less open.

To the regulatory components whose role definitions are found in legal statute can be added the private voluntary associations that develop "codes" and to some degree serve as a control over the distributors. Such distributors provide them with money, and they in turn provide surveillance and other services.

The regulatory subsystems draw definitions of permissible and non-permissible content from the general set of external conditions within which this extremely complicated system operates. Surrounding the entire structure as an external condition are our society's general norms concerning morality, and the expressions that these find in formal law. Similar, although less likely to be incorporated into law, are our general cultural norms and beliefs regarding what will be likely to entertain or otherwise gratify Americans.

Thus, we seldom see traditional Chinese opera but frequently see western horse opera. We seldom hear the strains of Hindu temple music but frequently hear the "strains" and other noises of the latest singer whom teenagers admire. If our interests run to more serious fare, we are likely to hear the music of a relatively small list of European or American composers who created their works within a span of about three centuries. Or we are likely to view ballet, opera, drama, and so on, of a fairly limited of artists whose products are defined by our society as classics or as innovative new approaches.

Each of the several media will fit into this general model of a social system in slightly different ways. A complete description of each of the media separately would be tedious. Indeed, each could well occupy the contents of an entire book. Two decades ago, Opotowsky attempted just such a detailed analysis of the television industry, although he did not use the social system concept.

To add to the complexity of this conceptual scheme, it must be remembered that although each medium constitutes a somewhat separate social system in itself, the media are also related to one another in systematic ways. Thus, we may speak of the entire set of communication media, including those which have not been specifically analysed in the present volume, as the mass communication system of the United States.

The structure of this mass communication system has been heavily influenced by the general social, political, economic, and cultural conditions that were current during the period when our mass media were developing and remain as important socio-cultural forces in the society within which they operate. Because of their importance for understanding our mass media as they are today.

Our free enterprise beliefs, our views of the legitimacy of the profit motive, the virtues of controlled capitalism, and our general values concerning freedom of speech constitute further external conditions (in addition to those related to moral limits and cultural tastes) within which the American mass communication system operates.

Within the system itself, the principal internal condition is, of course, a financial one. Most of the components in the system are occupational role structures, which motivate their incumbent personnel primarily through money. To obtain money, they are all ultimately dependent upon the most central component of all-the audience. Unless its decisions to give attention, to purchase, to vote, and the like, are made in favourable ways, the system would undergo service strain and would eventually collapse.

Almost any dramatic change in the behaviour of the audience would cause the most severe disruption in the system for any given medium. The consequences of attention loss to the motion picture theatre as a mass medium was shown to be severe.

Such disruptions are infrequent, but they do occur. The key to heading off dramatic changes in audience behaviour, of course, is to provide entertainment content that will satisfy and motivate the largest possible number of audience members to carry out their roles in accord with the needs of the system. Such content will, in other words, maintain the stability of the system. The ideal, from the standpoint of the system, is content that will capture audience members' attention, persuade them to purchase goods, and at the same time be sufficiently within the bounds of moral norms and standards are not provoked.

The entertainment content that seems most capable of eliciting the attention of the largest number of audience members is the more dramatic, low-taste content. Since the most central media system goal is economic profit, sex and violence or any other attention-getting and attention-maintaining content is functional in the sense that even though it may be of low-taste, it maximizes the size of the audience exposed to advertisements. In general, the larger the audience, the more the distributor and producer can charge for advertising. For example, ads in prime-time television periods cost substantially more than those aired during relatively low-audience-size periods, such as early in the morning.

The assumption made by many media personnel and advertisers that low-taste content appeals primarily to the relatively uneducated, who still constitute a majority of the potential audience, may be false. In an early study Wilensky found that educated people said that they preferred and exposed themselves to high-taste content more often than did the relatively uneducated. But when observations were made of what the educated and educated actually aid, there was little difference between their levels of exposure to low-taste media content.

There is a great deal of evidence to show that the relatively uneducated spend more time than the educated being exposed to the mass media. It may be misleading to conclude that they do so only because the uneducated relish low-taste content. The relatively uneducated majority also have relatively low incomes, which probably means they have less choice than their more educated and wealthier counterparts in how they spend their non-working hours. The mass media may be more appealing to the relatively uneducated and poor in large part because the media are relatively inexpensive forms of leisure. Moreover, as Baker and Ball point out, it is probably superficial to think that the only reason people in general spend time with the media is because of the inherent appeal of their content. Any number of need-fulfilments and gratifications, over and above those related to entertainment or staying informed, are provided by the media. Babysitting and companionship (even when it is electronic companionship) are examples.

When all is said and done, however, it is still true that low-taste content sells and sells big. This fact establishes it as the key element in the social system of the media. It keeps the entire complex together by maintaining the financial stability of the system. Critics who provoke public attention by denouncing media content or by proclaiming that a casual connection exists between media content and socially undesirable behaviour may temporarily receive some recognition, they may also achieve some temporary disturbance in the system, or if they are persistent enough, they may ultimately even displace some specific from of low-taste content from a given medium altogether.

Examples from the past are quiz shows that were found to be "rigged," and popular disc jockeys who were receiving "payola" (a fee for repeatedly playing a song to make it popular). In such cases the audience may be temporarily disaffected, low-taste content comes in such a variety of forms that the temporary or even permanent absence of one minor form does not alter the major picture. Critics have been complaining about newspaper concentration on crime news for a century, yet there has been no noticeable abatement in the reporting of such stories.

Critics of the soap opera may have breathed a sigh of relief several years ago when these programs at last disappeared from radio. Their joy must have been short-lived when such daytime serials turned out to be quite popular with television viewers, so popular in fact that soap operas now appear during prime evening hours. Analyses of the level of violent television content show that it goes down slightly after federal government investigations on the effects of television violence or widespread campaigns by voluntary associations (e.g., the P.T.A.), only to return shortly after the public outcry has subsided.

When a formula is discovered for eliciting attention and influencing purchasing decisions from any large segment of the audience, it will be abandoned by the media only with great reluctance, if at all. The broadcast ballgame, the war movie, the star comedian, the family situation comedy, the western thriller, the detective story, the adventures of the secret agent, the drama of the courtroom—all are beginning to rank with such time-honoured formulas as the sob story, the funnies, the sex-murder account, the sports page, and disclosure of corruption in high places as attention-getting devices that can bring the eye or ear of the consumer nearer to the advertising message.

In short, the social system of the mass media in the United States is becoming more and more deeply established. Some future change can be expected in the kind of content it will produce to maintain its own stability. At present, however, the function of what we have called low-taste content is to maintain the financial stability of a deeply institutionalized social system that is tightly integrated with the whole of the American economic institution, the probability that our system of mass communication in this respect can be drastically altered by the occasional outbursts of critics seems small indeed.

Far more likely than media system change brought about by periodic attacks on low-taste media content is media system change brought about by trends in the economic system such as the emergence of a "post-industrial" society. Because the

The best insights of modem science, too, confirm those of traditional religion and of non-theological humanism. As the Indian space scientist Yash Pal put it while speaking at a South Asian seminar convened in 1980 by the Indian Institute of Mass Communication : "It has become clear from science that myself, all my cells, all my constituents and those in this match-box or in this table, or in a piece of stone—that all this material at some time past was cooked together in the same star. Does not this have any implications for questions like our essential relatedness, about ecology? And does it at all conflict with the very beautiful, holistic inspiration of all the great religious teachers ?"

***Values of Non-religionism :*** Jawaharlal Nehru, moulder of independent India for nearly two decades, as Mahatma Gandhi had been of a whole generation of fighters for freedom, strove to reconcile in his own mind religion and science, tradition and modernity. But Nehru, for the greater part of his life, was more conscious of the negative features of religious tradition than of the positive, and was much attracted by modem technology. His close friend and colleague Maulana Azad, whom he chose as free India's first Education Minister, was unashamed of humanity's religious heritage though he was not opposed to technology (Azad held the portfolio also of natural Resources and Scientific Research).

***Values regarding Humanity :*** Like Mahatma Gandhi, Maulana Azad was in favour of instructing children in the humanist values which are common to all religions at their best. Writing a decade before independence, Gandhi said in 'Harijan' in response to a correspondent's query on the place of religious instruction in his Wardha Scheme of Basic Education : "I regard it as fatal to the growth of a friendly spirit among children belonging to the different faiths if they are taught that their religion is superior to every other, or that it is the only true religion. Fundamental principles of ethics are common to all religions. These should be taught to the children."

Speaking in similar strain in February 1947, a month after assuming the Education portfolio in the Interim Government, Maulana Azad said : "The religious instruction imparted in India in private institutions is of a kind which, instead of broadening the outlook and inculcating a spirit of toleration and goodwill towards all men, produces exactly the opposite results. The aim of all religious teaching should be to make men more tolerant and broad-minded. And it is my opinion that this can be more effectively done if the State takes charge of the question than if it is left to private initiative."

In advocating instruction in the essence of all religions as part of the curriculum, Maulana Azad was at one not only with Mahatma Gandhi, the great experimenter with the practice of religion, but with Dr. Kadhakrishnan, the renowned exponent of the philosophy of religion.

The Commission on University Education headed by Dr. Radhakrishnan expressed itself, in the report it drew up in 1949, in the same terms as Maulana Azad. Religious instruction in the universities was one of the issues remitted to the Commission, which included distinguished scholars and scientists. The report of the Commission referred to the Constitution of free India that was then being drawn up, and said : There is no State religion. The State must not be partial to any one religion. Each one is at liberty to approach the unseen as it suits his capacity and inclination. If this is the basis of our Secular State, to be secular is not to be religiously illiterate. It is to be deeply spiritual."

However, the Constitution that came into force in January 1950 contained provisions relating to religious instruction that were contrary to the advice of Mahatma Gandhi, Maulana Azad and RadhaKrishnan. Section (1) of Article 28 expressly prohibits religious instruction in any educational institution wholly maintained out of State funds. But, strangely, it is permitted in privately run institutions even if they receive aid out of State funds. And Article 30 reads :

> "All minorities, whether based on religion or language, shall have the right to establish and administer educational institutions of their choice."
>
> "The State shall not, in granting aid to educational institutions, discriminate against any educational institution on the ground that it is under the management of a minority, whether based on religion or language."

Here is a case of unilateral secularism. The majority of Indian students (necessarily Hindus) were to be denied religious instruction; but students belonging to the minority religions—of which Islam and Christianity are the largest—are allowed to be indoctrinated in their respective monotheistic faiths according to which there is no salvation except through the teaching of Jesus Christ and Prophet Mohammad respectively.

The prohibition of religious instruction in State-run schools and its permission in those run by religious minorities runs counter to other Articles of the Constitution which guarantee non-discimination between citizens on the ground of religion. The unilateralism is reminiscent of the Khilafat years, in the early part of the century, when Gandhiji called upon Hindus to support their Muslim fellow-countrymen's Fight to preserve the territorial empire and the spiritual suzerainty of the Sultan of Turkey over Muslims world-wide, but refused to ask for a quid pro quo from Indian Muslims. M. Asaf Ali, nationalist Muslim leader of Delhi, made a visit to Deoband, a centre of Muslim theological learning, to persuade the teachers and students there that Muslims in India would do well to reduce or eschew cow slaughter voluntarily, as a mark of respect for Hindu sentiment and a reciprocal gesture for Hindu support to Khilafat.

But Gandhi was against anything smacking of a bargain. He wanted Hindu support for the Muslim cause of Khilafat to be unconditional. It is another matter that his hopes of enduring Hindu-Muslim unity being forged thereby went awry. India was partitioned in August 1947 to constitute Muslim-majority areas into a separate State of Pakistan.

Maulana Azad returned to the subject of moral instruction in the course of an address to the Central Advisory Board of Education in February 1948. He said : "It was at first considered that religious instruction would stand in the way of the free intellectual development of a child, but now it has been admitted that religious education cannot altogether be dispensed with. If national education was devoid of this element, there would be no appreciation of moral values or moulding of character on humane lines."

Maulana Azad's warning has proved only too true. In the case of the majority of India's younger generation comprising those who are Hindu by the accident of birth, secular education has nurtured the pursuit of money and of pleasure, never mind the ethics of how they are secured. Jawaharlal Nehru was able to sense this danger by 1959 when, during the Azad Memorial Lecture, he said that 'the passion for riches, for acquisition, for more and more wealth tends to corrupt" and cautioned against the tendency to criminality and eroticism.

On the part of many members of the Muslim community, the constitutional sanction of indoctrination in a single religion in educational institutions run by religious minorities has kept alive and intensified the separatist mentality that resulted in the partition of India in 1947. Among the factors that have nurtured secessionist sentiment in Kashmir over the decades since the State acceded to India in 1947 is the continuous indoctrination of Muslim children in a fanatical version of Islam in madarsas run by the Jamaat-e-Islami.

This is grim proof of the soundness of the warning sounded by Maulana Azad in January 1948 : "What will be the consequence if the Government undertakes to impart purely secular education? Naturally, people will try to provide religious education to their children through private sources. How these private sources are working today or are likely to work in future is known to you. I know something about it and can say that not only in villages, but even in cities the imparting of religious education is entrusted to teachers who, though literate, are not educated. To them religion means nothing but bigotry."

Ecumenism is a term used by Christians for unity of the whole Christian world, transcending differences between Christian sects. A higher vision, that of a vast inter-religious ecumenism, inspired Gandhi, Azad and Radhakrishnan. Jawaharlal Nehru came to accept this when he said in the course of the Azad Memorial Lecture delivered by him in November 1959, less than five years before his death : Two great religions have influenced India—two emerging from her own thought, Hinduism and Buddhism, and two coming from abroad but establishing themselves firmly in India : Christianity and Islam.

Science today challenges the old concept of religion. But if religion deals not with dogmas and ceremonials, but rather with the higher things of life, there should be no conflict with science or *inter se* between religions, it might be the high privilege of India to help in bringing about this synthesis."

While Nehru thus finally arrived at the truth perceived earlier by Maulana Azad among others, it did not impel him to call for a reconsideration of the provisions in the Constitution relating to religious instruction in schools and colleges which run flatly counter to inter-religious ecumenism: these provisions, as we have seen, banish religious instruction from State-run schools but permit fanatical indoctrination in a single religion in private schools run by religious minorities—including those that are recognised by and given financial aid by the Indian State.

What Jawaharlal Nehru came to see in 1959 is being gradually recognised by Nehruites. G. Parthasarathi, a protege of Nehru who distinguished himself in the fields of diplomacy and education after initial grounding in journalism, said in the course of his convocation address at the University of Hyderabad in March 1987 : "Now that the concept of a core national curriculum has been accepted, it seems to me that consideration might be given to the inclusion in it of a course covering the development of human values the world over, and with special reference to India.

Such a course would cover the contributions made to the development of a humanistic outlook by the various religions, by outstanding thinkers, by Marxism and the different schools of socialist thought, as well as by modem science many of whose findings are supportive of the concepts of humankind's oneness and of the ecological relatedness of all life on earth."

Another Nehruite, Aruna Asaf Ali, approvingly quoted the above passage in the course of the Azad Memorial Lecture she delivered in 1989. She went further and called for a review and amendment of the Constitutional provisions pertaining to religious instruction in schools so as to promote the inter-religious ecumenism which the best Indian minds have commended through the ages, and of which recent advocates include Gandhi, Azad, Radhakrishnan and the later Jawaharlal Nehru.

Among the paradoxes of free India is that the noble concept of inter-religious ecumenism has come to be equated with and referred to as 'secularism'. This is a violation of the English language. As the Concise Oxford Dictionary tells us, secularism stands for, 'concerned with the affairs of this world; not sacred or monastic or ecclesiastical; sceptical of religious truth or opposed to religious education'.

Like much else in post-independence India, the confusion of thought about secularism has its origin in the development of Jawaharlal Nehru's ideas. Beginnings as a Marxist and an agnostic, he matured over the years to the advocacy, cited earlier, of inter-religious ecumenism. In between, for long years, he popularised the term 'secularism' to stand for his own vision of the good society. In a letter to Chief Ministers of States in 1956, he wrote : "We call our State a secular one.

The word 'secular' perhaps is not a very happy one. And yet, for want of a better, we have used it. What exactly does it mean ? It does not obviously mean a state where religion as such is discouraged. It means freedom of religion and conscience, including freedom for those who may have no religion. The word 'secular", however, conveys something much more to me, although that might not be its dictionary meaning. It conveys the idea of social and political equality. Thus, a caste-ridden society is not properly secular."

It is a pity that, along with Nehru, the Indian Press by and large failed to see the absurdity of constitutional provisions some of which ordain equal treatment of citizens irrespective of their religion, and Articles 28 and 30 which treat citizens differently precisely on the ground of religion. The Ramakrishna Mission seeking the status of a religious minority in order to avoid State interference in the educational institutions run by the Mission, and securing legal recognition as such in 1985 through a judgment of the Calcutta High Court, was a reduction ad absurdum of Article 30. The Press hardly said a word about the case. Nor has there been much notice taken of the Supreme Court's reversal, in the second half of 1995, of the Calcutta High Court's judgment in the Ramakrishna Mission case.

Nehru, again, saw no violation of secularism in his confining to Hindus the reform of marriage and family laws in the 1950s. As a result, it became an offence for a Hindu to practise bigamy or polygamy, while Muslims remained free to practise bigamy or polygamy. No wonder that the Muslim vote bank, virtually controlled by the community's fanatical and male-chauvinist leaders, remained available to the Congress party for decades.

It is not only the Congress that has followed the policy of

placating Muslim sentiment, while professing secularism, witn an eye on the Muslim vote. On 7th June, 1969, the Community Party of India (Marxist), then ruling the State of Kerala in coalition with the Muslim League, announced that it would carve out a Muslim-majority district of Malappuram, on the eve of a by-eiection there. Other secularists did not criticise the politically opportunist decision aimed at securing the Muslim vote. It was left to Kelappan, an aged Gandhian, to lead an unsuccessful protest.

Many Muslims in northern India became alienated from the Congress during the emergency regime of 1975-76 because of the strong-arm methods employed by Prime Minister Indira Gandhi's second son, Sanjay Gandhi, to promote family planning through sterilisation. This was among the factors leading to Congress defeat in the Lok Sabha elections of early 1977. The post-emergency Janata Party government soon fell, due to internal squabbles for power. After returning to power in 1980, Indira Gandhi issued instructions for implementation of a 15-point programme for upliftment of the religious minorities (meaning Muslims since the second largest religious minority, the Christians, are neither educationally nor economically backward compared to the generality of the population). The special programme, which has continued to be implemented by successive governments to this day, is reminiscent of the days of British rule when the alien regime showed solicitude for the minorities in an effort to keep them away from the national movement. The Press, by and large, found nothing wrong in special favour being shown to certain citizens on the basis of their religion.

Opportunism is no monopoly of political groups professing secularism. The Bharatiya Janata Party, which accuses others of appeasing Muslims and exploiting caste feelings, has not dared to question the concept of reservation in admission to colleges and in recruitment to government services and public sector undertakings for persons—irrespective of his or her merit—belonging to a particular caste (Scheduled or 'Other

Backward') or tribe. The BJP obviously values the OBC vote bank as much as every other political party does. It has been left to the judiciary to come to the rescue of a polity plagued by caste-based vote-bank politics, by placing a limit on such reservations and insisting on a means test by calling for exclusion of the 'creamy layer' which is to be found in every caste.

The Press neither noticed the BJP's call in 1989 for a system of proportional representation which will more truly reflect popular opinion in the legislatures, nor BJP's subsequent abandonment of this important item of electoral reform. Till the elections to the ninth Lok Sabha, the BJP had been securing fewer seats in the State Assemblies and the Lok Sabha than its share of the popular vote warranted. Thereafter, it became in many states a beneficiary of the prevailing electoral system of first-past-the-post.

When the Rajiv Gandhi government sponsored the disgraceful Muslim Women's Act following a howl of protest by Muslim male chauvinists against a Supreme Court judgment of 1985 which held that Muslims were as much bound as other citizens of India to provide maintenance to a divorced and needy wife, there was criticism of the opportunist legislation by a wide section of the Press. But thereafter the newspapers lost interest in the subject.

The Press, by and large, did not criticise the call by the Muslim League, emboldened by the Rajiv Gandhi government's retreat, for repeal of the Directive Principle of the Constitution which calls for enactment of a uniform civil code for all citizens. In 1995, when a Supreme Court bench reminded the government of the subject and asked what the government was doing about it. Prime Minister Narasimha Rao trivialised the issue by speaking of the difficulties of enacting a uniform marriage law when there were different practices in different communities, and different parts of the country, in the matter of marriage between cousins.

Few commentators told the Prime Minister that the issue is not about marriage between cousins, but whether bigamy should be legitimate for some citizens of India and a crime for others, depending on their religion; and that equal treatment of all citizens irrespective of their religion is what secularism—which Narasimha Rao frequently swears by—is all about.

On 16th March 1995, the Press Information Bureau of the Central Government put out a news item that the Finance Corporation for Minorities, which the Narasimha Rao government established after conferring statutory status on the Minorities Commission, would extend aid on concessional terms to members of minority religious communities whose household income is twice the poverty level as defined by the Planning Commission from time to time. Here was a virtual laying down of two poverty line definitions, one for the Hindu majority and the other for religious minorities. There can be no more blatant violation of secularism, yet the Press has hardly taken notice of it. True, the PIB's daily output is largely of publicity puffs, but it is surely the duty of the national news agencies which supply the staple of news to newspapers of varying political persuasion, and of the special correspondents of individual newspapers, to retrieve the few needles of significant information from the haystack of PIB's output.

In respect of these parodies of secularism, it was not to be expected that A.I.R. and Doordarhan, tightly controlled by the Government, would attempt critical discussion.

The failure of the Press in the cases—illustrative, not exhaustive—cited above perhaps arises from the fact that the intellegentsia manning the Press—belonging as they do to the same social, economic and educational background as the middle and higher levels of the teaching profession and the judiciary—share the general confusion of thought about secularism. Another reason could be that journalists, like academics, have been well looked after by successive governments—through Wage Boards in the case of the Press, as by the University Grants Commission in the case of the higher class of the teaching profession.

In any case, it is remarkable that the Press took hardly any notice when intellectuals sustained in comfort by the Establishment through such government-funded bodies as the Indian Council for Social Science Research, the Institute for Advanced Studies and the Indian Institute of Mass Communication, adopted a resolution at a gathering at Shimla in April 1987 which said : "Secular values should be actively promoted by judges, teachers and religious teachers." This extraordinary proposition would have been laughed to scorn anywhere except in India. Not surprisingly, intellectuals of that age, as well as the Indian Press by and large, have been in a state of amnesia about Prof. Mushirul Hasan who was expelled by Islamic mobs from Jamia Millia (a central university funded by the Government) in 1992. Me was thus punished for suggesting that reasoned discussion is a better way of countering the views expressed in a book (in this case 'The Satanic Verses' by Salman Rushdie) than banning it. Mushirul Hasan continues to be holed up in the campus of Jawaharlal Nehru University where his wife teaches.

So devoid of meaning has the term secularism become that (the then) President Shanker Dayal Sharma has described Guru Teg Bahadur, who put his religion above his life, as a 'secularist'. According to a Press release of the PIB on 17th December, 1993, Dr. Sharma said in the course of his statement on the anniversary of the Guru's martyrdom : "May his shining example of service and secularism and the glory of his sacrifice inspire each one of us to work for national unity."

Earlier, Prime Minister Narasimha Rao said in the course of his convocation address on 22nd November, 1991 at the Sathya Sai Institute of Higher Learning that the Sai Baba's "emphasis on five universal values of Sathya, Dharma, Shanti, Prema and Ahimsa is truly Secular in character, and these constitute the major bedrock of all the religons of the world."

No wonder that, in this climate of totally confused thinking on what secularism means, the Press did not report at any length, nor studied and discussed, the judgment delivered by the Supreme Court on 11th March 1994, upholding the dissolution of the popularly elected legislatures in four States following the demolition of the Babri Masjid in December 1992, on the ground that the Bharatiya Janata Party that ran the governments there was not committed to secularism.

In a medley of judgments that concurred on this central point. Justice A.M. Ahmadi (now Chief Justice) said in the course of his order : The term 'Secular' (in the Preamble to the Constitution) has advisedly not been defined, pre-sumably because it is a very elastic term not capable of a precise definition, and perhaps best left undefined." (SUPREME COURT CASES, 1994, Vol. III, page 77). Another Judge on the nine-member bench that decided the case. Justice B.P. Jeevan Reddy, remarked in the course of his order : "Both the expressions—'socialist' and 'secular'—by themselves are not capable of precise definition."

Our newspapers have hardly noticed the implications of the remarks of the two learned Judges quoted above, who held along with seven of their brother Judges that Secularism, though it is undefinable, is a basic feature of India's Constitution. Failure of the media to demand, and themselves to attempt, clarification of the concept of secularism has detracted from their social role as agencies of non-formal education.

The media and the general public will do well to ponder the advice given on this subject by Aruna Asaf Ali, heroine of the freedom struggle and a lifelong fighter for women's equality and economic justice. Pointing out that the Muslim League and the Bharatiya Janata Party claim to be secular, as do the Congress and the Left parties, she said in the course of an article in *'National Herald'*, Delhi, of 2nd October, 1993 : "Considering that all political parties have made a mockery of the concept of secularism, is it not time to drop the term from the vocabulary of our political discourse ? If what we want to advocate is equal goodwill on the part of the State towards all citizens of India irrespective of their religion, and civilised and humane treatment of each other by the citizens themselves, I would suggest that we find another word. Perhaps it could be humanism."

A document that has not received the public attention it deserves, since the media have taken hardly any notice of it, is the report of a Core Group on Value Orientation of Education, set up by the Planning Commission. The group, which was headed by Dr. D. Swaminathan, member of the Planning Commission, was formed as the result of the notice taken of the subject by the Commission while formulating the Eighth five Year Flan (1992-97). The Plan document said, in the chapter on education : "The significance of value education has been highlighted by several committees and commissions on education. The Planning Commission has recently constituted a core group on value orientation in education. The recommendations of the group will be considered for implementation in consultation with the Ministry of Human Resource Development, University Grants Commission, Association of Indian Universities and National Council for Educational Research and Training."

The core group's report, submitted in October 1992, says in the Introduction : "In post-independence India, in the name of secularism which was not correctly understood, hardly any serious efforts were made to promote value orientation of education." (para 2.06). This was a surprisingly daring statement to be found in a document emanating from the Congress establishment, even if the report abounds elsewhere in instances of equating—though it is linguistically absurd to do so—secularism with religious values. It is also of interest that most of the institutions where instruction is imparted in moral values, whose work is surveyed approvingly in the lengthy annexures to the core group's report, are associated with traditional religion, not secularism. They include : Sri

Sathya Sai Institute of Higher Learning, Prasanthi Nilayarn; the Banasthali Vidyapeeth, where the students recite 'Sarva Dharma Prarthana' on the lines advocated by Mahatma Gandhi; the Dayalbagh Educational Institute which was founded by the fifth guru of the Radhaswami faith, which seeks to promote an understanding of various beliefs so that students may develop an attitude of tolerance; and the Ramakrishna Institute of Moral and Spiritual Education, Mysore, whose B. Ed. course includes compulsory study of the major religions of the world.

Much of the report of the Planning Commission's core group consists of a recital of what earlier committees and commissions said on the subject. Of special interest is the following extract from the report of the Committee on Religious and Moral Education set up by the Union Ministry of Education in 1959, with Sri Prakasa as chairman : "Many ills that our world of education and our society as a whole is suffering today, resulting in widespread disturbance and dislocation of life, are mainly due to the gradual disappearance of the hold of basic principles of religion on the hearts of the people. The only cure, it seems to us, is in deliberate inculcation of moral and spiritual values from the earliest years of our lives."

Again, the Education Commission headed by Dr. D.S. Kothari said in its report (1966) : "Modernisation does not mean, least of all in our national situation, a refusal to recognise the importance of, or to inculcate, necessary moral and spiritual values and self-discipline. While a combination of ignorance with goodness may be futile, that of knowledge with a lack of essential values may be dangerous."

The weakening of social and moral values in the younger generation is creating many serious social and ethical conflicts in western societies, and there is already a desire among great Western thinkers to balance the knowledge and skills which science and technology bring, with the values and insights associated with ethics and religion at its best."

Two questions arise. Will politicians, engaged in a ceaseless battle for survival in, or capture of, power find time to implement the recommendations made by the Planning Commission's core group on value orientation in education ?

The recommendations amount to what we have described as the promotion of an inter-religious ecumenism. This raises the second question. Will the leaders of the two largest religious minority communities agree to compulsory instruction in the values common to all religions ? This will amount to an admission that Islam and Christianity are not the only true religions.

The Sufis of Islam cheerfully accepted the oneness of all religions. Thus saint Sarmad of Delhi, who hailed from west Asia, said that he had passed from Jewish faith into Islam and had wandered from Islam "into the garden of Sri Rama and Laxman". Sarmad's friend and follower, Dara Shikoh, translated some of the Upanishads into Persian. But Dara's younger brother Aurangzeb, a fanatic, caused both Sarmad and Dara to be put to death. And the dominant influence on the minds of Indian Muslims has continued to be the Shariat, and not Sufi teaching. Similarly, in the deeply humanist teaching of Jesus Christ himself there is no sectarian dogmatism, but Pauline churchianity has been a different matter. As for India's principal religion, while the history of Hinduism is not free of instances of sectarian pride and intolerance—as for instance on the part of the fanatical among Saivites and Vaishnavltes—Hindu polytheism has served to make intelligible at the popular level, and thereby to sustain, such humanist insights as that truth is one though the learned call it by different names, and that different faiths are only different paths that lead to the same goal.

It is this catholic strain in Hinduism that has made it possible for the people of India, most of whom are Hindus, to accept the democratic and egalitarian foundations of the Constitution which—aberrations like Articles 28 and 30 apart—treats all citizens alike.

The teaching of inter-religious ecumenism as a compulsory part of education will be as difficult to achieve, and for the same reasons, as a common civil code. But both are equally necessary for building a just and agalitarian society. The media can do a great deal, through sustained education of public opinion, to make this possible.

***Tradition and Culture :*** The hope of the mass media drawing on the best elements in each of India's religious traditions is considerably dimmed by their present performance, which Is subversive of our cultural heritage.

The threat to culture posed by the mass media was ably summed-up by the Parliamentary Standing Committee on Human Resource Development, in its twelfth report presented on 25th August, 1994. After considering the approach paper on a Rational Policy on Culture prepared by the Ministry of HRD, the committee said it was "deeply disturbed at the virtual absence of any reference in the Approach Paper to the impact of the mass media on cultural development, nothing in the recent past has had such dramatic and deleterious impact on our cultural traditions as the invasion of the mass media, both indigenous and foreign."

An important objective of the NPC is to evolve a creative response to this new challenge which alone will enable us to preserve our cultural continuity with the past, while rejecting the baneful and integrating the desirable in the influences which are entering our country through the new electronic technology. Should we fail to evolve a sufficiently creative response to this challenge, there is every danger of India succumbing to an imitative culture and losing its indigenous creative genius. It will avail us nothing if we attain material progress but lose our soul in the bargain.

> "There is no way in which we can shut ourselves off from the consequences of satellite technology. Retracting into a shell is not the answer. At the same time, passively succumbing to the invasion

is not the answer either. Even while emphasising the need for a creative response to this invasion, the NPC must see how we can avail ourselves of this technology to promote an understanding of our cultural heritage among the masses of our people at large, as well as take the message of India to the outside world."

"On the domestic front, this will require the conscious and deliberate use of the electronic media for the dissemination of our many rich regional cultural and linguistic traditions within the region and in the country at large. It will also call for the deployment of numerous local TV, Video and Radio Production centres, especially in remote and rural areas, for local communities to actively participate in Radio and TV programmes of their own making, instead of being reduced, as at present, to merely passive recipients of programmes produced, broadcast and telecast from elsewhere, many of which have little relevance to their lives. Such production centres, with responsibility delegated to grassroot bodies, would be the ultimate answer to the dangers of consumerism, commercialism, heedless Westernisation, and imitative cultural modes. This will also counteract the tokenism which now represents the media attitude towards both folk and classical culture. A few small slots in a crowd of commercial entertainment respect neither the artistes nor their public. The proliferation of channels on Doordarshan must be utilised to encourage both tradition and experiment in rural and urban art forms."

"At the same time, global satellite technology offers us an unprecedented opportunity of disseminating our culture to the world at large; it is a challenge to which our electronic media must rise, in concert, with the Department of Culture, whose duty it is to ensure that Indian global TV does not become a pale imitation of existing Western-dominated networks."

"The Committee recommends that the NFC should explore measures to make the mass media an effective instrument for the dissemination of culture. The emphasis should be on the production of serials, documentaries and films relating to important personalities, places, festivals, literature and the arts. The mass media should not promote superstitious and magical belief systems. Doordarshan should use innovative methods to attract attention to the classical arts. Children should be exposed to the diversity of India's cultural and linguistic traditions through translations into their mother tongues of the poetry and the songs of great patriots and poets."

The Committee expresses its serious concern over the ever increasing and reckless exhibition of violence, antisocial activities and obscenity through the cinema, the worst sufferers of which are the younger generation whose finer sensibilities are being coarsened and creative faculties dulled. The Committee, therefore, recommends that the NPC should address these issues and discourage these trends.

Among the glories of India's cultural heritage is the sensitive awareness of our forbears to the relationship between human wellbeing and the environment, exemplified by veneration of the *pancha bhoota* of air, water, earth, fire and the sky. It is tragic that the mass media did not bring out, over the decades of the heedless pursuit of industrialism and of profit for contractors and industrialists, the social cost in terms of the pollution of our rivers and denudation of our forests. Environment has begun to be discussed by the media only after the subject became a fashion in the industrially developed countries of the west. This is one of the many instances of the imitativeness of western culture on the part of most of our media practitioners, arising from their ignorance of and consequent lack of pride in our own cultural heritage.

## Guiding Theory

***Guidelines for Press :*** In an annexure, listing guidelines on the right to privacy, the Council pointed out that the Indian Constitution does not expressly declare any right to privacy unlike certain global instruments to which India is a signatory, like the human rights charter. Even so, there is a school of thought which holds the view that the right to privacy is a fundamental right emanating from Article 21.

According to the Press Council, the law of defamation covers certain limited aspects of privacy. Certain countries have, therefore, enacted privacy laws which go beyond the range of defamation or reputation to protect personal interest, grief and the personality or psyche of the individual.

The guidelines laid down by the Council specify that for journalists writing about people in terms of human interest, the litmus test must be in public interest—the person being a public person by some reasonable definition (politician, sportsman, scientist or anyone in the public eye by virtue of his position, achievements or notoriety) and a person whose actions fall within the domain of public interest, as an example or warning to others. Even then, the publication must be justified by the legitimate public interest, not a prurient or morbid curiosity.

The personal and family or social life of a public figure or one who adopts a position of moral leadership can legitimately be open to public scrutiny where the private conduct can adversely affect or influence the proper discharge of his/her public functions and he/she may be setting a bad example where seen as a role model by others.

Any private activity liable to result in the commission, of a crime or result in evasion of criminal liability or in seriously antisocial conduct may also be legitimately exposed in the public interest.

While all individuals are equal, certain vulnerable categories like children, women, the aged, the mentally retarded or handicapped and the sick require added protection.

Rapes and molestation of women, sexual abuse of children etc. are fit cases where privacy should be respected and the identity, photographs or sordid details of the offence should not be publicised to those unconcerned with law enforcement or with administrative jurisdiction in the matter.

A discharged convict has a right to a fresh start in building his/her life anew. It would be an invasion of privacy to recall his/her earlier crime to damn a redeemed criminal in the absence of any public interest consideration.

It would also be an invasion of privacy to name the family or associates of a wrongdoer when they are totally innocent of the crime and no public interest is involved. Suggestive guilt by association would be unfair to the privacy of others.

Even in cases where the reports are legitimate and proper, but the means by which the information has been gained entails an unwarranted intrusion into the privacy of an individual, such reporting is to be eschewed. Such intrusive reporting may be by gate-crashing into a home or hospital room unnoticed to write about an accident or illness, or publishing casual conversation overheard or something told in confidence or in a privileged gathering.

Interception of mail, phone tapping, bugging, photographing people in their homes without their consent or by using telephoto lenses would be invasion of privacy. Breach of fair practice by one journal would not justify publication by another.

*The Times of India* published the regret on September 27,1991 with the following note from the Editor :

'The Press Council has directed this paper to publish

> the gist of its decision of how the murder of the two nuns in Bombay in November 1990 was reported and has asked us to express our regret, which we now are doing. We are deeply sorry if our report has hurt the sentiments of a section of our readers. However, in the light of the Press Council's findings, we will now review several issues of journalistic ethics which this case has given rise to — Editor.

The Illustrated Weekly of India in its issue dated May 18, 1986, carried an article by its correspondent S.M. Abdi entitled, 'Shocking: The strange escapades of J.B. Patnaik' (Orissa Chief Minister). It dealt with deviant sexual life of the Chief Minister.

This article was followed by another captioned: 'Why is J.B. being allowed to gag the Press? The second supported the first.

The first article carried photostats of FIR of complaints against Patnaik. Soon after it was published, Patnaik filed a suit for damages of Rs 1 crore against The Illustrated Weekly of India.

In the suit filed in the Orissa High-Court, Patnaik asked for details about the documents, source of information from the writer of the article and the editor and publisher of the Weekly.

Even as the case was pending in the High Court, the editor and the publisher moved the Supreme Court against the order of the lower court arguing that the application for better particulars etc. amounted to seek disclosure of evidence which was not permissible under Order 6 of the Civil Procedure Code and no journalist could be forced to disclose his source of information.

Advocates for the petitioners also submitted that what was before the court was a libel suit and if anyone of the objection raised was proved, the suit would be decreed.

It is strange that this landmark in journalism should be

attributed to The Illustrated Weekly of India. Magazine journalism came of age in India primarily due to this journal. Under Khushwant Singh's editorship in early seventies, the Weekly gained unprecedented heights. Magazine reports had never before been taken so seriously. Also the magazine had never sold so well. The seeds of the magazine revolution, which swept India in the late seventies and the early eighties, were sown in the offices of the Weekly.

It was the Weekly success story which led to the launching of Sunday and India Today in mid-seventies.

It was the first magazine to send its young reporters for field assignments. Investigative reports and human interest stories became the byword for magazine journalism.

As described earlier, the events of 1977 and the subsequent developments saw magazines emerge as a dominant force on the Indian media scene. Indepth reports and investigative stories became the preserve of the magazine. The dominance of the magazines over newspapers continued till mid-80s.

By mid-80s, the newspapers had begun to overtake the magazines in the field of indepth and investigative reporting. Sunday editor M.J. Akbar, who emerged on top of the scene after starting as a brilliant reporter for the Weekly under Khushwant Singh, started concentrating on daily newspapers. Slowly the glamour days of the magazines faded out.

With the sole exception of India Today, which showed a steady upward trend in its circulation figures, magazines by and large suffered considerable loss in circulation. It is said the Weekly story on Patnaik came at this juncture. It started publishing a number of sensational stories, each accompanied with a mark of exclamation.

Soon after the story about Patnaik appeared, Patnaik brought the full force of his office to harass and humiliate Pritish Nandy. He was arrested and interrogated. He was made to appear before the courts time and again and barring a brave but solitary exception, even senior lawyers of the state were reluctant to come to Nandy's help. All those who had filed affidavits against Patnaik retracted.

The Weekly maintained the posture that it had committed no wrong, in fact, done public service by exposing a chief minister who had been using his office for purposes other than administration.

After three years of legal battle, The Weekly's will wilted. It agreed before the Supreme Court to tender an apology to the chief minister. The text of the apology was filed before the apex court, and sealed till it was published by The Weekly.

The apology was published by The Weekly in its issue dated August 27 - September 2,1989. It ran as follows:

We Bennett, Coleman and Company Ltd., Pritish Nandy, Editor of The Illustrated Weekly and S.N.M. Abdi, special correspondent of The Illustrated Weekly, had published two articles under the captions, 'The strange escapades of JB Patnaik' and 'Why is J.B. Patnaik being allowed to gag the Press,' in the issues dated 18-24 May 1986 and 3-9 August 1986 respectively, based on information available to us. Subsequently, we found that the information on the basis of which these articles were written was not true and was politically motivated. We regret the damage done to Mr. Patnaik s reputation and offer our apologies to him.

Commenting on the Weekly-Patnaik episodes, Khushwant Singh said that he would never have published this kind of an article. He said he had the same kind of material sent to him, when he was the editor of the Weekly, by a senior member of the IAS. It was accompanied with documentary proof as well as a confidential report of the services tribunal which had recommended his dismissal. But he refused to publish it.

He said his view was that a person's private life should be his own. A public figure's private life could only be exposed if there was a clear evidence of misuse of power.

An eminent freelance journalist Nikhil Chakravarty said that an apology did not add to the credit of any newspaper or journalist. Therefore, before writing a story, we should exercise a sense of responsibility not only in relation to the question of privacy but on any other issue. He said 'my point about this particular case is that it should not have dragged on for three years. When the case was launched then if those who were responsible for the story found that it could not be substantiated, then they should immediately have moved up and issued a contradiction.

The question of code of conduct has been hanging fire for decades. If you want to have a code of conduct for journalists you cannot have it in isolation from the code of conduct for politicians or public life as a whole. Even if one were to have a code of conduct it will be very difficult to enforce.' *Navbharat Times* Editor Rajendra Mathur said that first it was difficult to prove a case like this when the allegations were made against the chief minister in his home state. Second, there was the question of expenses because the case could go on and on and Bennett and Coleman could not fight these cases in a very pedestrian way.

He thought what could have been awarded as damages if Patnaik had won, half of it or perhaps two-thirds would have been spent in litigating the case. All this might have influenced the decision to apologise.

Inderjit, editor, INFA said: 'When a publication like *The Illustrated Weekly* carried a cover story on Patnaik, I was little shocked. Having been associated with *The Times of India* group for almost ten years, these are not the kind of cover stories one normally carried. I felt that the editor of the paper would have good reason and solid facts to back up the story. Now that he has agreed to apologise I do think that the facts could not back up the story. Therefore, I am a little distressed by this development. It was not in keeping with the character of *The Times* Group. It was scurrilous and highly defamatory.

It is possible as some people suggested that it was not easy to get the required evidence, it was also suggested that people in Orissa were afraid of the consequences, it was also suggested that people who had given sworn affidavits had resiled, but these are the hazards of our profession and all these factors should have been taken into consideration before publishing the story...'

*The Times of India* Editor Dilip Padgaonkar offered the following comments:

> '...I would say, as a rule, a public official had a right to privacy, but if that privacy is explored without malice for public good, the Press should be allowed to do so. In this particular case, the article is not the kind I would have published in *The Times of India*, but if the editor thought it necessary to expose certain aspects of private life of the public official concerned I would have given him the benefit of doubt because the person in power and authority has a far greater room for manoeuvre to get things done to bring subtle or harsh pressures to promote his interests.

I may not agree with the decision of the editor to offer to apologise, but I understand why it was done. If you are going to enter into a very hazy legalistic area and if at the end of it all there would be no victors of any kind then why go into it? This can be one line of argument. I have known people who have filed suits because of intrusion into their privacy and then they find that if they submit themselves to interrogation, then there will be worse defamation.. .not many people want to subject themselves to this.

...principles are involved and my hope was that certain professional bodies such as the Editors Guild would take up this matter. I certainly intend to do so because if this becomes a precedent—an out-of-court settlement of this kind—then I am afraid that sooner or later—sooner rather than later—we might end up by curtailing an important area of Press freedom.'

It is worthwhile comparing what happened in Goa in September 1989. Goa Legislative Assembly Speaker Dayanand Ganesh Narvekar, allegedly molested a clerk, Sumita Holdankar. The matter leaked out. Credence was given to it by a political opponent, the leader of the Maharashtra Gomantak Party, Mr. Ramakant Khalap. The latter insisted that the story of molestation was true and that if it was proved to be false, he would quit politics.

The matter was taken up by Goa's English paper, *Gomantak Times.* The paper demanded the resignation of Narvekar. The daily reflected popular sentiment for soon the cry was taken up by others as well.

It is not that efforts were not made by interested parties to silence Sumita. *Gomantak Times* published stories of how attempts were made to buy Sumita Holdankar's silence. Someone, apparently, gave her Rs 11,000 to buy jewellery. *Gomantak Times* published photostats of bills. Sumita still has to explain how she was bribed.

Demands for Narvekar's resignation gathered momentum. The Gomantak Kshatriya Marathis Samaj, which comprises people belonging to the Kharvi and Pagi communities and of which Dayanand Ganesh Narvekar is a member, launched a strong attack on him. Over 6,000 young people from all over Goa converged on Panaji, the capital, to demand Narvekar's resignation.

The protest rally convened by the Students Action Front was addressed by Sumita who braved the wrath of the Speaker. Subsequently, Narvekar resigned.

But in the case of *The Illustrated Weekly* none among the journalist's community came out openly to support it. The key witness disappeared or refused to give evidence against Patnaik. The lawyers in Orissa, with the sole exception of one Ranjit Mohanty were not prepared to take up this case because of the fear of retribution from the Chief Minister.

There might be few politicians whose personal lives are completely above board. The U.K. Prime Minister Harold Macmillan's life was in a mess with his wife Dorothy carrying on for years with another man; so was Lloyd George, US President Franklin Delano Roosevelt, had an affair with a friend of his wife, Eleanor.

S. Gopal, son of India's President S. Radhakrishnan, has written about his father's liaisons and the affair of Jawaharial Nehru with Lady Mountbatten has been talked about for years now with everyone from Mountbatten's official biographer Phillip Ziegly down to others less knowledgeable trying to put a kind face on the subject. Only Nehru's personal secretary, late M.O. Mathai, had the temerity to suggest that the emperor had no clothes. But the important thing about these happenings i& that they never arose during the life time of these individuals.

The scandal involving Christine Keeler (U.K. Society girl) and former UK Minister John Profumo is an extreme case. John Profumo had to resign not because he was carrying on with Christine Keeler, but because Keeler also had a Soviet Official as a friend to whom it was suspected, she might' have passed on secrets. Profumo had to quit in public interest.

It is doubtless that the life style of a public official has a tremendous bearing on the administration, but this can be exposed only if it is in public interest to do so.

It is also true that in India, unlike in the West, the public officials do not lead a distinct private and public life. It is invariably mixed up. This, perhaps, requires a close tab on them.

Taking into account the increasing tendency to publish defamatory news in the newspapers and magazines there is a need to strengthen defamation laws in the country. The Press Council indictment of newspapers publishing defamatory news is not a sufficient deterrent to prevent such publications. The Editors Guild and other Press associations should ponder over this problem and suggest steps for self- regulation.

But the move on the part of the Rajiv government to pass Defamation Bill was to gag the Press and stop it from exposing misdeeds of public men.

***Bill of Defamation :*** The idea to enact the Defamation Bill was conceived by the government sometimes in early 1987. It was around this time that media exposures on Bofors, Reliance Industries, and Ajitabh Bachchan's alleged purchase of flat in Switzerland surfaced.

The immediate provocation was the revelations involving Lalit Suri allegedly getting a Rupees Six Crore commission from a Japanese firm on a pipeline deal. This story was carried by *The Statesman.*

On August 29, 1988, the Lok Sabha passed the Defamation Bill putting unprecedented curbs on the freedom of the Press in the post-Independence era, barring the Emergency period. The Bill sought to bring the following changes in the old law.

***Old Law***

(1) Prima facie onus of proving defamation with the complainant.

(2) Defamation cases to be tried in the judicial magistrate's court.

(3) No deadline for clearing the case.

(4) No minimum imprisonment.

(5) Matters termed grossly indecent, scurrilous and intended for blackmail not covered by law.

(6) No penalty for criminal imputation.

(7) Ten grounds to prove innocence including publication in good faith.

(8) Government departments treated on par with others.

(9) No pretrial penalty.

(10) Specific exemption from personal appearance.

(11) No provision for summary trial.

***New Law***

(1) Entire onus of proving innocence on the accused. The prosecution would have the right to lead evidence in rebuttal.

(2) The cases to go directly to the second stage Sessions Court.

(3) 90-day limit for the final judgement.

(4) Minimum imprisonment of one month on first offence, three months to five for subsequent offence. The imprisonment could be up to five years for subsequent offences.

(5) All these terms ware included in the Bill without specific definitions, making it possible to twist their meanings to support trumped up charges. The bill created a new offence of publication of grossly indecent or scurrilous matter intended for blackmailing. The terms grossly indecent or scurrilous were not defined. The bill explained that it was not scurrilous to make true imputations against any person provided it was for the public good, but the fact that it was good for the public had to be proved by the accused.

(6) Criminal imputation was made an offence.

(7) No ground to prove innocence in the case of criminal imputation.

(8) No exemption at all. The editor, printer and publisher to be personally present at every hearing of the case which would proceed on a day-to-day basis.

(9) Provision for summary trial and the proceedings to be held in camera.

The bill was rushed through and passed in a matter of nine-hour acrimonious debate in the Lok Sabha which resulted in the opposition walkout. The government did not bother to consult any professional body of the journalists during the time of the formulation of the bill.

The Home Ministry proposed a policy paper on the Defamation Bill. The then Home Minister Chidambaram played an active role in its drafting and instead of sending the paper to the Cabinet for approval, it was directly sent to legislative wing of the Law Ministry. In mid 1987 when the furore over defence scandals such as Bofors and HDW deals was at its peak, the Home Ministry approached the Cabinet with a comprehensive Bill.

The Cabinet appointed an 8-member group of ministers including P. Shiv Shankar, Vasant Sathe, H.K.L. Bhagat, Chidambaram and H.R. Bhardwaj, with Home Minister Buta Singh as its Chairman. The group met at least 20 times to finalise the bill. The final approval was given on August 8,1988.

The Bill evoked angry reaction from the journalists, constitutional experts and lawyers. It soon snowballed into a nationwide agitation.

On September 5, 1988 in an unprecedented show of unity, various sections of the Press from all over the country came together at a rally in Delhi against the proposed Defamation Bill. The journalists were joined in the rally by proprietors, freelancers and press workers. The 800-strong protestors marched down India Gate to Boat Club carrying placards.

Among the prominent personalities present at the rally were Ram Nath Goenka, Proprietor of *Indian Express,* Mr. Rajaji Rao, editor and proprietor of *Eenadu* (A.P.), Mr. Girilal Jain, former Editor, *The Times of India*, Mr. C.R. Irani, Managing Director, *The Statesman*, Mr. Arun Shourie, editor, *The Indian Express,* Mr. N. Ram, Associate Editor, *The Hindu*, Mr. Prem Bhatia former editor, *The Tribune*, Mr. M.J. Akbar, editor, *The Telegraph*, Mr. Aroon Purie, editor and proprietor *India Today*, Mr. Khushwant Singh, Mr. Kuldip Nayar, Ms Amita Malik, Mr. Gour Kishore Ghose, veteran journalist from Calcutta and winner of Magsaysay award, Mr. S. Nihal Singh, former editor of *The Indian Post* and *The Statesman.*

Mr. Ramkrishana Hegde and Mr. Biju Patnaik, also put in an appearance to express solidarity with the journalists.

With the exception of the English daily, *The National Herald* and its Urdu counterpart *Qaumi Awaj* all newspapers and news agencies observed a day's token strike on September 6 as part of the protest at the proposed Defamation Bill. On September 11, seven thousand lawyers practicing in various courts in Delhi, except the Supreme Court abstained from work against the Defamation Bill.

While expressing their solidarity with the agitated journalists, lawyers also warned the government against undue delay in withdrawing, what they said, the draconian Bill which was said to be the worst statutory aggression and onslaught on the freedom of speech and expression.

In pursuit of their struggle against the Defamation Bill, newsmen on September 7 walked out of a Press Conference being addressed by Union Minister for Information and Broadcasting and Parliamentary Affairs H.K.L. Bhagat.

Bhagat's plea that the government was prepared to reconsider all aspects of the Bill could not satisfy the journalists who maintained that they could not offer any cooperation on the issue with the sword of Damocles hanging over their heads.

On September 8, the entire Pune Press and the correspondents of Bombay newspapers boycotted the felicitation of Congress Secretary and barrister V. N. Gadgil. The latter was to be felicitated by Maharashtra Chief Minister Sharad Pawar on his first visit to the city after becoming Congress (I) General Secretary.

To meet out this threat from the journalists, the government worked out a strategy. Meetings were arranged with senior journalists known to be pro-Rajiv, but most of these journalists advised the government against the enactment of the Bill. Rajiv's media managers then tried to create rift among journalists by inviting some of them on the television.

Later, Bhagat wrote personal letters to journalists, inviting them for a dialogue with a 7-member committee constituted by the Prime Minister. But to the government's surprise, all the organisations, except three which are pronouncedly pro-Congress-I rejected the invitation.

Faced with this situation, Prime Minister Rajiv Gandhi and his advisers desperately tried to evolve a face-saving formula.

Shortly after his return from Punjab on September 21, 1988, Rajiv Gandhi summoned the ministerial group for a discussion at his residence. The meeting lasted for over three hours and Rajiv decided to withdraw the Bill.

On September 22, 1988, Rajiv Gandhi announced the Defamation Bill's withdrawal with the following statement.

The Defamation Bill, 1988 was brought forward to protect the individual from defamatory speeches, writings and actions and to provide adequate and timely redress to the aggrieved. The Bill seeks to codify the existing law on the subject and to take it forward in some areas.

Defamation as defined in the Bill is not an issue between government and the Press but an issue between individual and individual, between a person aggrieved and a person accused. The Bill attempts to reconcile the rights of an individual with the right to freedom of expression of another.

A free Press is an integral part of the inner strength and dynamism of our democracy. Without a free Press, there can be no democracy. The imperishable values of our freedom struggle have gone into the making of the Press in India. We uphold this legacy. We shall continue to do so. Our commitment to this freedom of the Press is total. We have no intention of curbing in any way, the freedom of the Press.

The freedom and rights of the individual are equally sacred. It is this that makes the issue of defamation a serious issue.

The bill seeks to resolve the issue in accordance with the basic principles of our Constitution and the laws. It has, however, aroused misapprehensions and misgivings. The Press and section of the public have expressed their concern.

We are alive to these concerns. We draw inspiration from Mahatma Gandhi, Jawaharlal Nehru and Indira Gandhi, who always responded to democratic expression of opinion. We, therefore, offered an unconditional dialogue on the subject. Some organisations and individuals have responded to this offer.

We feel, however, that there should be wider and fuller national debate in keeping with our heritage and traditions.

The issue of defamation remains. It is our earnest hope that the concerned citizens, jurists and media will participate in the national debate on the issue of defamation. In course of time, government may, if necessary, make suitable forum to carry forward the dialogue in a spirit of understanding and cooperation. A solution based on national consensus will strengthen the institutions of our public.

The Central Government has made every effort to manage the Press after managing the other two organs of the government successfully—the Parliament and the judiciary. The Press by and large in India is pro-establishment. Even then the government is not satisfied and wants to choke a few discordant voices in the Press. The passage of this Bill would have scared the Press to do whatever little investigative reporting they are doing. In fact, there was no need to enact such laws if the Press Council in India is adequate to deal with defamation cases.

It is worthwhile examining the laws pertaining to the freedom of the Press and the right to privacy.

The mechanisms that have been evolved in truly democratic countries for achieving the above objectives are generally twofold. One is to make defamation a crime punishable with imprisonment or fine or both. The other is an action in the courts of law for the Tort of defamation in which damages can be awarded.

It is well known that in countries that have followed the civil law system, like France, have favoured the system of subjecting the defendant or respondent to penal punishment.

In those countries where the Anglo-Saxon system of jurisprudence prevails, like the United Kingdom, the USA, Australia and India, there are provisions for imposing penal punishment and/or claiming damages in civil courts.

Although criminal action can be taken in Britain, this is done in very few cases. In the UK there was some thinking whether the law of criminal libel should be drastically reformed and whether a new statutory offence of criminal defamation should replace the old offence.

It was proposed that the offence should be triable only on indictment and the penalty should not exceed two years imprisonment or a fine or both.

In fact, the British Law Commission had made it clear in its report that the offence which it had in mind is the character assassination type. When the Faulk Committee in England considered defamation in 1971, the British Press Council was of the view that criminal libel would have no relevance so far as the Press was concerned.

In the US one hardly comes across any instances where penal punishment has been awarded in defamation cases. But in civil actions the damages that are granted are so heavy that every newspaper has to think twice before publishing a libellous article.

Any student of the law of defamation has to understand its basic object and aim. The question immediately arises as to when interference with an individual liberty can be allowed.

The answer given is that such interference would be permissible when the individual actions cause harm to other members of the society. What kind of harm should the law then punish. As defamation deals with harm, it is necessary for the person who has published a defamation matter to justify the publication by invoking the fundamental right of freedom of expression which would include freedom of the Press as guaranteed by Article 19 (a) of our Constitution.

This raised the point that if something has been done for public good or in public interest or its truthfulness established, the harm to reputation of the person defamed should not attract any such consequences as may be penal or may involve payment of damages.

These as regarded as some of the basis of the defamation laws.

In the US, the decision of the US Supreme Court in *The New York Times*—Sullivan case (1964) has brought about revolutionary changes, especially in cases of action against public officials. In Sullivan case, the court ruled that even erroneous statements about public officials were protected by the constitutional mandate unless a libellous statement had been published with full knowledge of falsity or reckless disregard or its truthfulness.

In Australia, the position seems to be similar to that in the US where if one is wise one would make sure that all assets are in somebody else's name. For if one wants to discuss anything which is even slightly controversial, however small one is, one will be sued for defamation and one will be out of business or bankrupt within months.

Indeed it would not be wrong to say that criminal libel is becoming outmoded in defamation laws even in those developed countries where freedom and privacy of the individual are zealously guarded and highly prized rights.

In most of the countries the right of an individual to privacy has been recognised and it has close connection with defamation. Although privacy has been defined in the US, the best definition appears to be the one given by Thomas Colley. Privacy has not been recognised as a Tort either in India or Britain.

The Second Press Commission in India did not recommend any legislation on the subject. The Commission considered that Section 13 (l) (c) of the Press Council Act, 1978 should be amended by adding the words 'including respect for privacy.'

In our country, any law of defamation has in the first place to pass the test of constitutionality. Article 19 (1) of the Constitution confers on every citizen the fundamental right to freedom of speech and expression.

The Supreme Court has left no one in doubt that freedom of the Press is included in the above provision. The ambit and the scope of the provision is no less wide than what has been conferred by the First amendment to the American Constitution.

Clause 2 of Article 19 indicates the parameters of the right guaranteed under clause (1). Thus, existing or future laws can be made imposing reasonable restrictions on the exercise of the right in the interest set in clause (2) which includes defamation.

One of the most important steps taken for the purpose of preserving the freedom of the Press and of maintaining and improving the standards of newspapers and news agencies was the establishment of the Press Council in 1966 by an Act of Parliament. The Act was repealed in 1976 and there was no Press Council in existence till the end of March 1979.

Our Press Council being a statutory body derives its powers from an Act of Parliament. It has 28 members and a chairman. It is completely independent and the manner in which its chairman and members are nominated is such that no executive or outside interference is possible.

## Global Norms

In France the law relating to privacy has been developed largely through interpretation of Article 1382 of the Civil Code of 1859 by the courts on case-by-case basis. There was a spurt in this process during the fifth and sixth decades of the twentieth century as a response to the increasing invasions of personal privacy by the Press. The principles thus evolved, by courts, were embodied in the Law of July 17, 1970. Article 9 of this codified law provides that 'each person has the right to have his privacy respected'.

The law of 1970 does not provide a general definition of 'privacy'. This has been left to be spelled out by the courts. In general, family, personal, and sexual matters are all covered by the right of privacy. 'Public interest', 'good faith', and 'truth' do not in themselves, furnish a good defence in an action for violation of privacy.

In Germany, the Penal Code punishes, as criminal offences, certain grosser invasions of privacy, namely:

(a) trespassing into another person's home, and in certain other private places;
(b) recording private conversation without permission;
(c) eavesdropping using bugging devices;
(d) obtaining certain private information (such as medical records) without permission, and
(e) obtaining any private information which is stored in a computer.

To the above, there are certain exceptions, e.g., pictures within the scope of contemporary history; pictures of public processions, and pictures created for genuinely artistic purposes.

German Civil Courts have, through an interpretation of the Constitution, devised the concept of the 'right of human personality'. Pursuant to this concept, the courts provide a civil remedy in actions for defamation and invasion of privacy in a number of situations, which include:

(i) Where a newspaper publishes inaccurate personal infirmation about a person and then refuses to correct it;
(ii) Where one person makes use of another's picture without his consent in order to advertise the products; and

(iii) Where someone publishes the past misdeeds of an ex-offender, where it is not in the public interest to do so.

Like Denmark, in the Netherlands, apart from defamation, a number of invasions of privacy are criminal offences. These include: trespass into another person's home, to eavesdrop on private conversations, and to take photographs of people on private property, without their consent; publication of such photographs is also an offence.

Several provinces of the Canadian Federation have enacted torts of privacy. The British Columbia Privacy Act has much in common with the laws on the subject enacted by the other Provinces. This Act of 1979 provides that it is a tort, actionable without proof of damage, for a person wilfully and without claim of right, to violate the privacy of another.

Eavesdropping and surveillance are specifically but not exclusively, cited as means by which privacy may be violated. However, it is not a violation of privacy to publish material that is of public interest or (in) fair comment on a matter of 'public interest'. Unauthorised use of a person's name or portrait is also a tort under the Act.

A similar approach to the subject of privacy has been adopted by the Saskatchewan Privacy Act, 1979.

The Canadian Federal legislation on privacy (relating to information about individuals, held by public bodies) provides by contrast an exhaustive definition comprising 18 paragraphs, of private information. It also includes a general public interest provision to cover matters falling outside the specific criteria. This definition has been widely criticised as too long and confusing.

Professors Philip Meyer and Ruth Walden of the University of North Carolina, Chapel Hill, have conducted research in ethics of journalism. They find that the laws governing the Press in United States of America are frequently confusing and subjective, particularly in the area of privacy law. Walden notes that with a few minor exceptions, there is no federal law governing invasions of privacy by the media. Essentially, every state has its own law. There are 50 different privacy laws as they relate to the media. Nevertheless, since Warren and Brandeis article of 1890, intrusion upon an individual privacy has gradually come to be recognised as a tort throughout most of the United States, even though its definition and application vary from state to state.

According to experts, the tort appears to cover the following four kinds of invasion of privacy, though they are considered distinct rights having little in common:

(a) intrusion into an individual's physical solitude;

(b) publication of private matter violating the ordinary decencies;

(c) putting someone in false light; and

(d) appropriation of an individual's name or likeness (normally for commercial purposes).

It is proposed to elaborate these categories a little.

***Intrusion :*** Intrusion upon the solitude and private life of an individual is prohibited as an actionable wrong. Unauthorised wiretapping, telephone tapping, room bugging, snooping, making illegal searches and breaking into private records of an individual and like acts, without the consent of the individual concerned, are considered torts falling in this category.

This legal wrong is committed as soon as the intrusion takes place whether or not the private facts gathered are published. Intruders are liable for this tort regardless of what use is made of the purloined material. This was so held by a California Court in Dietemann Vs Time-Life Magazine Inc, (1971).

However, the whole area of the law relating to intrusion upon privacy has not yet come out of the grey zone. Some kinds of intrusions through new sophisticated devices are hard to define. For committing this tort, it is not necessary for the intruder to enter upon private property. He may commit intrusion from outside, remaining at a distance, with the use of some snooper aids as telephoto lens, hidden microphones etc.

'While the public interest', noted Don R. Pember, 'Is the key to defending most privacy suits, it has very little to do with intrusion'. It seems that in U.S.A. public interest defence, normally, does not avail against intrusion.

***Publication of Private Information :*** This category has been defined as 'the disclosure of private, embarrassing, non-newsworthy facts about an individual'.

This may take the form of deceptive or illegal means of obtaining information such as trespassing or unauthorised use of cameras. 'Gossip substances of private conversation, and details of private tragedy or illness', particularly when their publication is repugnant to good taste and sense, are legal wrongs of this category. Truthfulness of the information published is no defence to a suit when this tort constitutes the cause of action.

An example of lapses in ethical standards, akin to this type of infringement of personal privacy, is furnished by the publication of a story in *The New York Times.* In the second week of April, 1991, in which not only the alleged Palm Beach rape victim, who has accused a member of the Kennedy family of the criminal act, was blamed, but also the details of the woman's past, including her alleged 'wild break' in high school, her mother's divorce, and her 17 tickets for speeding and careless driving, were given.

*The New York Times* further reported, 'She gave birth to a daughter by a local man she did not marry. In 1989 she had a brief affair with the son of a once prosperous family He was the father of the child, friends say. . . .' Another acquaintance, Nathaniel Read said: 'She liked to drink and have fun with the never-do-wells in cafe society.'

The publication of this story is reported to have brought *The New York Times* into the centre of an embarrassing public debate of its unusual foray into tabloid journalism. The editors of the paper had to face sharp protest from members of its own staff. One woman employee said that 'we don't understand why you have got *New York Times* reports peeping in windows'. Another staffer said the paper had 'crucified' the woman.

*The Times* editor also faced criticism over the publication on the front page of the newspaper recently, on Kitty Kelley's biography of Nancy Reagan, which contained unsavoury and fallacious allegations against the former First Lady. The Executive Editor of *The New York Times* was reported to have admitted that Kelley piece was a 'mistake' and that 'the story did not live up to our standards'.

The primary defence to an action for this kind of invasion of privacy, is that the published material is newsworthy, that is to say, it is of wide public or general interest. A Newsworthy formula has been devised by American Courts for this purpose. According to this formula, the nature of the story, the status of the subjects, the intimacy of the revelations, and the degree of embarrassment to the plaintiff are all weighed against each other. Publication of information about public officials or public figures, such as Ministers, legislators, entertainers, labour leaders, sport personalities, even "some editors, journalists and broadcasters, normally qualify as newsworthy. But publication of the same kind of information about private persons who are not public figures might not so qualify.

The kind of invasion of privacy, according to some scholars, is an outgrowth of category (d) Appropriation. For constituting a tort under this category, it is not necessary that the published material should be defamatory or has been presented in a derogatory manner.

It is sufficient if the representation of the published material gives a false impression, even though the impression is not unfavourable, of the plantiff. Photographs, rather than stories are the common source of 'false light' actions in tort. Truth of the report is a valid defence to such an action. The defendant can also use the First Amendment as a defence and maintain that the plantiff has failed to prove that the material /story was published by the defendant with actual malice knowing it to be false, or in publishing it the defendant exhibited reckless disregard for the truth of the story.

This includes the unauthorised use of individual's name or likeness for trade or advertising purposes. Appropriation is the least ambiguous and the oldest of these four kinds of torts, stated above. The law relating to all the above categories of invasion of privacy, in the USA, is being still developed by their Supreme Court through its adjudications in a manner which seeks to strike a proper balance between the right to freedom of speech and freedom of the Press on the one hand, and the right to individual privacy, on the other. The overall position in USA has been summed up by Calcutt Committee (UK), thus:

> 'Generally speaking, the Press is free to publish almost any true material about public figures on the basis that virtually all human activity reveals the character of the person concerned. In some states, however, the publication of truthful but embarrassing information about individuals who are not public figures, can give rise to a cause of action. The Supreme Court has yet to rule on the constitutionality of this. Where the material published is untrue, some states provide redress on the grounds of false light. Cases on such grounds have been upheld by the Supreme Court.'

Although the English Common Law does not recognise the invasion of privacy as a tort in all cases in which the courts in USA do, yet the development of the law in USA had its impact on British scholars and jurists. Salmond in his Law of Torts, 15th Edition, adopted the view of Dean Prosser, one of the outstanding exponents of this concept. Salmond identifies four distinct kinds of torts recognised by American Courts.

No general right of privacy has been recognised under Common Law of the United Kingdom. However, as invasions of privacy by the media, particularly by the tabloid Press, increased, complaints against these intrusive forays were voiced by several sections of the British public. At the advent of the 7th decade of the Century, Younger Committee on Privacy was set up to study the problem and suggest remedial measures. In its Report rendered in July 1972, the committee recommended, by a majority, against statutory right of privacy for the reason that there was before it no compelling evidence, of a substantial wrong to be tackled.

It noted that since in complaints of invasion of privacy there may be a conflict of interest between the need of the public to be informed and the need to respect the individual's privacy, the balancing of these interests in each case should be left to the judgement of the Press Council. It recommended that the Council should insist that its adjudications be published with equal prominence to the original item.

It further recommended that the Council should explore the possibility of codifying its adjudications on privacy to give readier guidance to busy practising journalists and to the interested public and to keep the codification up-to-date. Consequent upon this, the Council began codifying its general adjudications but remained opposed to the publication of a formal code of practice.

In 1976, U.K. Press Council issued the following declaration of principles on privacy, setting out the rules for guidance of editors in deciding when to publish stories about people's private lives:

(i) The publication of information about the private lives or concerns of individuals without their consent is only acceptable if there is a legitimate public interest overriding the right of privacy.

(ii) It is the responsibility of editors to ensure that inquiries into matters affecting the private life or concern of individuals are only undertaken when in the editor's opinion at the time a legitimate public interest in such matters may rise. The right to privacy is, however, not involved if the individuals concerned have freely and clearly consented to the pursuit of inquiries and publications.

(iii) The public interest relied on as the justification for publication or inquiries which conflict with a claim to privacy must be a legitimate and proper public interest and not only a prurient or morbid curiosity. 'Of interest to the public' is not synonymous with 'in the public interest'. It should be recognised that entry into public life does not disqualify an individual from his right to privacy about his private affairs, save when the circumstances relating to the private life of an individual occupying a particular public position may be likely to affect the performance of his duties or public confidence in him or his office.

(iv) Invasion of privacy by deception, eavesdropping or technological methods which are not in themselves unlawful can, however, only be justified when it is in pursuit of infirmation which ought to be published in the public interest and there is no other reasonably practicable method of obtaining or confirming it.

(v) The Council expects the obtaining of news or pictures to be carried out with sympathy and discretion. Reporters and photographers should do nothing to cause harm or humiliation to bereaved or distressed people unless it is clear that the publication of the news or pictures will serve a legitimate public interest and there is no other reasonably practicable means of obtaining the material.

Editors are responsible for the actions of those employed by their newspapers and have a duty to ensure that all concerned are aware of the importance of respecting the legitimate claims to personal privacy.

The Third Royal Commission on the Press headed by Lord McGregor, in its report of July 1977, adopted an approach similar to that of the Younger Committee. In the Commission's view also, legislation was not necessary because the Press Council could be its appropriate substitute. It, however, recommended that the Press Council should formulate a comprehensive code of conduct for the Press.

During 1988 and 1989 there occurred a number of glaring invasions of personal privacy by a section of the 'British Press, particularly the tabloid Press. As a result, the Press came under severe criticism for intruding upon accident victims and other patients in hospitals, for using stolen private photographs or correspondence and for publishing scurrilous details of individuals' private lives. Matters reached a climax when a million pound out-of-court libel settlement was made following stories in *The Sun* about Eltson John's private life.

In the course of discussions in the 1988-89 session of Parliament, on two private Members' Bills, one introduced by John Brown, MP, and the other by Tony Worthington, MP, on protection of Privacy and Right of Reply, respectively a number of cases of such unethical practices indulged in by the Press were cited.

This led to the appointment by the government of the Committee under the Chairmanship of Sir David Calcutt to consider what measures (whether legislative or otherwise) are needed to give further protection to individual privacy from the activities of the Press and improve recourse against the Press for the individual citizen, taking account of existing remedies, including the law of defamation and breach of confidence, and to make recommendations.

Following the appointment of the Calcutt Committee, there were two major developments. In November 1989 Newspaper Publishers Association, formulated and declared a code of practice. Thereafter, on March 13, 1990 the Press Council in U.K. adopted a revised code after discussion with the interested parties, including Newspaper Publishers Association (NPA).

Para 5 directs Newspapers and journalists serving them to use 'straightforward means to obtain information or pictures. The use of subterfuge can be justified only to obtain material which ought to be published in the public interest and could not be obtained by other means.'

As per para 7, newspapers and journalists serving them were required to avoid intrusion into personal grief and to carry out inquiries with sympathy and discretion.

Para 10 provides that save in exceptional circumstances newspapers should not, even where the law permits it, identify children under the age of 16 as victims, witnesses or defendants involved in cases concerning sexual offences.

Para 11 forbids newspapers to identify victims of rape, or publish material likely to contribute to such identification.

Para 12 provides that newspapers should refrain from publishing pictures which needlessly exacerbate grief or cause distress.

Para 15 directs journalists making inquiries at hospitals or similar institutions, to identify themselves to a responsible official before entering except in very rare cases where information which ought to be disclosed could not otherwise be obtained.

*Committee's Role* : The Calcutt Committee accepted that there is little possibility of producing a precise or exhaustive definition of privacy or for that matter public interest. It felt that working definition of privacy, however, is nevertheless needed as a yardstick against which to measure complaints and solutions. It, therefore, adopted the following working definition:

> Privacy could be regarded as the antithesis of what is public hence everything concerning an

> individual's home, family, religion, health, sexuality, personal legal and personal financial affairs. The formulation 'the right to be let alone' is too simplistic. There is a mismatch between what an individual might regard as private and what might be regarded as such by his neighbours, including the Press....
>
> ...our formulation is the right of individual to be protected against intrusion into his personal life or affairs, or those of his family, by direct physical means or by publication of information.

The Committee emphasised that individual privacy is not to be considered in isolation. It must be weighed alongside freedom of speech and expression. In balancing these two factors, the Committee preferred to be guided in its approach by what the European Court of Human Rights, when interpreting Article 10 of the Convention, in its judgement in *The Sunday Times* vs United Kingdom (1979-80) 2 EHRR 245: (the Thalidomide case) emphasised that it was faced not with a choice between two conflicting principles but with a principle of freedom of expression that is subject to a number of exceptions which must be narrowly interpreted.

'Thus, the Committee professedly started from a position that freedom of expression is preeminent. Certain exceptions protecting individual privacy may then prove to be necessary.

The Committee conceded that it is not possible to devise a simple criterion of what constitutes a justifiable intrusion into an individual's privacy, it may have to be recognised that not all people are entitled to expect the same degree of privacy. A distinction may have to be drawn between what is justified in respect of public figures and what is justified for other people. Nevertheless, a public figure should not be required to surrender his right to privacy over every aspect of his life when he takes up public office or pursues a career which brings him into the public eye.

The committee emphasised that 'Public interest' in bald terms is not helpful in determining whether an intrusion is or is not justified.

In general terms, the Committee accepted that any conduct which impinges upon the public, might reasonably be made public. An individual who publicly claims to practice certain special or religious principle or adopts a position of moral leadership, can reasonably be subject to greater public scrutiny than his fellow citizens.

The committee opined that (generally) the revelation about the private life of a public figure are justified only:

(a) to protect the health or safety of the public, or

(b) to expose crime or seriously antisocial conduct, or

(c) in his behaviour if his private life adversely affects his public duties or is so hypocritical that the public is likely to be seriously misled.

The Committee concluded that just as it is impossible to define privacy other than in terms of a series of general values, so what constitutes an unwarranted intrusion into an individual's privacy can only be set out in terms relative to that person's status and conduct in the context of what is socially acceptable at the time. It is inevitable that decisions will be based on a series of value judgements. 'We consider', said the Committee, 'that every code of practice likely to be of practical use in newspaper offices must take account of these complexities.'

A number of witnesses urged that the Calcutt Committee to recommend the introduction of a statutory tort of infringement of privacy. There was also a suggestion that the civil law might be evolved in relation to privacy by courts on case-by-case basis. In this context, the Committee observed:

> 'A Common Law right to privacy could possibly develop in Scotland, where there is more general concept of Culpa (wrongful behaviour) compared

> with the more narrowly-drawn English torts. But in its judgement on March 16, 1990 in Keyer Robertson and Sport Newspapers Ltd., the Court of Appeal clearly ruled out the development of such a tort in English Law. Any remedy of this kind would now have to be provided by Statute.' The Committee then quoted from the judgement of Glide-well and Legatt L. JJ. in the said case where this point was raised.

After examining the five Bills introduced on this topic from time during the period 1961 to 1989, as also the draft Bill produced by Justice and the Natural Council for Civil Liberties and all other material and suggestions before them, the Committee concluded:

> '... an overwhelming case for introducing a statutory tort of infringement of privacy has not so far been made out and that the better solution lies with the measures set out elsewhere in this report. We, therefore, recommend that such a tort should not presently be introduced.'

The Committee made it clear that they were making their recommendation on the assumption that the improved scheme for self-regulation of the Press recommended by them in Chapter 15 of their report, will be made to work.

The Committee recommended: 'The Press should be given one final chance to prove that voluntary self-regulation can be made to work. However, we do not consider that the Press Council even if reformed as proposed in its internal review, should be kept as part of the system. We, therefore, recommend that the Press Council should be disbanded and replaced by a new body, specifically charged with adjudicating on complaints of Press malpractice. This body must be seen to be authoritative, independent and impartial. It must also have jurisdiction over the Press as a whole, must be adequately funded and must provide a means of seeking to prevent publication of intrusive material. We consider it particularly to emphasise the break from the past. The new body should, therefore, be called the Press Complaints Commission.' (Hereafter called PCC.)

It is further recommended by the Committee that the PCC should publish, monitor and implement a comprehensive code of practice for the guidance of both the Press and public. The PCC should operate a hot line for complaints on a 24-hour basis. The PCC adjudications should in certain cases, include a recommendation that an apology be given to the complainant. The precise form of the apology, including whether it should be given publicly or privately, could also be prescribed.

The PCC should have an independent Chairman and not more than 12 members, with smaller subcommittees adjudicating on complaints under delegated powers. Appointments to the PCC should be made by an Appointment Commission with explicit freedom to appoint whoever it considers best qualified. The Appointments Commission itself should be independently appointed, possibly by the Lord Chancellor.

Complaints Committee should have delegated power to release adjudications subject to a right of appeal for either party to the full Press Complaints Commission before publication.

The PCC should not operate a waiver of legal rights. If the industry wishes to maintain a system of non-statutory self-regulation, it must demonstrate its commitment in particular by providing the necessary money for setting up and maintaining the PCC.

The Calcutt Committee has recommended that the following acts should be criminal offences in England and Wales:

(a) Entering private property without the consent of the law ful occupant, with intent to obtain personal information with a view to its publication;

(b) placing a surveillance device on private property without the consent of the lawful occupant, with intent to obtain personal information with a view to its publication; and

(c) taking a photograph or recording the voice of an individual who is on private property, without his consent, with a view to its publication and with intent that the individual shall be identifiable.

The Committee has further recommended that it should be a defence to any of these proposed offences that the act was done.

(i) for the purpose of preventing, detecting or exposing the commission of any crime, or other seriously antisocial conduct; or

(ii) for the protection of public health or safety, or

(iii) under any lawful authority.

The Committee further suggested that the individual having a sufficient interest should be able to apply for an injunction against the publication of any of these criminal offences or, if the material has already been published, for damages or an account of profits. It also recommended that further considerations should be given to the extent to which the law in Scotland needs to be extended to cover the proposed offences and civil remedy and how this might best be done.

The other important recommendations made by the Committee, are as follows:

*Legal Restrictions on Press Reporting*

(a) The statutory prohibition on identifying rape victims in England and Wales should be extended to cover the victims of the sexual assaults (such as procurement of intercourse with a woman by threats, or by false pretences or by administering drugs, intercourse with girls under 16 or with mental defects, incest, buggery, indecent assault on female or male etc.).

(b) In any criminal proceedings in England and Wales,the court should have the power to make an order prohibiting the publication of the name and address of any person against whom the offence is alleged- to have been committed, or of any other matters likely to lead to his or her identification. This should only be exercised if the court believes that it is necessary to protect the mental or physical health, personal security of the home of the victim.

(c) After consulting the Press and the broadcasting authorities, Press Complaints Commission should is sueearly guidance on jigsaw identification.

***Right of Reply***

(d) A statutory right of reply should not be introduced.

***Tort of Infringemen t of Privacy***

(e) A tort of infringement of privacy should not be introduced.

***Statutory Complaints Procedure***

(f) If the Press fails to demonstrate that non-statutory self-regulation can be made to work effectively, a statutory system for handling complaints should be introduced.

(g) If maverick publications persistently decline to respect the authority of the Press Complaints Commission, the Commission should be placed on a statutory footing. It should be given sufficient statutory powers to enable it to require any newspaper, periodical or magazine to respond to its enquiries about complaints and to publish its adjudications as directed. It should be able to recommend the payment of compensation.

(h) The Government should set the budget for any statutory Press Complaints Commission and provide the money which it should then reclaim from the industry. The industry should set up a funding body which would apportion the cost between and collect the money from, various industrial bodies or individual publications.

***Press Complaints Tribunal***

(i) Should the Press fail to set up and support the Press Complaints Commission or should it at any time become clear that the reformed non-statutory mechanism is failing to perform adequately, this should be replaced by a statutory tribunal with statutory powers and implementing a statutory code of practice.

(j) There should be two separate triggers for the replacement of the Press Complaints Commission by a Press Complaints Tribunal.

(k) A Press Complaints Tribunal should perform two distinct functions. First, it should attempt conciliation and investigate complaints. Second, where necessary, it should resolve disputes by ruling whether there had been a breach of the code of practice. This should be reflected in its structure and procedures.

(1) The Press Complaints Tribunal should be able to award compensation. Unless the complainant can show financial loss, the amount of compensation should be limited by statute. This limit should be periodically reviewed.

(m) In privacy cases, the Press Complaints Tribunal should be able to restrain publication of material in breach of the code of practice by means of injunctions. No injunction should be granted if the publisher could show that he had a good arguable defence.

(n) The Tribunal Chairman should be a judge or senior lawyer appointed by the Lord Chancellor. He should sit with two accessors drawn from a panel appointed by the Home Secretary.

The Calcutt Committee has also proposed a code of Practice for the Press. Since infringement of privacy cannot be considered in isolation from other norms of ethics.

*An Assessment :* Some aspects of the Calcutt report have been the subject of worldwide criticism. The chief target of criticism is that part of its recommendations as a result of which the new body i.e., The Press Complaints Commission which has replaced the erstwhile British Press Council has not been entrusted with the responsibility to preserve the freedom of the Press. This recommendation rests on the specious argument that defending the freedom of the Press and adjudicating on complaints are distinct functions which sit uneasily together, there being an inherent conflict between the two.

Mr. Blom Cooper, Chairman of the erstwhile Press Council, maintained that the twin functions are not merely compatible but also interlocked. He submitted that in this respect the report of the Calcutt Committee was fundamentally flawed. In support of the view that these twin functions were inextricably linked with each other, Mr. Blom Cooper referred to a passage in a speech delivered by Lord Devlin, the first independent Chairman of the British Press Council, that to censure effectively misconduct by the Press, it is essential that the Council seeks to preserve the established freedom of British Press and work as to maintain its character in accordance with the highest professional standards.

At the international Conference held in Stockholm on 11-15 June, 1991 on the occasion of the 75th anniversary of their Press Council, delegates from several countries assailed this recommendation of the Calcutt Report and consequent debarment of the new Press Complaints Commission from entertaining complaints of infringement of Press freedom. Eminent among those critics included, Mr. Olle Stenholm, former Chairman of the Swedish Newspaper Publishers Association, Mr. Kenneth Morgan, Director of the British Press Complaints Commission and Professor David Flint, Chairman of the Press Council of Australia.

All of them were firmly of the view that preserving Press freedom and maintaining Press standards, were inseparable as two sides of the same coin. Professor David Flint described the British experiment in setting up the Press Complaints Commission as an ill advised attempt to divorce Press freedom from Press responsibility.

Since Mr. Kenneth Morgan was the best informed person about these developments in UK it will be worthwhile to refer to some of the points made by him in his speech.

In his opinion, the main contributory cause of the death of the British Press Council, was 'that characteristically English disease, obsession with privacy and obsession with privacy in two paradoxical senses'.

Explaining the background of this development, Mr. Morgan said '...the British have no law at all protecting personal privacy. In, say the last twenty years, there has been recurrent concern among politicians, but among others too, about whether she would have such laws, particularly to curb intrusion into people's privacy by the Press, or rather part of the Press, bent on gratifying other peoples' curiosity. The developing chorus of criticism at newspapers during that time has not been directed at all newspapers though its effect may be felt by all of them....

'It is a paradox that while condemning newspapers' focus on private lives, the public rushes out in millions to buy these very newspapers. The argument of proprietors and editors—and it has some force—has been that the sales figures demonstrate that they have been giving readers what they want, whatever politicians, pundits and moralists may say they ought to have. Wearing its Press freedom hat, the Press Council shared the Publishers' antagonism towards new legislation which would be likely to inhibit proper investigation and inquiry by the Press as well as curbing the improper intrusion into private lives at which it is aimed.

Mr. Morgan further reported: 'The Council's view like that of many similar bodies elsewhere, was that while new restrictive laws were undesirable, individuals had a moral right to privacy about their private lives and affairs which editors ought to recognise. The right extended not only to wholly private citizens but also to the people in public life unless what they were doing in private bore directly on their ability or fitness for their public role.

Mr. Morgan lamented that while the Calcutt Committee's report adopted many of the Press Council's own proposals, it suggested the Council's abolition and replacement by the Press Complaints Commission having no role as the Press Council had in defending the freedom of Press. The lopsided suggestion by the Calcutt Committee in Mr. Morgan's view 'was the most significant central flaw in a report which contained many valuable suggestions'.

Mr. Morgan criticised the Calcutt proposal to create the new criminal offences of which in practice only journalists could be guilty.

He further disclosed that the new body, PCC has a code of practice to enforce but not one of its own making. The code, 16 points running from accuracy through privacy and harassment to protection of confidential sources was devised for the newspaper and magazine industry by a Committee of editors led by Miss Patricia Champan, editor of *News of the World*. Commenting on this code, Mr. Morgan said: 'It cannot be denied that a code of this type presents problems. It is to be applied in the spirit not merely in the letter but it is taken to be comprehensive and it thus restricts criticism of conduct which was not thought of by the authors of the code. We cannot all hope to be as farsighted as the Almighty at Sinai when trying to envisage possible human frailty and sin or editorial responsibility. The code will require extension or its restriction of what complaints may be made will have to be relaxed as the years go by.'

Incidentally, these comments are in line with the view consistently taken by successive Press Councils of India, that it is neither necessary nor feasible to formulate a rigid exhaustive code of conduct for journalists. In Press Council of India's view, any attempt at framing a code of this kind would result in a mere enunciation of a few basic principles only in general terms which would be of little help in applying them to individual cases: Because of their elusive, variable nature, these moral principles cannot be reduced into rigid formulas. Ethics being dynamic principles, abhor Procrustean approach.

Questioned as to whether the new Press Complaints Commission on probation was working more effectively than the erstwhile Press Council in ensuring high professional standards of newspapers on self-explanatory basis, Mr. Morgan felt that it would be difficult to devise a more severe test of the new system in Britain than that this commission faced in its first month. He illustrated this point by referring to the complaint of Ms Clare Short, MP, before the PCC, alleging infringement of her right of privacy by the *News of the World*.

The complaint 'combined a minefield of issues which are, some of them both in public interest, of interest to the public and crucial to the operation of a system of self-regulation of the Press running alongside the law'. Facets of that single case included:

The question arose whether the private life of a politician, and a leading woman politician at that, was a legitimate subject for newspaper inquiry and report?

The suggestion in the newspaper report was that nearly twenty years ago she had a relationship with a man with a serious criminal record who was eventually shot dead in the street in what may have been a gangland killing. Did the newspaper, as she asked, 'to crawl over' her private life of long ago, invade the privacy of her former husband, a former psychiatric patient, and intrude on the privacy of her present husband, himself a former Member of Parliament and a seriously sick man? Was what emerged an information which ought to be disclosed in the public interest or no more than information which might interest the public?

Should newspapers publish pornographic or near nude pinup pictures? Was this newspaper pursuing Ms Short as part of a vendetta because she had led a campaign to ban by law the publication of page-3 type pictures, an art form made famous by its sister newspaper? Part of Ms Short's complaint was the way the newspaper reported a speech she made about it and newspaper ethics in Parliament. Part of its case was that she misused her privilege in Parliament to attack the paper and its reporter. She complained of a breach of Parliamentary privilege.

Was the *News of the World's* source for some of its material about Ms Short's private life, information from disaffected members of the West Midlands Police Serious Crime Squad whose record she had attacked in the House of Commons? She complained about this to the Chief Constable and the Police Complaints Authority.

Could the new Press Complaints Commission be expected to deal with her complaint against the paper when her lawyers were already in correspondence with the paper and a legal action looked imminent? The old Press Council had asked complainants to waive their legal rights. The new Commission was not going to do that. Then the overall question that arose was: Could the self-regulating Commission hope to deal fairly and squarely with all these issues on a complaint that the *News of the World* broke the industry's own code on privacy and accuracy? The editor of the Paper, Miss Chapman, was a member of the Commission and Chairman of the Committee which framed the code.

The Commission dealt with these issues, upheld the complaint and the *News of the World* published it's condemnation fairly and in full, taking up a whole page. 'The new Commission has no more sanctions, no more penalties at its command than the old Council. Its greatest strength has in two factors—commitment and fear. Commitment by newspaper and magazine owners and editors to support it and make it work and fear of the threat by government and opposition of what will befall the Press if the test of the last chance is failed.'

# 2

# Media, as Career

In the modern context, newspapers cannot compete with radio or TV in being first and fast with news. They can, however, serve independently and as supplementary to these media by giving more balanced account of news alongwith backgrounds, better interpretative, investigated and thorough reporting and coverage, wider variety of reading material and shades of opinions in their columns. Magazines deal more with opinion interpretation, incisiveness and colour. Noticed or read by the elite and policy makers, leaders of parties and professions, as also by workers, farmers, students and housewives, they can influence public opinion and more so the policy makers. Today, the press is not merely observing and reporting but asking, pursuing, investigating, doubting, demanding and sometimes even biting.

It is far more vigilant and rancorous about fundamental and civil rights, corruption, economic exploitation and social abuses. Modern newspapers illuminate the mind through their cartoons, illustrations, graphics, features and human interest writings. They highlight or underline particular events by their headlines, leads, cutlines and column boxes. Their searching interviews, columnist writings and editorials furnish better comprehension of complicated events and affairs.

Reader columns in newspapers tie in readers and provide noticeable columns of public grievances. There are also engagement columns, notices, fitting advertisements, etc. for those who need them. Notwithstanding occasional bias and slants in reporting and writing, their concentrated urban approach and obsession with political and sensational news, professionally competent and disciplined dailies and magazines command comparatively better respect, credibility and acceptability than any other media. Even grassroots media, community papers and other small professional or specialised periodicals are dear to readers, though for different reasons. Thus, newspapers today occupy a prestigious position in the galaxy of media with their roles varying from the 4th Estate to the 5th Estate, from an informer to a critic, from a narrator to a commentator, from an investigator to an analyst, from a mentor to a teaser, from a peace preacher to violence or racialism baiter.

In developing countries the press has a special role to play as a social monitor, a constructive critic, the stimulator of debates on public issues and a medium of feedback while balancing the wheel of the Governmental structure. A great social vitaliser and the right arm of liberty, it is also a big enemy of tyrants and an exposer of public corruption. The media is also an interpreter of public events and a professional forum for investigative and interpretative journalism. It acts as a watchdog of a sleeping democracy and a public university for the masses. "A people without reliable newspapers," said Harold Laski, "is sooner or later a people without the basis for freedom."

## Historical Knowledge

In India, Independence constituted a turning point in the history of the Indian Press. It brought to a close the era of journalism as a mission and the media was left free to become a business or an industry. Refashioning the Press was part of the larger enterprise of refashioning society. The partition of the country made the Muslim League-dominated newspapers to quit or lapse. Consequently the Urdu and Bengali press suffered the most. Some of the important Urdu papers from Lahore sought to find a new home in Delhi, Amritsar and Jalandhar. The Anglo-Saxon group of papers lost their punch, homogeneity and *raison d'etre* as a group. Comparing the Indian press then with the contemporary press in the West, there was no national newspaper in India which could play the role of an activist or act as the voice of the nation. There was not a single daily in the country with a circulation of even one lakh. The Times of India printed 94748 copies, the Hindu 69748, the Statesman 65032 and the Hindustan Times 48141 copies.

The circulation of these big papers was in fact a pittance of the circulation of some foreign newspapers of the time: Le Petit journal selling more than a million copies per issue since 1886; in 1900 the daily Mail, London crossed the seven figure mark; in 1979, the Japanese Yomiuri Shimbun sold over 13 million copies per day in a nation of about 110 million. In Britain with a population of about 55 million the Sun sold four million copies a day. The position of Indian language dailies was still lower. *Swadesamitran* with 39509 copies was considered a top-notch language daily; then followed *Sakal* (27262), *Mathrubhumi* (25736) and *Andhra Patrika* (23086). There were no worthwhile dailies in several states and languages. The capacity of newspapers, therefore, to influence public opinion for good or bad was of a limited nature.

Another feature of the Indian press was its concentration. Our of a total of 330 dailies, five owners controlled 29 papers and 31.2 per cent of circulation, while 15 owners controlled 54 newspapers and 50.1 per cent of the circulation. The Telugu daily Andhra Patrika, selling 23086 copies accounted for more than 50 per cent of the circulation in its language area. The diffusion rate which is an index of media growth was 7 per thousand.

The circumstances after the partition were alarmingly unsettling, but despite handicaps the Press in general increasingly turned its attention to the numerous constructive tasks ahead. The news started being presented and interpreted from that angle. Gradually newspapers strove for improved professional techniques and conveniences. Important or big newspapers began to enlist the services of special correspondents and seek more facilities of various kinds. Feature writings got impetus.

Some eminent journalists like M. V. Kamath, Khushwant Singh, Kuldip Nayar, Dom Moraes, Arun Shourie, B. G. Verghese, A. G. Noorani, Shoba Kilachand, Abu Abraham, etc., achieved distinction by writing their sparkling by-lined columns in big English newspapers and magazines. The language newspapers too inducted equally famous personalities. In fact, some newspapers became popular because of these columns.

Most papers also followed the technique of writing behind-the-scene stories based on current affairs. That made newspapers more readable and in turn attracted more readers. Starting from R. K. Karanjia and Baburao Patel and passing on to Khushwant Singh, M J. Akbar, Ashwini Sarin, Neera Chaudhary, Pritish Nandy, Aroon Purie, Chaitanya Kelbag and Vikram Vohra emerged enterprising people journalism, which talked about not only political shenanigans and scoops but also focussed on prominent personalities, their life-styles, fads and habits. Couched in chatty, masala style, these writings made newspapers readable and provocative.

Journalists like Khushwant Singh gave a package of religion, sex and politics including jokes and made-up stories, which made some magazines and newspapers more poplar and caused an increase in their sale. M. J. Akbar's redressing of the Telegraph and Pritish Nandy's revamping of The Illustrated Weekly of India as a feature magazine, are other promotional devices to give a new look to publications and boost their circulation.

Journalistic ranks have expanded and management has shown signs of improvements. The result of these developments was a rise in circulation. As for the various language press, the increase in circulation was a cumulative result of the increase in formal education, rise in purchasing power caused by growing industrialisation, trade and commerce, the information explosion caused by the spurt of new planned programmes, acrimonious politics and class, caste and communal clashes, expansion of communications and transport facilities, the awakening caused by general elections, mass media and advertising expansion. Consequently the circulation of some dailies and weeklies touched record levels.

Quantitatively the press grew enormously both in terms of dailies and periodicals and their circulation (average number of copies sold or distributed free per publishing day). The number of all newspapers-covering any printed or cyclostyled periodical publication like dailies, weeklies and other periodicals-rose from 4769 and 1952 to 19937 in 1982, with a few periods of steep ascents like in 1970, 1979 and 1981 when there was a rise both in terms of number and circulation. Since the sixties the number of dailies quadrupled from a modest 330 to 1334 and periodicals of all categories and periodicity also expanded four times from 4439 to 18603. The circulation of all reporting newspapers depicts the same scale of having rocketed from over 1052000 to 50094000-more than five times, and of dailies from 2.5 millions in 1947 to 14.84 millions in 1982, indicating a six-fold expansion. The spurt in the circulation of periodicals during the last three decades was more pronounced and rose from 8 million to over 35 million-nearly four and a half times. This phenomenal expansion in number and circulation of periodicals is popularly known as the periodical or magazine explosion.

This quantitative stride has some important implications. The first is that now newspapers and periodicals are published by more States and Union Territories than in the sixties. Blanks where no newspaper is published are only Arunachal Pradesh and Lakshadweep and thin areas are Nagaland, Andaman and Nicobar, Goa, Daman and Diu, Mizoram, Pondicherry, Meghalaya, Tripura, Manipur and Himachal Pradesh. So even today, at one end of Press development are heavyweight States and Union Territories like Maharashtra, West Bengal, Uttar Pradesh, Kerala, Delhi and Tamil Nadu where a large number of newspapers with sizable circulation originate; at the other end are blank or thin areas in this respect. Similarly there is a wide variation yet in the circulation of dailies per thousand population (an important criteria to judge whether a place is below or above UNESCO's minimum norm of 100 copies per thousand or population). The range among the States differs from 44.14 copies in Kerala and 24.71 in Maharashtra to 3.62 copies in Nagaland, 2.72 copies in Sikkim and 1.95 copies in Assam. Among Union Territories the scale moves from 116.22 in Chandigarh and 48.36 in Delhi to 0.95 in Mizoram and 0.01 in Dadra and Nagar Haveli.

The second important feature of this growth pattern is a revelation of much faster rate of development in languages than in English. In fact a silent revolution has been taking place in the course of which the two century old dominance of the Press in English has been overcome by the Indian language Press in terms of both number and circulation. And it is not merely that the total circulation of all Hindi Newspapers including dailies has surpassed that of English newspapers, but the number and circulation of language newspapers as a whole has gone up. Also, in areas outside metropolitan cities, language newspapers have generally eclipsed every other English newspaper issued from these areas. The rate of growth of newspapers in Malayalam, Bengali, Kannada, Punjabi and Telugu is conspicuously high. In comparison, however, the share of Tamil, Urdu, Marathi and Gujarati in the total circulation chart has recorded a downward trend.

It is interesting to note that the circulation of some Indian language newspapers has reached spectacular proportions The Anand Bazar Patrika in Bengali with a circulation of 416514 copies retains the pride of place as the largest circulated single daily in 1981 followed by another Bengali daily, Jugantar with a circulation of 314018 copies. Among periodicals Malayala Manorama, a Malayalam weekly from Kottayam, has the largest circulation.

**New Method**

Another notable trend in the Indian press is towards localism. Purely local interest newspapers appear to be gaining ground at the expense of regional or national dailies. Pune affords a significant example. Three local Marathi dailies Sakat, Kesari, and Tarun Bharat not only compete with two big dailies originating from Bombay but command around 90 per cent of the total circulation of the five dailies in Pune. Similarly the dominance of the English daily Tribune of Chandigarh has not been surpassed by prestigious national English dailies coming in from Delhi.

Newspapers in India continue to be largely an urban phenomenon. Even in that respect there is a concentration inter se. Over 30 per cent of the newspapers are located in the four metropolitan cities. State capitals account for nearly 17 per cent. Other big cities with a population of over one lakh contain 30 per cent of the total. There are eighteen cities which account for 50 per cent of the total number of newspapers in the country. Only a handful of rural newspapers exist (which devote 40 per cent of their contents for rural areas). Dailies are completely urban. But the analysis of publication of newspapers bring out one significant point that more newspapers are published from cities and towns other than metropolitan cities and state capitals.

The reason is that except English papers which are largely concentrated in the four metropolitan cities, Hindi papers are published mainly from medium towns (with a population of one lakh and more) while the press in Assamese, Bengali, Kannada and Tamil are mostly concentrated in the State capital towns.

Location may be a matter of convenience or the question of availability of printing facilities. But circulation pattern is a better norm of judging how far medium serves the rural people. Dailies coming from big cities claim more than nineteenths of the total circulation of dailies in the country. The Press Commission's study of 11 dailies (4 big, 5 medium and 2 small) reveals that rural circulation of these papers varied from 9.75 to 21.96 per cent in the case of nine papers and in the case of Dinamani of Madras and Yugadharma of Jaipur, Nagpur and Jabalpur it stood at 63.56 per cent and 57.45 per cent respectively. The average rural circulation of these papers was 22.28 per cent.

In 1981, the number of newspapers stood at 19144. A sample of the reporting newspapers to the RNI shows that while the circulation of 453 newspapers owned by joint stock companies was more than 19.6 million (that is nearly 38.4 per cent), nearly 65 per cent of the newspapers are owned by individuals, but their share in the total circulation is only 36.2 per cent.

The way a press actually functions is influenced largely by the news values which prevail among journalists. And that is reflected in the gatekeeping function of the practitioners, including various forms of information or knowledge control or the selection and highlighting of news stories and their projection, headlining, backgrounding and interpretation.

Joseph Pulitzer, publisher of the St. Louis Post-Despatch and the New York World once instructed his staff to look for news stories that are original, distinctive, dramatic, romantic, thrilling, unique, curious, quaint, humorous, odd and apt-to-be talked about. To these may be added newness, the prominence of persons or places concerned, the proximity of the event to the place of publication, the human interest involved and timeliness. These constitute some of the attributes of good newscasting according to Western standards.

The Second Press Commission of India finds that most of the commercial newspapers in India do not pursue these guidelines. Rather they imitate the cheap, though currently known as popular journalism of the West by highlighting news about petty politics, politicians and their pourings, flooding their news holes with stories of crimes, violence and aberrations and displaying creaking headlines and sensuous illustrations and ads. Equally questionable is the sense of "human interest" which often find reflection in the reporting of foreign news and photographs, foreign serials or syndicated features. The desi (local) contents are hardly flattering. These comments seem to be rather harsh, but it is very much our journalism today.

The Commission maintains that objection is not against reporting dirty politics, sensational events or crime and tension which in any way form a part of news flow. Rather it is to the preoccupation with them to such an extent that the readers are not supplied the information and discussion they need to discharge their responsibility to society, or to make judicious decisions or exercise wisely their franchise right.

The disproportionate picture of coverage in the Indian press is revealed by another study of the Second Press Commission. According to this study, Assamese dailies devoted the maximum of edited space-37 per cent-to political items and news regarding conflicts and tension, perhaps because of the controversy in the State on the issue of foreign nationals. Tamil, Punjabi, Hindi, Oriya and Telugu , dailies also devoted a large amount of space ranging from 41.6 to 31.6 to such items. These items occupied 23.7 per cent of the space in English dailies, the least for any daily.

Items devoted to economic development and , Government matters occupied 40.5 per cent space in Oriya dailies which was the maximum for any language. Hindi dailies devoted 29.0 per cent and English dailies 36.5 per cent space to such items. Assamese dailies devoted the least-19.6 per cent-space to such news.

In Sindhi dailies, news items on unrest, law and order and

courts occupied 21.2 per cent of the space. Hindi dailies gave 1735 per cent and English dailies English dailies devoted the maximum 9.9 per cent space to sports, while Hindi dailies gave 6.0 per cent. Sindhi newspapers had the least amount-1.00 per cent-of space given to such items.

Gujarati dailies had the maximum 22.5 per cent-space devoted to items on entertainment and culture. The percentage was 18.4 for Hindi and 6.4 for English dailies. The least space 5.8 per cent given to such items was in Oriya dailies.

Items of interest to woman and on social and human interest matters occupied 13.4 per cent of the space in Sindhi dailies. Hindi dailies gave 5.6 per cent and English dailies 4.1 per cent space to such items. The least space-3.0 per cent-give to such items was in Assamese dailies.

According to a random survey conducted by PR unit of the Council of Scientific and Industrial Research (CSIR) the space devoted to science news in Indian newspapers varies from .63 to 10.65 per cent of the total news content. The Hindu, Economic Times and Financial Express were found to be leading in the coverage of science news.

These analyses depict the need of a serious attempt on the part of the reader and professionally oriented newspapers to give deeper thought to the problem of giving a balanced coverage and adoption of healthier professional norms in selecting and projecting news in their columns.

Perhaps more distressing is the coverage of human interest stories culled out from western newspapers. That only shows the trend and mentality even of our best gatekeepers of newscasting. The Press Commission has quoted the selection of the following news stories and photographs by five leading English newspapers published in Delhi as illustrations of this unedifying trend, "(i) a 22-cm story of 2nd December 1980 (AP report from Leeds, U.K.) under the headline "Girl escapes attack by "ripper"'; (ii) 3-column photograph of 3rd December, 1980, showing two policemen on their night patrol talking to a young woman out alone on a Leeds Street near where the mass murderer, known as the Yorkshire Ripper, claimed his 13th victim; (iii) whole of the first page of the weekly section of a newspaper of 14th June, 1981 devoted to the first instalment of "The Yorkshire Ripper Story'; (iv) a 16-cm story (AP report from Los Angeles) on 25th June, 1981 under the headline 'Rapist on parole held again'; and (v) front-page 9-cm story (UNI report from Nairobi) on 6th November, 1981 about a Kenyan African who had 40 wives and wanted more."

This perversity is at its worst in film magazines in India and elsewhere in the Third World, continued the Commission's report. How morbidly these magazines pack their pages with rumours, gossips and speculative and unseemly exposures of the private lives of film stars, instead of dilating on professional aspects of the media or carrying critical articles of film appreciation.

Newscasting or reporting about development or rural affairs is no better. There too the trend is in giving more importance to what is wrong than what is right, to conflicts rather than to resolving them, to airing grievances than to getting redressals. It is no wonder then that the maximum output of the press in development or rural reporting consists of a miscellaneous succession of stories and images which have no relation to the actual lives of rural people or even to poor and weaker sections in urban areas. And what happens in such situations is that generally simple science, relevant technology, activating success and human interest stories or field based reports, which are the heart of development reporting, go by default.

Apart from this low rating of proper news values even techniques and quality of development reporting, except in a few newspapers and magazines, is poor, says the Commission, Readers hardly get a feeling of participation in the reported events, programmes or social change. Again, interpretative or in-depth journalism is as a low ebb yet.

According to the Commission, all investigative reporting is no development reporting, but the latter is essentially investigative. Apart from it one may add that it should also be interpretative, educative, expository and promotional in nature. It has also to be venturesome and innovating-professional qualities born out of commitment to public interest, fundamental duties and regard for the public weal.

The actual news values displayed by professional gatekeepers or reporters in the bulk of newspapers today is however wide off these marks. According to a Magsaysay Award winner, India's editors or reporters even don't read public documents properly. Some of them plagiarize, add a few words of their own to it and call it a scoop. Even if they read a newspaper file, they call themselves investigative journalists. Most editors have competent staff, but they don't use it to good account.

There is need, therefore, to give news values a different orientation in the interest of higher professionalism, social health and national development, argues the Press Commission. It urges the organisations of publishers, editors and journalists to evaluate, on a continuing basis, the concept and contents of healthy news culture in the light of changing socio-political ethos.

It reinforces Hutchins Commission's observation that journalists today should not regard only events as news, but also social and economic processes. Many activities of utmost social consequences lie below the surface of what are conventionally regarded as reportable incidents. In the Indian context these could be: Induction of new farming technology or participatory management in factories, adoption of new sources of energy like solar or gobar (cow dung) gas, introduction of new designs of low-cost housing, etc.

The Press Commission further holds that if conflict is news but not resolution of conflict, if the unusual and the bizarre is news rather than the normal, if news is what happened just a while ago (even if the event was not significant) and not a significant happening of a week or a month earlier which has only now come to light, the portrayal or reality in the press is bound to be distorted. Added to this aberration is often the slanting or hoisting of news done on the dictates of the personal or business interests of owners and pressure groups.

The former Prime Minister, Mrs. Indira Gandhi, in her theme address at Namedia in December 1983 also adverted to this unhealthy news sense displayed by our newspapers. She said that many journalists consider it smart to initiate the popular Western definition of bad news being good news and are bored by constructive and developmental activity. In this connection she cited a recent survey by the Press Council which showed that only two per cent newspaper space was devoted to social issues.

Is this what really interests readers? she asked. Are they content to remain ignorant of what is happening in various spheres, of what deepens their understanding, what helps them discharge their duty as well-informed citizens? she added.

To rectify this aberration, what is actually required is the sharpening of news sense and social sensitiveness among media practitioners. They should also develop the ability to interpret events and trends in the context of various disciplines and cultural milieu of the region.

Should journalists alone be the gatekeepers of news? Should the desk personnel or reporters be allowed to have a free hand in selecting, interpreting, shaping, displaying, timing, withholding or repeating news, or should be consumers of news also be permitted to have a say in the matter? The Press Commission has preferred to follow the existing practice of leaving the discretion in these matters to journalists, government information officials and media managers. The commission also wants editors to have the final say in the acceptance or rejection of advertisements especially those which border on or cross the line between decency and obscenity or those which promote the notion of women as sex objects and run contrary to the social or news value of their newspapers.

The practice in the West however varies. In free marketing democracies like Japan, USA, West Germany and France, newspaper publishers seek to follow the 'serve and sell' policy of giving the bulk of news and editorial matter according to the ascertained demands, tastes, needs and feedbacks of readers. In some countries like Japan even incentives are offered to make housewives buy a particular brand of paper. On the other hand, in socialist countries or authoritarian states, the party guardians or autocratic rulers and their agents act as the censors of reading material, determining what will go and what will not.

As mentioned earlier, freedom of the press is not merely a professional right that is inherent in journalists or publishers. Ideally these interests have to be reconciled: those of the publishers, readers and society. Feedback surveys or ballots, readers' columns, opinion polls, interviews and direct contacts with readers, policy makers and public representatives can bridge the gap partly. Suggestion and public opinion columns, panel discussions, direct mail ballots and coupons, publisher's letters, professional seminars and magazines as also the ombudsmanship of the Press Council can further fill in the void.

In the absence of regular readership and public feedback mechanism or other safeguards, however, the claim of journalists to be sole censors or arbiters appears to be presumptuous. When newspapers are controlled by big business or are influenced by vested interests or pressures, they run the risk, says the Commission, of becoming vehicles of expression of these internal and external influences. It is not, however, difficult as research and comparative studies bear out, to remove the dichotomy and gulf by delinking and diffusing ownership and control and by adopting a package of readership feedback mechanism and research, public representative consultation process and norms, codes and guidelines for gatekeeping evolved by the professional bodies. Some of these suggestions have been recommended by the commission itself. What one may conclude is that by taking some of these measures newspapers can become people's universities and development activists without compromising their professional standards, social responsibilities and communication role as free public informers, educators and custodians of public interest. And perhaps in this direction lies the future development of journalism in India.

As described earlier there has been an increase in the number and circulation of periodicals since 1970. Today we see glossy and attractively produced Magazines which can compete with any of their Western counterparts in excellence. The gross circulation of any one of these periodicals, however, has not yet touched a seven figure-a phenomenon common among many advanced countries. Nor have any of these magazines come anywhere near even a; single multi-editioned magazine like the Reader's Digest which publishes over 31 million copies in 17 languages.

In the group of Indian periodicals which appeared in 1981, monthlies constituted the largest ingredient followed by weeklies, fortnightlies, quarterlies and annuals. In terms of circulation also monthlies had an edge over others.

**Growth in Number**

The maximum number of periodicals are brought out in Hindi followed by English, Bengali and Urdu. In terms of circulation too Hindi periodicals maintain the top position (27.6 per cent). Then come English periodicals (20.6 per cent) and Tamil (10.9 per cent). Among the Indian languages Malayalam has the maximum circulation of weeklies as well as of other periodicals per 1000 of the linguistic population (1979 figures). Kashmiri comes at the bottom with hardly any circulation. Fifty-seven periodicals have a circulation of one lakh or more copies (1980). Five of them have a circulation exceeding 3 lakhs. The two top have circulation exceeding 5.5 lakhs.

The Registrar of Newspapers Report categorises, the journals into 21 groups according to the contents. The Second Planning Commission Report however, divides them into ten categories : (1) News and current affairs journals: (2) opinion journals; (3) farm journals; (4) economic and financial journals; (5) science journals; (6) literary and cultural magazines; (7) women journals; (8) children journals; (9) sports journals; and (10) film journals. According to the Commission's calculation, news and current affairs journals constitute the largest group.

The Illustrated Weekly of India, India Today and Link are the mast bearers of this group. A feature of the growth of such periodicals in recent years has been the emergence of investigative reporting in some of these journals and also a marked increase in circulation of such journals since 1977. Some top journalists, however, consider this type of investigative reporting, at least in a few of these journals as muck raking or gutter reporting; but a few better reports have proved to be earth shaking or stunning revelations. Qualitatively the coverage in India Today, Gentleman, the Illustrated Weekly of India, Sunday, Probe, Celebrity, Imprint, Sunday Observer, etc. is commendably supported by interpretative graphics and illustrations.

Literary and cultural magazines constitute the second largest group. The bulk of these magazines particularly those with a large circulation, however, follow a formula of mixed contents in order to appeal to different tastes and thereby attract more readers. Kumudam, a Tamil weekly, is a leading illustration of this group.

Opinion journals are distinct from news magazines as also from journals of entertainment for leisure time reading. They are generally imbued with social concern and a sense of purpose. Seminar and Mainstream are illustrations of this category.

Covering nearly three-fourths of the country's rural population there are only 345 farm journals (1979 figures).

Shetkari and Gramsevak belong to this group. The number of copies of farm journals per 1000 rural literate population is only 1.5 per cent, a discouragingly low figure. Some weaknesses of these journals are that they use heavy terminologies in explaining technical information and they do not engage experts to write or report for them. It is probably because they cannot afford it.

Hindu Survey of Indian Industry, Business World, Business India and Udyog represent the economic and financial category of journals. The number of these journals is not sizable in the aggregate, though some of them are fast sellers. Their number, however, had taken an upward trend since 1952 and so also their circulation.

The growth of science journals to which belongs also a better seller like Science Today was evidently noticeable during the eighties but not significantly or adequately enough. Although the number rose from almost scratch and so also the circulation of these journals, their development is not as much as it should be according to its need. To popularise science and technology and inculcate scientific temper among the people is an imperative need. But the existing journals in this category cannot perform this task satisfactorily. This misgiving was also expressed by the Press Commission.

The number of women journals is still small despite an increase during the eighties. *Vanitha,* a Malayalam monthly from Kottayam has the highest circulation in this group. One dimension which distinguishes these journals from their Western counterparts is what a Press Commission Study points out that these journals consistently seek to direct women's energies into a narrow channel and to define their concerns, preoccupations and aspirations within an arbitrarily imposed feminine framework.

The covers of these magazines generally feature a brightly dressed woman, baring some parts of her body. Apart from these aspects, these journals depict women's mental faculties and behaviour in a way as if they can fit only into a male-dominated social relationship. The study says that readers get an impression that the outside world belongs to men and that the issues which arise there do not affect woman except indirectly through the men related to them. The trend, however, is now changing for the better.

Despite some increase in the number of children's journals, their position in the market is very thin. The position of Indrajal Comics in this group is the highest. Most magazines in this section only provide entertainment in the for of light reading. Some also carry informative articles including those on current and sports events, but the number of such articles in an issue is not more than two or three. One regrettable trend noticed by the Press Commission in children's magazines is an effort to depict sex and violence in a bid to increase circulation. Instead of resorting to originality and creativity, which can help to sell the magazines also, their sponsors are trying to lean on cheap circulation gimmicks.

Sports journals had a low rate of expansion of circulation upto 1975, but thereafter they started showing progress. Sports World today crosses five figures. Qualitatively they do not reflect the latest trends in sports journalism.

Film journals indicated an increase in number since the sixties, but professionally and circulation-wise their record does not show much improvement. Only Filmfare an English fortnightly from Bombay, touches a respectable figure. A study for the Press Commission says that the bane of many film journals is the lack of professional standards. Many of these journals resort to gossip and scandal about alleged peccadillos of film stars. It is an interesting finding that many articles in such magazines are written by PR men in the pay of film producers of staff and therefore attacks on some film stars are deliberate or -tendentious.

As an activist in the all round development of Indian society, development journalism can be a faithful ally of the whole process. This brand of journalism is, however, not merely economic or financial journalism. Neither is it a government mouthpiece. It doesn't imply polishing up press releases issued by the PR Departments. It is a positive, forward looking, field based, two way participatory and development promotional reporting and writing. It is pragmatic, result and action oriented and barefoot type of journalism. To this end, it has to be bold and venturesome investigative or expository reporting involving issues, problems and exercises of social significance or public interest. But the perspective is not to write merely what is wrong, but also what can be the right thing and how it can be brought about.

It should probe into the reasons for success or failures at different places under different conditions of various development programmes. Development Agency's National Adult Education or National Rural Employment programmes, Marginal Farmers and Agricultural labours Project, etc. affect the lives of common people such as small farmers. It is indeed a sad reflection that newspapers in India have not adequately taken up this type of dynamic journalism or reporting. It has not undertaken initiative in reviewing or reporting in depth development activities nor reporting incisively about socio-economic programmes or about the green and white revolutions that are taking place in rural or remote areas.

The Press Commission draws attention particularly to one defect in this area of development reporting. It finds that many newspapers today depend heavily on official hand-outs or briefings and not on field work or direct observation preferably participant observation. Instead of venturesome reporting in so far as it is oriented to social and economic issues like the exploitation of Harijans, tribals or contract labour the trading in human flesh or delays and corruption in public administration, they feel contended in loading their stories with big and small statistics. They fail to help the readers know how the beneficiaries feel or react about the claims and achievements of different development programmes.

The Commission points out yet another omission in development reporting. This relates to the praiseworthy performance of non-official agencies and workers in fields like education, leprosy relief, etc. Indeed it is a poor reflection on the professional standards of newspapers that they do not take initiative in India in reviewing such activities.

Rather they themselves become aware of them after some non-officials have been honoured with international or national awards. Surely, the free press in developing countries should be more socially conscious and enterprising than what our press actually is. Also, there is a need for the big and small media to operate as change agents, watch-dogs or gatekeepers in the process of socio-economic development taking place in various parts of the country.

At the moment only a few language newspapers especially in Oriya, Telugu, Marathi, Malayalam, Bengali and Hindi are devoting an increasing proportion of space to development coverage like that of health, family welfare, industry, science and technology, agriculture, education and public utilities. This conclusion is based on a study entitled "Percentage of front page space devoted to different themes in daily newspapers."

Another study of the Commission reveals yet another healthy trend among some language newspapers (Bengali, Kannada and Malayalam dailies) besides English which were reporting regularly on development topics and socio-economic issues. Topics covered in such reports include the condition of tea garden labourers, problems of drought and irrigation, dowry deaths, ill-treatment of women, plight of under trial prisoners, living conditions of slum dwellers, and the like.

This is a welcome development which needs to be emulated and encouraged also in other newspapers which have set their heart on serving rural people. This task, however, will warrant social aptitude and barefoot qualities on the part of reporters and communicators and their ability to understand, interpret and report on socio-economic issues in terms of the problems, needs, experience and language frameworks of rural readers.

**The Press**

Press freedom provides the oxygen in a climate of a healthy democracy. It is a matter of common experience that the press can do well and perform its professional work smoothly if it operates in the open and competitive information market and does not itself throttle or vitiate the process of collecting, selecting and presenting the news objectively and truthfully. The Press commission had therefore underscored that it is only on this type of free press that people can largely depend for the primary data of their political thinking.

It is because of the freedom both from black laws or menacing pressures from without and the irresponsible journalism from within that the Fourth Estate can function as a watch-dog, ombudsman, constructive critic, public investigator and expositor, philosopher, guide and even an entertainer of the society.

Press freedom is conceded by the constitution, but not as a separate entity or a special privilege. It is included in the individuals' right to freedom of speech and expression. The government, however, has resented the licentiousness shown by a few newspapers in always criticising the ruling party and only harping upon what is wrong about things. All our governments have preferred press freedom to be linked with social and fundamental responsibilities and the obligation to report objectively.

Taking into consideration the constraints of the Indian model of democracy and socialism and the objectives laid in the Preamble of the Constitution or its Directive Principles of the State Policy, the second Press Commission has advocated that the Press should be neither an adversary nor an ally of the Government, but a constructive critic. To be a mindless adversary or an unquestioning ally would be to abdicate judgement, states the report of the Press Commission. It further stresses that journalism is a public utility service and not merely an industry.

Whereas a doctor may cause harm only to a few dozen or at the most a few score patients during the full span of his career, a dishonest or unprofessional journalist can poison the minds of hundreds of thousands or millions of his fellowmen. It is true that journalism has to be a viable business if it is to be free from want and patronage, but a special plea for its fundamental duty and its responsibility to the society and readers is not far stretched. The Press Commission has therefore urged that in the changed circumstances today, the protection of the freedom of the issuer of news alone is not enough; the freedom of the consumer (readers and public) must also be protected.

The press is a great social asset, for it has to serve the entire community of varying minds with its raw material for thought, as also to act as a watch-dog by exercising its role to warn and curb forces of repression, corruption and divisiveness.

It is possible to have a free but responsible press and good, responsive and democratic government at the same time. In fact, the freedom of the press is the mother of all other freedoms. This freedom can be used to create a brave new world or to bring about universal catastrophe. It is imperative for the society and government to protect journalists and assure them conditions for working unhindered or undertake unrestrictedly investigative reporting strictly for professional purposes. 'More journalists are killed or kidnapped, victimised or persecuted than members of any other profession,' says Sean MacBride, Chairman of the International Commission for the Study of Communication Problems.

They certainly need protection and perhaps a special status,' he adds. In India these suggestions need special consideration for instances abound when journalists were murdered or manhandled by terrorists, agents of politicians or infuriated mobs or were sacked by their proprietors at the instance of political barons or some other wire-pullers.

Press freedom is very fragile. It can be weighed from two sides; (1) the external and internal pressures, and (2) draconian or vexatious laws. The press has to be protected both ways.

The pressures could be six-fold: (1) physical attacks on the editor or the offices of the newspaper or its employees by the aggrieved or angry mobs, (2) obstructions posed in the expression of political opinions not to the liking of trade unions and newspaper employees, (3) interference in the editorial autonomy by proprietors with a view to protecting their own business interests, (4) pressures from advertisers (5) interference by the functionaries of the government through selective and politically motivated exercise of powers under the law and through extra legal action, and (6) inducements or favours sought by the journalists themselves. To give protection to the press in these respects the Press Commission and many other authorities have advocated the expansion of the jurisdiction of the Press Council to be able to look into these complaints.

The legal areas in which press freedom is sought to be augmented comprise immunity regarding disclosure of sources of information, defamation, contempt of legislatures and courts and regarding a few limitations ordained by the Press and Registration of Books Act 1867, Post and Telegraph Act, Industries (Development and Regulation Act) 1951, etc. To this end, the second Press Commission has suggested certain amendments in the existing press laws to expand reasonably the scope of press freedom and at the same time underscored the need to protect the right to privacy of the individual and prevent newspapers from indulgence in free style of character assassination.

Beside the promotion of products and services, advertising has a great role in sustaining the newspaper industry and free press. Press advertising as a factor of newspaper economy is therefore taken very seriously by newspaper managements of modern times. Any restrictions imposed on advertising space or expenditure or newsprint supply would naturally evoke resentment among big and medium papers.

Till the second half of the sixties the advertisers and big advertising agencies in India depended primarily on dailies for extensive advertising. Thereafter a clear cut differentiation began to emerge that while daily newspapers should be used primarily for advertising capital goods, employment and trade notices and for institutional campaigns and periodicals should be employed for sustained advertising of consumer goods. In fact the sudden increase in advertisement revenue after the sixties enabled leading Indian periodicals to improve their production standards and editorial content, thereby attracting a wider readership. Even for the bulk of other periodicals, income from advertisements became the mainstay of their economy.

**Value of Publicity**

Today advertisements occupy a substantial proportion of space in newspapers. It is, however, only the big general interest magazines, and comparatively the English dailies attached to newspaper chains, and combines of large business houses who usurp the lion's share in the cake of advertising revenue. A trend to rectify this imbalance has been sought by the government by pursuing a liberal policy of giving special rates of government advertisements to language news papers besides augmenting their newsprint supply and granting them rebate from excise duties, etc. But still the big and medium dailies and periodicals, not withstanding competition from radio TV commercials, continue to have edge.

Notwithstanding the maximum of 40:60 space allotment suggested for advertisements by the first Press Commission, the space given to advertising has been actually increasing in big newspapers. According to data given in the annual reports of the Press Register there was no paper in 1965 which gave 60 per cent or more space to advertisements and there were only 10 papers which devoted 50 to 59 per cent space to advertisements. In 1981, three big and medium and 37 small papers started devoting 75 per cent or more space to advertisements. And 5 big 25 medium and 112 small papers used between 50 and 74 per cent of their space for advertisements.

The percentage of space devoted to advertisements was generally more in the case of dailies that periodicals. However, the average space devoted to advertisements was found to be 39 per cent in the case of dailies 27 per cent in the case of weeklies and 31 per cent in the case of monthlies. According to ORG survey, 77 per cent of the total advertising revenue income and 51.8 per cent of the space was accounted for by big newspapers with a circulation of 50, 000 and above.

This, a small chunk of big newspapers have an economic or competitive edge over the bulk of small and medium newspapers in the country. On an average the share of advertising revenue to the total income was merely 52 per cent in the case of big papers and a little over 26 per cent in the case of medium papers. The bigger dailies, particularly the big English dailies were usurping a disproportionately larger chunk of advertisement revenue in 1981 and therefore were in a position to offer more pages on the same selling price. Even from the point of view of the resale price, the big papers provided a benefit to the customers.

The second press Commission therefore felt that the prescription of a price-page schedule with fixed news to advertising ratio is absolutely necessary for the existing newspapers. In view of the need to help small and medium newspapers overcome disadvantage of lower advertisement incomes and smaller number of pages the Press Commission recommended a specific ratio of 60 per cent for big papers. A bold and fair suggestion, but its validity is a matter of speculation.

***Production with Quality*** : In India as has been already seen, good production did not brother the pioneer journalist in the past. Photo journalism and colour reproduction were at their embryonic stage.

The opinion advocacy or adversary Journalism of those days with low print orders did not lend themselves to competitive or marketing urges in terms of variety or innovativeness in design or production. Things, however, started changing for the better during the 1950s and 1960s. The vocation became a business of industry and subjected to: marketing and advertising pressures for better looks and attractive layouts and typography.

The challenge of utilising resources optimally, effective economies in costs and ensuring speedier delivery schedules, motivated the owners to resort to modern printing technology for their papers. By this time the Indian printing scene was also exposed to the new trends in the West where two types of technological revolutions were sweeping the scene. Web offset and electronic printing technologies involving photo composition or computer controlled teletype setting or electronic typewriters were replacing the conventional hot metal linotype and monotype composing processes. For a' multilingual developing country like India these two technologies suited immensely, though they were costly. Among the obvious advantages of these technologies to Indian publishing in languages are the superior and consistent quality of letter image, elimination of the use of scarce material such as lead and the unlocking of capital invested in lead type faces.

During the last two decades, the big chain English newspaper publishers or language newspapers bringing out multi-editions and affected by competition have been gradually reeling towards sophisticated and modern technologies of various shades. So is the trend with some of the class A and class B printing houses where big magazines and medium newspapers are being printed as job work. For instance, three giants among the Malayalam press Malayala Manorama, Mathrubhumi and Kerals Kaumudi are in competition to get into the faster and the latest printing processes. Of these three big Malayalam papers Kerala Kaumudi was the first to install the transmission link, a process by which composed matter can be sent column by column within two transmission points, thus enabling the resident editor to choose matter of local importance in his edition. This is an improvement on the facsimile transmission method employed by the Hindu which results in a comparatively more rigid similarity between all editions of the paper. Another high technology gadget that distinguishes Kaumudi is the tele-photo by which any major event occurring anywhere in the world can be splashed within a few hours in this paper.

There are today many language newspapers especially in Urdu, Hindi, Gujarati, Marathi and Telugu which have resorted to one or the other of the modern technologies. This is enabling them to offer colour printing as also modern layout and typographical designs to their advertising clients and readers- a significant landmark in language journalism.

The Hindu, was the first newspaper in India to install the latest computer technology both for printing and type setting processes. Instead of hot metal composing on stereo plates, a feature common to most of the other big dailies, typesetting in this paper is done by a typesetter working on one of the 24 video display units in an air-conditioned office. The type text is stored in one of the two computers and on editorial command, a laser camp photo typesetter produces bromides of the text and advertisement copies which are set and designed into complete pages, according to layout plans.

Each page is then photographed by an automatic computerised camera to obtain a negative. This is then printed by contact on to a thin polymer plate under high intensity lights. After etching, which takes only minutes, the plate is ready for printing the headquarter's edition. The images of these of these pages are then sent at the rate of seven minuted a page by facsimile transmission to Bangalore, Hyderabad, Coimbatore and Madurai for simultaneous printing of regional editions. Recently the Indian Express, telegraph and Aaj installed computerised photo typesetting systems.

*The Illustrated weekly of India* an allied magazine of the Bennett Coleman and Co. now uses electronic technology in colour separation and automatic processing of film negatives as also adopts a sophisticated printing process of in-depth colour printing known as photogravure.

The Weekly's photogravure machine has nine units and it can print an 80-page at the rate of 90000 copies per hour. It can also control paper tension and colour alignment. Folding and stitching is done automatically.

Another illustration of the latest technology-based printing press was the opening of a new unit called Mayar printers at Okhla Industrial estate where the new electronic dot generating colour scanner, the process camera, film and plate processors and photo typesetting units have been installed. This plant is fully computerised.

Apart from these sophisticated presses, according to the Press Registrar's Report of 1981. 366 dailies have their own publishing arrangements. Also 398 dailies have their own composing arrangements. In these units however the printing technologies used are predominantly relief, stereo plate flat-bed, lithography and offset and for composing mono, lino, inter type and hand composition systems with a sprinkling of photo composition. To help modernise the printing industry the government has assured all possible help. In the existing situation, there seems to be three options open for must of the newspaper publishers: (1) to continue with the old technology, (2) to obtain secondhand reconditioned equipment or to resort to the manufacture of such machines locally, or (3) to take a leap into the new technology. At the 21st All India printers Conference, eminent overseas speakers advised Indian Printers not to hesitate in making up their minds in favour of adopting the new technology for it is like a moving train. The longer one takes to make up his mind, the harder it is to jump in later on.

The old technologies, however, cannot be discarded like the village cart. Some experts have suggested that India should continue to have an appropriate mix of old and new processes in such a manner that the adoption of the new technology by existing processes may allow them to survive initially for such period as they would choose to replace the old technology altogether. The Press Commission has left it to each publisher to decide what technology would suit its requirements best. Newspapers, particularly those which want to grow, should have an open mind and a progressive outlook while selecting proper technology.

It has further recommended that the proposed newspaper development Commission should special attention to the development of printing and other technologies suitable for the Indian press, especially for Indian language and small and medium newspapers. The Press Commission own preference was how ever for new electronics technology which has a clear advantage so far as composition in Indian script is considered. To meet the immediate requirement of small and medium newspapers it suggested that these units should be allowed to important, rebuild or recondition machines available abroad.

Till the time new production technologies sweep printing scene in the country, the well produced Hindu, Malayala Manorama, Times of India, India Today, Gentleman and Illustrated Weekly of India will coexist with hundreds of shabbily produced small papers, though liable to serve useful function at the grassroots level.

The Indian media scene presents a picture of congested basti with an overcrowding of small newspapers. In a total number of 1914 units, only 17$ belong to the category of big newspapers and the rest to the category of small papers. Although small newspapers have increased in number their share the total circulation has declined markedly during the last quarter century. In the daily press, the big paper have a share of 54.3 and medium 25.4 per cent of the circulation. In a country like India where three quarters of the people live in small towns and villages, mofussil newspapers, invariably small ones with circulation ranging from a few hundreds to 15000, have distinct role to play in the process democratizing communication than big newspaper. Their functioning is however handicapped, their circulation in the rural areas is circumscribed, their economy is depressed and the their impact is reduced.

People who have experience of publishing large and small daily newspapers testify that small newspapers can still grow more if they make themselves useful the local community by conveying information of local relevance and interest and seek to bag rural advertisements, rather than compete with the state capital or metropolitan newspapers ineffectively. Eve at the present stage of development in our country newspaper serving one or more districts with common cultural and economic features likely to be successful.

The reassuring examples of community newspapers the USA and critical newspapers in the UK are appropriate. The development of such newspapers will reduce the disparity between India's large rural population as compared to the small circulation and readership of newspapers in rural areas. Even if it is conceded that newspaper readership per copy is higher in rural papers, the rural reach of the Indian press is so limited that it should call for concern and attention, says the Press Commission. In this connection, extension of educational opportunities for children and illiterate adults and gainful employment for the youth, women and rural people is very necessary.

***No Proof of Another Relation :*** The soul of a people is in the press. But the press at times in the hands of a few financial magnates who may murder its soul by corruption or narrowness of commercial interests. The question has often been raised in India as to how the economic independence of the press can be preserved from crippling and subservience to commercial and financial interests of the controlling groups. In this connection the second press Commission feels that newspapers controlled by the big business are liable to become vehicles of expression of the ideologies of their owners. To curb this trend, the Commission has suggested the delinking of the press. To this end the Commission recommended a law should be enacted preventing, in phased from, a person carrying on the business of publishing a newspaper to have any direct or indirect interest beyond ten per cent in any other kind of business.

Similarly it wanted that any other business person from outside having a business in excess of ten per cent elsewhere should not have permission to dominate any publishing concern. Other remedies suggested to obviated interference or nomination of unprofessional proprietors are the prescription of price-cum-page schedule and fixing of news to advertising space ratio of 40 to 60 in big papers.

This proposal of delinking has drawn the heaviest fire from four dissenters in the press Commission, who have characterised these recommendations as discriminatory and detrimental to the economics of big newspaper publishing. Whatever be the legal or professional implications of these proposals and that certainly needs to be further probed into there is no doubt that the media at small places should be allowed to play their role effectively. The proprietors of big papers should not be permitted either to injures healthy journalism at the grassroots level or poison the functional autonomy of working journalists.

An equitable, balanced, multilateral and evenly distributed spread of information is a vital condition for the growth of a well informed citizen. It can have meaning only if the system at all levels reflects and smoothly transmits news dealing with the life and problems of people.

India today has four main news agencies and a number of other non-wire news and feature agencies. The four main agencies are Press trust of India , United news of India, Samachar

Bharati and Hindustan Samachar. The first two supply news in English and the other two operate through the media of Hindi and other Indian languages.

PTI started operating in 1949 after taking over Reuter's business in India as well as the interest of the Associated press of India. It is the biggest Indian news agency, employing a 1300-strong editorial and technical staff. Its news service is carried over a teleprinter network of over 60,000 kilometres in length. More than 200 newspapers in the country subscribe to PTI service, besides AIR, Doordarshan, Central and State Governments, commercial establishments, universities and public institutions. PTI has arrangement with Reuters Agence France press of France the united Press International of USA and some other technical news agencies. PTI has also its own correspondents at selected places abroad.

The UNI started its operation in 1961. Within a decade it had spread its teleprinter network over 25000 kilometres. At present, UNI has 50 branch offices and a network of 50000 kilometres of leased teleprinter lines. It gets its reports from correspondents as also from half a dozen foreign news agencies AP, DPA, ANSA, Tass and few others. The agency has also launched a weekly background Service, Agricultural Service, Economic News service to cater to the special needs of newspapers, periodicals and other subscribers.

Hindustan samachar and Samachar bharati mainly serve the language press. The former, India's first multilingual agency, was started in 1948. It became a workers cooperative in 1957. A second Indian language agency, Samachar bharati, came into existence in 1967. In 1970 the agency became almost a public sector company when five state governments bought more than 50 per cent of its shares.

The small agencies provide news of local interest and significance. Specialised agencies in photographs, cartoons and other visuals seek to enrich reporting and make newspaper contents more attractive and interesting, more explanatory and understandable. India's news agencies need to be streamlined and their efforts need to be directed towards rural areas and the needs of small newspapers operating in mofussil areas. At present our news agencies are hardly equipped to report social and economic changes taking places in the countryside. The press Commission has therefore laid stress on the starting of small news agencies especially in languages. These would offer two way news and comments in different perspectives. The commission also desires the emergence of more agencies specialising in photographs, cartography and other visuals. It envisages the scope for pooling and federating systems for ensuring a countrywide dissemination of the more significant stories of success and failures in rural areas. The other need it has stated is to evolve teleprinters in various languages.

Among the non-wire news-feature agencies which have made a mark are Indian news and feature Alliance, public Opinion Trends which specialises in dissemination pertaining to neighbouring countries, the cartographic News Service and Pan Asian newspaper alliance, a photo agency, Some other non-wire agencies provide news and analysis in specific perspectives.

Since 1976 the non-aligned countries representatives have taken note of the persistent and serious disparities and imbalance in the global information situation and its adverse effects on non-aligned countries. Dependence on big international agencies made these agencies the arbiters of world reality for; developing countries. This accounted for much of the biased reporting in the Western media about developing countries. There was hardly any news; about developing countries unless it be of disaster or: disturbances coups, murders or sex. The stupendous tasks of development or changes being brought out in villages and towns found no mention. Some of the Western media even used reporting as an adjunct to project the foreign policies of their countries; and in certain cases even for acting as cover for intelligence agencies.

Information ministers of the non-aligned countries who met at new Delhi between 8-13 July 1976 therefore stressed the need to liberate their information and mass media from the colonial legacy and expressed their collective determination to rectify this situation. To give practical shape to this the Non-Aligned News Agencies pool was set up on 13 July 1976. The basic philosophy of the New pool, as stated by Shri H.K.L. Bhagat at a three-day international Seminar on improving News Pool held on 25-27 April 1984 in New Delhi, was the right of each country to participate in the global process of communication on an equitable and just basis.

It is a system of news exchange based on professional cooperation, equality, coordination and collective- self reliance among the 87 Pool partners. This pool transmits more than 60000 words around the world each day. India is currently having direct communication links with Belgrade, Djakarta, Bahrain, Havana, Colombo, Hanoi and Kuala Lumpur through satellite and with Dhaka and Islamabad through terrestrial link. The Press trust of India operates the non-aligned news agencies pool from India. The working of this Pool has however raised some misgivings. Critics of the pool allege that no thought has been given to ensure internal democratisation, objectivity and credibility. The government control can lead to controlled versions of news.

The supporters of the pool on the other hand argue that it is not an inward looking closed circuit system of information. The objective is to supplement and not to supplant the existing translational news agencies. The setting up of the Non -aligned news Agencies Pool is only an attempt at greater flow of developmental news among the non-aligned countries. To this end, the creation of a full-fledged Third World news agency to disseminate the non aligned point of view on a global scale was suggested at the Namedia meet held in New Delhi between 9 and 12 December 1983. The conference also asked non-aligned nations to do much more than what they have done so far to increase the flow of information among their own people and among non-aligned countries by reducing tariffs and developing news agencies. They also urged professionalists to intensify their endeavours to widen and strengthen the base of free and balanced flow of communication and evolve commonly acceptable norms to improve the news pools credibility and utility.

**Forces of Opposition**

The Second World War years culminating in the Quit India movement and the 1942 disturbance saw the nationalist press going through a period of acute stress and strain when it fought hard for mere survival and the odds were against it. It found itself in a desperate situation in which, on the one hand, it had to function under severe restrictions imposed on it by the alien Government and, on the other had to discharge its duty to the people and the nation, which under the leadership of Gandhi was making one last and final attempt to free itself from foreign yoke.

It was difficult to imagine that the Indian press would have survived the ordeal if the occasion had not produced a leader of the calibre of Kasturi Srinivasan, managing editor of *The Hindu,* who was acting as the spokesman of the Indian press, negotiated with the government and tried to soften the rigours of the Government onslaught on the nationalist press. His efforts were not entirely successful and even he was led, at one time, to organise a black-out of government news and speeches in the Indian press in protest against their attitude. Not all the nationalist papers and Gandhi himself were satisfied with his work and accused him of letting down the national cause. But all without exception recognised his sincerity and integrity and his keen desire to make it possible for the press to live under the most dire circumstances.

When World War II broke out in September, 1939, the Viceroy, Lord Linlithgow, announced that India was at war and sought the cooperation of all parties in the war effort. The Congress demanded a declaration of British war aims, especially about India's constitutional future. The nationalist press supported the Congress demand and said that Indo-British relations would improve and there would be greater enthusiasm for the war effort if India's independence was recognised.

The newspapers representing the Moderates questioned the wisdom of raising the constitutional issue at a time of grave crisis for Britain and advocated cooperation in the war effort. They believed that freedom would come at the end of the war by the mere force of events. The Anglo-Indian press with some exceptions, was sympathetic to the demand for declaration of war aims but they urged Hindu-Muslim unity as a preliminary to constitutional changes.

Linlithgow was not favourably disposed to the Congress demand. He wrote to the Secretary of State, L.S. Amery, after the fall of Singapore: "I am carrying here almost single-handed an immense responsibility. Indeed, I do not think I exaggerate to affirm that the key to success in this war is very largely in my hands." Linlithgow thought the grant of political concessions would imperil the present and the future. There was no possibility of giving satisfaction to the Congress leaders, he said, and he described them as "entirely ruthless politicians." "India is hopelessly and, I suspect irremediably", he wrote, "split by racial and religious divisions which we cannot bridge and which become more and more acute as any real transfer of power by us draws nearer." He concluded that since India was so vital to the success of the Allies he would rather face such troubles as might arise from a continuation of the status quo "than those that might arise as a result of making concessions which are ill-advised and dangerous and on which we might have to go back for reasons of imperial security."

Soon after India was declared at war, the Government of India appointed a chief press adviser and chose Desmond Young, formerly editor of the *Pioneer*, for the post. It was the time when the Congress Ministries in the various provinces had resigned in protest against the declaration of war without the consent of the people's representatives and Gandhi had launched his individual *Satyagraha* movement to oppose the war effort. The Government of India issued an order under the Defence of India Rules without consulting the chief press adviser, prohibiting the printing and publishing of any matter "calculated directly or indirectly to foment opposition to the prosecution of the war to a successful conclusion or any matter relating to the holding of meetings or the making of speeches for the purpose directly or indirectly of fomenting opposition to the aforesaid."

**Existence of Dissent**

The Indian press protested against the order and said they had already accepted and honoured the principle of consultation in regard to publication of news items that might affect the war effort. A delegation on behalf of the Indian and Eastern Newspapers Society met the Home Member, Sir Reginald Maxwell, and was told that the order had been issued only to prevent the "exploitation of newspapers" for anti-war propaganda. The arrest of Jawaharlal Nehru at this juncture posed a problem to the newspapers of how much prominence could be given to it in the news columns and made it a live issue.

Editors of Indian newspapers decided to meet in Delhi to consider the situation and thus was born the All-India Newspapers Editors' Conference in November 1940 which was to play a vital role during the war years as the spokesman of the press in the confrontation with the Government. Kasturi Srinivasan, managing editor of *The Hindu* was unanimously elected president of the conference and his election was welcomed both by the government and Gandhi. Srinivasan told his fellow editors that no self-respecting editor could submit to the government order and he asked them to make it clear that they would not be a party to the curbing of normal political activity in the country in the name of war. He said the press had a right to publish news and it must be allowed to function freely.

The government should leave it to its own sense of responsibility to act in the best interests of the nation. He said that the government was attempting to exploit the newspapers to help them to control the political movement in the name of war effort. "The charge that the *Satyagraha* movement is pro-Hitler and, therefore, all publicity to it is fomenting anti-war activity is manifestly unjust and cannot be accepted", he said. Even as he finished speaking, a message was handed to him which said that the impugned government order had been withdrawn.

It was also disclosed that the government had agreed to establish press advisory committees in Delhi and the various provincial capitals, whose advice would be sought before any action was taken against any newspaper. The conference appointed a Standing Committee to be in touch with the government on matters relating to the press. The Standing Committee urged the government to standardise procedures for consultation and taking penal action against any papers after warnings had been issued following consultation with the local press advisory committee. Not all provincial Governments were cooperative and in U.P., the government took a long time to appoint an advisory committee and when one was appointed its recommendations were not accepted, as for example in the case of the *National Herald*.

A feature of the Newspaper Editors' Conference was that it was representative of all classes of newspapers, including British owned newspapers which were also represented on the Standing Committee. "The British element", says a writer, "showed marked adaptability and genuine interest to restrain bureaucratic excesses and defend the reasonable rights of the press." There was division among the editors as between editors of Congress papers and editors of independent papers and it was to the credit of Srinivasan that he managed to hold them together by his tact and patience.

Gandhi in a letter to editors of Indian newspapers in February, 1941, said that two statements of his carried by news agencies were suppressed by newspapers as they were not passed by the press adviser. The Statements related to continuance of the civil disobedience movement and payment of fines by *Satyagrahis*.

The statements were not passed as they were considered prejudicial and incitement for anti-war civil disobedience. Gandhi said: "We have become so used to the press gag that we hardly know that there is a partial paralysis of the press. In the name of war efforts all honest expression of opinion if it is opposed to war efforts conceived by the official word, is effectively suppressed unless an enterprising editor or publisher risks the loss of his press. Thus, my own effort, if my honesty be not questioned, is the true effort to end all war and, therefore, in no way anti-British or Pro-German."

Gandhi said he had to issue statements from time to time for the conduct of the campaign and to keep it within restraint. "I do not want", he said, "to extend the scope of civil disobedience beyond the present limit. But I do not know that I can exercise that restraint if the press abdicates its function publishing relevant news. I therefore, appeal to the press not to succumb to the gag but to assert its independence by publishing all the *Satyagraha* news in its fullness. Of course, it is open to the editors to criticise and condemn the movement or the statements that may be issued.

Editors may signify their disapproval of the gag by either publishing the offending statements and risking prosecution or even confiscation of the press or by stopping publication of their papers altogether by way of protest." Gandhi added: "I need hardly draw attention to the fact that I represent unadulterated non-violence whose spread can do nobody any harm. It is false and cruel to suggest that I could have anything in common with Nazism or Fascism because I happen to oppose imperialism."

**The Trouble**

Gandhi's letter followed a controversy started by his secretary, Mahadev Desai, who had accused the president of the Editors' Conference of having given an assurance to the government that they would not hinder the war effort. Srinivasan denied that any assurance had been given as suggested. He said that the press should not commit suicide but fight for its liberty "as it is by fighting and not by surrendering or resigning that one can get whatever one wants or wishes to achieve."

On February 4, 1941, the standing committee of the A.I.N.E.C. adopted a resolution moved by P.D. Sharma and seconded by Sir Francis Low *(Times of India)* requesting the government "ordinarily not to ban publication of statements issued by Mahatma Gandhi and in cases where they are inclined to take such a step, they should consult the Central Press Advisory Committee before passing any order thereon."

The A.I.N.E.C. faced a crisis in its ranks in 1942 when the Congress passed the "Quit India" resolution in August. Some of its members closed down their papers in accordance with Gandhi's suggestion who himself stopped the *Harijan*. Gandhi's speech at the All India Congress Committee in Bombay was not published in full by newspapers because news agencies themselves decided not to use all of it.

The Government imposed severe restrictions on the press in the wake of the August disturbances. These included registration of correspondents, limitation on the number of messages on the disturbances to be published, limitation of headlines and the space to be given to news of disturbances and precensorship with regard to certain categories of news. In U.P., the government issued an order prohibiting the printing or publishing of any matter in any newspaper in a type larger than that of a specimen given in the official gazette notification or in a line of continuous type wider than half of the breadth of the printed page of such publication.

The A.I.N.E.C. considered the new situation at its meeting in Bombay in October, 1942, and Kasturi Srinivasan, who presided, said: "We do not seek to minimise the fact that we have been unable to influence in our favour certain provincial governments. But as against this I may say that war or no war, we did assert our right to give expression to our grievance in the political field and have brought the government to realise the necessity to keep off from interfering with us in that respect." Referring to the precensorship and other restrictions imposed on the press, he said; "Freedom of the press in part of the larger freedom of the country and until the country is free, the press has necessarily to work under the limitation arising from factors and forces that are imposed on it. I have no doubt in my mind that the public do require the press to continue to function, to serve them within the limits of even the diminished opportunities.

There is unmistakable evidence that the people do not desire to be starved of news. They want papers to publish and discover ways and means for themselves to serve as best they can. The problem we are confronted with today is to decide what attitude the Indian press should take in the light of the demands of the government. There is no question of our willing submission to any proposal which in our opinion is derogatory to the profession or in any way prevents us from functioning as responsible newspapers."

Srinivasan suggested a formula for acceptance by the government which was endorsed by the conference. The formula was an assurance of exercise of self-restraint on the part of the editors and the withdrawal of restrictions by the government in return. The conference while adopting the formula advised editors to observe restraint in the presentation of news of disturbances and to avoid publication of news that might encourage illegal or subversive activities. On the basis of this resolution, the government withdrew the restrictions on the press and the papers which had earlier closed down resumed publication.

But not long after, another crisis brought forth fresh confrontation between the press and the government. Towards the end of 1942, Prof. Bansali, a Gandhian, in the Central Provinces (now Madhya Pradesh) went on an indefinite fast in protest against alleged atrocities by British troops against women in two villages. The C.P. Government issued an order prohibiting newspapers from publishing news of the fast and also the ban itself. Neither the president of the A.I.N.E.C. nor the Standing Committee was consulted before the issue of the order. The Standing Committee of the conference which met in Bombay in December to consider the new development was told that the government was unlikely to accept any demand for the withdrawal of the order.

The committee thereupon decided to non-cooperate with the government. It called upon newspapers to suspend publication for a day as a "protest against a recent order passed by a certain provincial government involving a flagrant breach of the agreement reached with the A.I.N.E.C." It also recommended to the newspapers "not to publish until the order is withdrawn (1) all circulars from Government Houses (2) New Years honours list (3) all speeches of members of the British Government, the Government of India and provincial governments except portions thereof which contain decisions and announcements."

***Steps to be Remembered :*** It was a historic decision and probably the only occasion when Indian newspapers as a body had defied the alien government in direct action. In accordance with the editors' decision, the New Year honours of 1943 were blacked out by Indian newspapers and speeches of ministers and officials shared the same fate. The Delhi chief commissioner served a precensorship order on the *Hindustan Times* and the Madras Government retaliated against *The Hindu* by withdrawing facilities to its reporters. The nationalist papers suspended publication on January 6,1943, as decided upon by the A.I.N.E.C. The confrontation with the government ended on January 13 when it was announced that the C.P. Government had withdrawn the offending order relating to Prof. Bansali's fast and that it had also conceded Bansali's demand for an enquiry into alleged excesses of troops, Bansali broke his 63-day-old fast and Srinivasan advised newspaper editors to withdraw the ban on publication of official news and circulars.

When Srinivasan laid down office as president of the A.I.N.E.C. in January, 1944, tributes were paid to him for what he had done to preserve the unity of the press and to maintain the rights and privileges of the press in its confrontation with the alien government. Devadas Gandhi, editor of the *Hindustan Times* and one of his bitter critics, said when Srinivasan took over the presidentship of the A.I.N.E.C, it was an occasion when he had to take up "virtually the managing editorship of the entire press in India." There was every possibility at that time of the press as a body being completely wiped out of existence. "Thanks to Srinivasan's protecting wings the press had not only not been wiped out of existence but the whole conspiracy to do so had been shattered once and for all." Sir Francis Low, editor of the *Times of India* said if one knew something of the differences that cropped up in a body of so many widely divergent interests, one would have some idea of the will and ability with which the retiring president handled, he would not say refractory, but a pretty mulish team. It was difficult indeed to get them all to see alike, but despite divergences they did find unity—unity in diversity.

While the Indian press had to fight for its rights and to stay alive, it had also to undergo various hardships inevitable in times of war. The worst of it was the lack of newsprint available quantities of which were controlled by the government. Newspaper owners formed an association called the Indian and Eastern Newspaper Society which negotiated with the government for a fair share to all papers in the allotment of newsprint Newspapers were forced to reduce the number of pages and *The Hindu* published eight pages for a long period. The prices also were increased. The papers were obliged to impose on themselves other austerities at a time when there was a great demand for news and people were prepared to pay any price to get a newspaper. It took a long time even after the end of the war for the newsprint situation to improve and for the newspapers to resume their normal size and meet the increased circulation.

Indian journalists had always nursed a grievance that Congress leaders were more willing to talk to foreign journalists than to their own countrymen and that they practised discrimination. For instance, when Gandhi was in prison in 1930, he gave an interview to George Slocombe, correspondent of the *Daily Herald* of London, who was able to get Gandhi's terms for settlement with the government. His dispatch, which was also published in *The Hindu* by special arrangement, hit international headlines. Slocombe wrote: "Two things seemed to be as clear as crystal during the five hours I spent with him: his burning love and his burning hate. He loves India as he loves all mankind. He hates British domination in India as he hates evil."

### Ne Suggestions

Gandhi conveyed a new offer of settlement to the British Government through another British correspondent, Stewart Gelder, to whom he gave an exclusive interview in 1943. The offer was, however, rejected by L.S. Amery, secretary of state, who said it was not free from "obscurities and reservations". Indian correspondents covering the Simla Conference of Indian leaders convened by the Viceroy, Lord Wavell, in July 1945, failed to get any information from any of the leaders attending the conference on what took place and why it failed. "Everyone appeared to be dumb", wrote one correspondent, "and mystery surrounded every face and even number one newstakers and expert readers of faces failed in a manner in which they have never failed before." Some of the correspondents who were worried by the deceptive faces at Simla and also the practice of top Indian leaders favouring foreign correspondents for exclusive interviews, approached Jawaharlal Nehru one evening and put this question to him.

The issue had become more insistent because in Simla one foreign correspondent, Preston Grover of the Associated Press of America was successful in getting interviews from Gandhi, Nehru, Azad and Jinnah. Nehru denied the charge that Congress leaders had an inferiority complex and that they preferred the white skin to the brown. He said there were certain "special circumstances" for such exclusive interviews to foreign journalists. There were very few men in the political life of India who were known outside India to the rest of the world. Naturally, the outside world wanted to know their views on serious matters concerning India and these few leaders also wanted publicity for India in the foreign press and so whenever opportunities offered themselves, they welcomed them.

Indian journalists were interested in day-to-day Indian politics while foreign journalists were interested in different problems concerning India. Whenever they met him or Gandhi they asked questions in which Indian journalists were not so much interested because they knew their views on those subjects.

In 1946, popular ministries took over in the provinces and the interim Government led by Jawaharlal Nehru was formed at the Centre some months later. The relations of the provincial governments run by the Congress with the press were smooth in the beginning but deteriorated with the outbreak of communal riots and industrial strife. Ordinances were issued giving special powers to the governments to deal with the press and there was a storm of protest from the press. Pandit Gobind Vallabh Pant, chief minister of U.P. spoke of the government's problem in tackling the press.

"If papers", he told a deputation, "go on expressing ideas which are not likely to raise but to drag down sections of the community, what would you advise us to do? If we are asked to intervene then your methods as you can easily understand can be only those which are available to us under the law.

These methods are not to our liking. I have already told you that we have taken pretty good care not to make use of them."

***A Great Problem*** : On the eve of the partition of India, riots broke out in the Punjab and there were unimaginable massacres and atrocities and millions of people were uprooted from their homes. The trouble was aggravated by writings in the press and one of the worst offenders was the *Dawn*, which was the Muslim League organ published from Delhi. The Chief Minister of Punjab, Dr. Gopichand Bhargava, complained to Vallabhbhai Patel, home member in the Interim Government, in November, 1946, that the *Dawn* was publishing objectionable articles and requested that action be taken against it. Patel replied that press reports indicated that the press in Delhi had come to an agreement on the question of treatment of communal news. The government, he said, was not satisfied with it but they were prepaid to give it a fair trial. "My policy is", he said, "to watch for the time being but to act swiftly if the arrangement appears inadequate or defective journalists.'

There were very few men in the political life of India who were known outside India to the rest of the world. Naturally, the outside world wanted to know their views on serious matters concerning India and these few leaders also wanted publicity for India in the foreign press and so whenever opportunities offered themselves, they welcomed them. Indian journalists were interested in day-to-day Indian politics while foreign journalists were interested in different problems concerning India. Whenever they met him or Gandhi they asked questions in which Indian journalists were not so much interested because they knew their views on those subjects.

In 1946, popular ministries took over in the provinces and the interim Government led by Jawaharlal Nehru was formed at the Centre some months later. The relations of the provincial governments run by the Congress with the press were smooth in the beginning but deteriorated with the outbreak of communal riots and industrial strife. Ordinances were issued giving special powers to the governments to deal with the press and there was a storm of protest from the press. Pandit Gobind Vallabh Pant, chief minister of U.P. spoke of the government's problem in tackling the press.

"If papers", he told a deputation, "go on expressing ideas which are not likely to raise but to flag down sections of the community, what would you advise us to do? If we are asked to intervene then your methods as you can easily understand can be only those which are available to us under the law; these methods are not to our liking. I have already told you that we have taken pretty good care not to make use of them."

On the eve of the partition of India, riots broke out in the Punjab and there were unimaginable massacres and atrocities and millions of people were uprooted from their homes. The trouble was aggravated by writings in the press and one of the worst offenders was the *Dawn*, which was the Muslim League organ published from Delhi. The Chief Minister of Punjab, Dr. Gopichand Bhargava, complained to Vallabhbhai Patel, home member in the Interim Government, in November, 1946, that the *Dawn* was publishing objectionable articles and requested that action be taken against it. Patel replied that press reports indicated that the press in Delhi had come to an agreement on the question of treatment of communal news. The government, he said, was not satisfied with it but they were prepared to give it a fair trial. 'My policy is", he said, "to watch for the time being but to act swiftly if the arrangement appears inadequate or defective."

On November 28, the Viceroy, Wavell, wrote to Patel that Punjab governor had written to him expressing concern at the "tone of the last few issues of the *Dawn* which published an "inaccurate and inflammatory" account of the Rohtak disturbances and other articles likely to stimulate communal hatred in Punjab. The government had ordered the arrest of the Rohtak correspondent of the *Dawn*. The governor wanted immediate action to stop publication of communal articles as those complained of. Patel replied that the editor of *Dawn,* who had signed the convention on publication of communal news, had not implemented it properly. He agreed that action was most urgent and suggested that an ordinance might be issued vesting in the government special powers to deal with the situation.

Later, in a letter Sir John Colville, acting governor-general, Patel informed him that on Wavell's suggestion he had convened a meeting of editors of import local papers and members of the Central Press Advisory Committee He told him of the mischief that was likely to result from the almost unrestrained manner in which certain papers were publishing and commenting on news of a communal character.

Patel said a code of voluntary restrictions had been evolved at the meeting of editors and had been in operation for a month. He, however, felt it was not being observed either in letter or in spirit by some newspapers. Patel said he found it distasteful to control the press by taking powers under ordinance. In his address to the All India Newspaper Editors Conference he had emphasised the importance of maintaining the liberty of the press but he stressed the obligation which that liberty involved. "In ordinary times, the government can afford to give more latitude to the press but in the prevailing communal tension in the country when a slight deviation from the path of responsibility and rectitude is likely to cause untold harm, I feel that the freedom of the press will have to be controlled as a matter of painful necessity". He said that the Governments of Punjab, Bihar and Bengal had issued ordinances and taken action against several papers.

Patel had no peace from the *Dawn.* On April 22,1947, he wrote to the Viceroy, Lord Mountbatten, drawing his attention to a report in the *Dawn* on Radio Pakistan. The paper, he said, had exhorted its readers to tune into an illegal radio stations, "the clear aim of which is to promote direct action by nefarious means and fits ill with the Gandhi-Jinnah Appeal (for communal harmony)". The report mentioned by Patel said new radio station has lately come in the air (not AIR) which operates underground. It begins and ends its programme with the slogan, 'Pakistan Zindabad'. Listeners in Delhi can hear it on metre band at 8.30 a.m. and 8 p.m." The *Dawn's* report was also noticed by Rajaji, who was also a member of the Interim Government. Rajaji wrote to Patel that if it was "not taken presumably notice of it will lead on to utter and wholesale defiance." Patel informed Mountbatten of the campaign carried on by the *Dawn* against him and AIR and said enquiries which he had made had shown that "as usual the *Dawn* is cent per cent off the track and the whole article is a tissue of lies and misstatements I need hardly say that the days of this kind of journalism are numbered."

Jawaharlal Nehru was not happy either with the writings in the press. He wrote to Patel late in 1947 that the chief minister of U.P. had complained to him that newspapers were presenting news of the happenings in the Punjab in a haphazard way, which was creating great excitement. The chief minister had wanted to know if something could not be done to tone down the presentation of news so that a calmer atmosphere could prevail. Nehru said: "I am afraid our press is not very helpful. The recent statements published about the position in Hyderabad have not helped us. Again, the news about Mountbatten's going to London and somebody also taking his place had no basis in fact, so far as I knew."

Incidentally, *The Dawn* distinguished itself by making *a faux pas* on Mountbatten's picture published in its front page. Narrating the incident Alan Campbell Johnson, press attache to Mountbatten said: "I went round to Mountbatten's suite and had a discussion with the viceroy-designate.... He showed me the morning's masterpiece on the front page of the *Dawn*. It was a photograph of Ronnie Brockman (of Mountbatten's staff) and Elizabeth Ward, Lady Mountbatten's private secretary, in which they are of course described as " Lord and Lady Louis arriving."

Mountbatten in a letter to Nehru in 1947 clarified his views on censorship. This was in reply to a letter from Nehru in which he had referred to questions put to him on censorship by British and foreign, press correspondents at a press conference. Mountbatten said if there was to be censorship, the question arose whether it should be military or political censorship, and who was to impose it. Military censorship followed certain well prescribed lines—the banning of reference to place, names, number of casualties etc., which might, affect the security of military forces on operation. Political censorship involved the stopping of news which the government felt to be obnoxious or inaccurate.

It would be virtually impossible to set a limit to the government's discretion in the matter. Mountbatten felt it would be impossible to impose censorship conditions which could be regarded or would be accepted by the press as being purely military. If the complaint was about inaccuracy the best solution, he thought, would be to increase the amount of factual background for the press and to maintain as much personal contact as possible with correspondents. He proposed that an Indian official should give the reports in the Map Room which should be previously passed by the Ministry of Information and that a daily summary should be issued under the aegis of the ministry. Mountbatten's observations came during the Punjab disturbances which were widely covered by foreign correspondents.

Patel who was shown Mountbatten's letter, wrote to him: "There is no desire on our part to have any censorship, more especially of foreign messages. I entirely agree with you that any censorship at the present moment would defeat its own purpose and do us harm. It is true that many of the messages sent by the foreign correspondents have been inaccurate and sometimes tendentious. Nevertheless, I am quite clear that there should be no censorship of the press. I am making it clear to the Communications Department that no message from accredited press correspondents should be stopped or censored."

# 3

# Media in Practice

The rapid development of industrialisation gave rise to new technologies which were instrumental in bringing about a change in the process of communication. The process of communication was fast and receipts of communication and the feedback were ensured. Mass Media and Communication technologies have become integral parts of our life and our society.

***System of Functioning :*** Media are used to add new information to human knowledge and keep on upgrading it. Ignorance can not be eradicated without adequate information supply. The overall development is directly related to education. Media enable the spread of education through conventional as well as unconventional methods. The desire to have access to media increases the level of education and knowledge among the population.

Increase in media use increases the level of education. Thus, people's demand for education has given rise to the need for greater access to informations which has further boosted the media hardware production causing an unprecedented growth in the economy. This, in turn, has stimulated the expansion of communications industry including media industries.

The mass media has monopolised the leisure industry. Transactional media giants have started invading the continents via the sky, using satellite slots. The competition for audience attention has become fierce.

Mass media have also played a leading role in shaping, guiding and reflecting the public opinion. These functions of media help to establish democracy. Use of media in a democratic polity creates critical awareness among the people. The media may not be able to perform these functions unless the access to them is ensured to a large section of our population.

Access to media means access to facts and documents which help one acquire information and knowledge. In comparison with individuals, media have more access to sources of information due to their reach and institutional character. Media power makes access easy.

Media access is important in the political sphere. Access to media is access to public opinion, so essential to protect and preserve democratic institutions. It is advantageous to both the leaders and masses. Leaders can address masses depending upon their convenience. They reach widely dispersed masses simultaneously through the electronic media in particular.

**Freedom of Press**

As technological innovations improved, as the spread and reach of the press expanded, attention was focused on diffusion of information upholding the right of the public to the freedom of information. Originally, the freedom of information meant the people's right to information. In simple words, it was the right to know whatever affected the individuals themselves. New information technology has posed new dangers to the freedom of media person as well as media consumers. In theory, everybody enjoys the right to freedom of expression, but the huge capital needed for investment in new media of mass communication, has negated the whole concept since only the very-well-to-do, the elite can afford to launch the media ventures.

India is a classic example of communication contradictions. Certain media are allowed in the private sector while others are controlled by the Government. Newspapers in India have traditionally uphold the freedom of press. In India, with a low literacy level, the influences of print media are limited to the urban centres. Further, most Indian newspapers being privately owned, are supposed to guarantee free and unbiased reporting. Several defects have been identified. Most of the largely circulated newspapers are owned by big business and industrial houses, and thus political interests take precedence over any other human interests. A study conducted by the IIPA, Delhi, revealed that out of 54 dailies selected, 27 newspapers were owned either partially or totally by business and industrial houses and controlled about 50 per cent of the total circulation. For the purpose of unbiased and objective performance, delinking the ownership of newspapers from large industrial houses was suggested.

However, inspite of all this, the Indian Press enjoys credibility with reading audiences. Public opinion is reflected either in the editorials or letters to the editor published in newspapers. But, with 85% of the population totally unexposed to the press and its accessibility limited to just the elite, it is questionable how accessibility to the media can be a criteria for its high credibility. Further, how can editorials or letters to the editor from the literate few, constitute feedback of the entire nation.

Government controlled electronic media are anathema to the very concept of an open society. Frequent political interference has eroded the credibility of both AIR and Doordarshan. Added to this, bureaucratisation has affected professional aspects of their functioning. These two powerful media can cross the barriers of illiteracy and their reach is the reason why political authorities keep a stranglehold on them.

A community is an assembly of people in an identified geographical area. A community's development hinges on effective communication. The increased use of local media makes communication a vital input of every community development programme. Community participation in media programmes accentuates free flow of information. Consequently, the democratic process acquires more meaning and relevance. Community participation in mass media can be both at the level of decision-making and management.

The mass media are very important component of society. Their use in a developing country like India is considered most crucial in the challenge to mobilize people for development activities. Therefore, there must be a communication policy. The policy should give direction to the programmes which are channeled through various mass media networks.

## Critical Problems

The mass media systems may fail to perform their functions when unplanned use of such technology creates problems. For instance communication resources can be concentrated in a few centres alone. The mass media may be misused by the owners to exercise their power, or the media content may be manipulated to give as a result of the communicators biases. All these problems forced the formulation of a viable communication policy. If the policy itself becomes outdated in the face of technological developments, it will have to be suitably changed.

Traditionally, communications research in India has shown a remarkable orientation towards social problems. Studies on propaganda techniques, attitude change, effects of mass media, personal influence, diffusion of innovations, flow of information, media uses and gratifications and the economics of communication have been motivated by practical problems faced in society. These studies focus on the need to understand the role of communication in those problems and the desire to apply the knowledge gained from research to solve them.

In spite of a great deal of empirical research, no systematic knowledge about the nature, frequency and origin of communication problems in India is available. However, the situation is changing now. Demands are being made for improving existing regulations, resource allocation principles, institutional arrangements, and defining the rights and responsibilities of professional communicators, commercial communication organisations and the bureaucracies. A communication policy must give importance to these issues. The policy, in effect, is built on the body of knowledge developed by research.

***Press View :*** A Policy is a set of principles, rules and guidelines to help in the tackling of problems which may be faced by a society in any particular field. A communication policy is formulated in response to the challenges of new communication technologies. We can define communication policy as action-oriented principles, outlining objectives and means of achieving objectives, focusing on what needs to be done and what is to be avoided in dealing with current and anticipated communication problems in society. The policies are formulated on authoritative guidelines.

Given the centrality of communication in modern society, one should rightly expect that communication policy would have a distinct and independent role to play. It would take into account the problems that crop up when using communication in varied activities. Communication policy should be based on an understanding of the totality of communication problems. Such a policy should aim at achieving society's goals and expectations regarding the applications of communication.

The priorities according to which the developed and the developing countries formulate their policies differ, sometimes even contradict each other. The technologically advanced countries like USA and Japan are concerned with mobilizing world markets for their communication goals and services.

The developing countries like India, on the other hand, are concerned with building and expanding their communication systems with indigenous and appropriate technology. One major objective of their policy is to eliminate the vestings of colonial dependency. A major thrust area of communication policy of developing countries is the implementation of viable alternatives to the one-way flow of information into their societies. Most of the developing countries are busy waging a constant battle against poverty, malnutrition, illiteracy and indebtness. Thus, communication development receives scarce priority in their national objectives.

The mass media can be tools of cultural enrichment, national cohesion and advancement. The media policy makers in India first have to bridge the gap between ground realities and ideal situations. Certain paradoxes exist in the field of communication which need to be considered by policy makers. Some of these realities are elucidated here-

(a) Whereas there is an urgent demand to realise the right to equal access to information, there is a widening of the information gap between the richer and the poorer sections of society.

(b) There is misappropriation of the mass media for commercial and political purchases, when the need of the hour is to apply the media to the task of propagating culture, education, information and leisure time entertainment.

(c) There is predominant use of media to impose foreign values.

(d) In India, by and large, the communicators don't desire to find out the reactions of the audience to their programmes.

(e) The increase in the number of channels is not matched by any corresponding increase in the standard of programming.

(f) While communication satellites remove the barriers to information and education across the national boundaries all over the world, the same technology pave the way for cultural imperialism and new communication colonialism.

The Doordarshan has always suffered from the dichotomy between policy pronouncements and the continuous drift and departure from them in actual practice. In developing and democratic country like India, access to television and the social benefit accruing from it, is a crucial test of the social relevance of such an expensive medium. The importance of utilising TV is not just for the idle entertainment of the elite but for the uplift of the poor. But in effect and in actual practice, the purchase of a TV set is seen as wholesale investment in entertainment which obviates the bother and expense of going to an auditorium or a stadium.

From inception, broadcasting in India has been looked upon as a public service for the promotion of social objectives. The concept of advertisements for the promotion of consumer goods was also considered incompatible with the prevailing philosophy of the "socialistic pattern of society". In a developing country like India, radio and TV should be viewed as a national resource for the uplift of the masses. It is only through a strong media network that the eight kind of information and education can be imparted to the people. But the media in our country, like elsewhere in the world, have buckled under the pressure of commercial interests. Mindless entertainment with little or no educative value defeats the very purpose of building up a strong media network.

The press in a democratic country plays a vital role in creating, moulding and reflecting public opinion. It is a fundamental institution of our society. Though the press in

India is free, it suffers from many ills. There are a few in-built handicaps such as vast geographical area, illiteracy, poverty, multiplicity of languages and absence of adequate communication facilities. Some other bottlenecks exist like –

(a) the linking of ownership of newspapers with other industrial or commercial enterprises.

(b) limited newspaper ownership with closely held share interest.

(c) Urban-oriented expansion of newspapers leaving the vast country side population untouched.

(d) inadequate and expensive newsprint.

(e) the lack of local advertisement support.

Man's greatest invention is language. The invention of the script has helped mankind to preserve human thoughts and learning. It has helped society to conquer both space and time. An important product of the script was the book. The books helped older civilisations like the Chinese and the Indian civilizations to preserve heritage. Books spread ideas which set people thinking, as a prelude to individual and group action. For this reason, they met opposition from guardians of political and religious doctrines.

Plato argued that wise men alone could rule and the state would control education. For Machiavelli, the security of the state was supreme. Hegel regarded state as embodiment of morality. John Milton (1608-1674) in Areopagitica gave a solid reason for the freedom of the Press. In his essay on liberty (1859) John Stuart Mill (1806-1873) proclaimed that liberty was the right of the individual.

Today freedom of expression and speech are internationally reorganised rights. The league of nations made the first organised attempt at the international level to proclaim rights of speech and expression by launching a series of conferences. In just a few years of its birth, the United Nations approved the UN Declaration of Freedom of Information (1946) and the Universal Declaration of Human Rights (1948).

With the gaining of independence, freedom of speech and expression were recognised as fundamental rights and were included in the Indian Constitution. They are provided in the Article 19(1) of our constitution. Article 19(2) provides reasonable restrictions on freedom of expression.

In U.S.A., freedom of the press was very clearly recognised for the first time in the Virginia Bill of Rights in 1776. Unlike U.S.A., Britain has no written constitution. But it has been the fountain of all philosophy concerning freedom of speech, expression and the press, as John Milton did most of his work in Britain. The rights of free speech, expression and the press are in a constant process of evolution.

In general press freedom means freedom, unless specifically prohibited by law, together, print and publish information and to set up technologies in pursuit of such objectives, to claim and gain access to information. In practice, freedom of the press means freedom of the owner of a newspaper. Journalists enjoy only that much freedom as is given to them by the owner of their newspaper/magazine.

From the beginning, freedom of the press was sought and obtained on the ground that it was a prerequisite to democracy. The press demand freedom because of the functions they discharge for the benefit of the society. In today's context, freedom of the press is only an extension of the citizen's right to freedom of speech and expression. It is the press alone which can thwart the attempts of any government to deny this right to the citizen. Today, the press, the electronic media, wherever they operate privately, have information-gathering networks spread all over the world. They are the eyes and ears of the people everywhere.

In connection with the limitation, the very first thing is that the right of the freedom of the press is only an extension of the citizen's right to freedom of speech and expression. Therefore, all those laws imposing restrictions on this right of the citizen apply to the press too. It has no special privilege that the citizens do not enjoy in this area. In all western societies and in India, the constitutions as well as the general laws of the countries, set the limits for the exercise of freedom of the press. It goes without saying that with regard to freedom, the press is not on any higher footing than the ordinary citizen. Since the press is also a business and an industry, all those laws which apply to business and industry, also apply to newspaper organizations.

The theory of responsibility is simple that everyone is responsible for the consequences of his actions. 'No Rights without responsibilities'. Therefore, freedom of the press is also linked with responsibilities.' At least, the freedom should not be abused. When we say that somebody is responsible, we mean that he has a duty to do something, when we say someone is accountable, we mean that if he fails to do what his duty is, he is accountable to some person or institution. Thus, the right to freedom of speech and expression carries with it, a duty not to disturb public peace. If he so disturbs it he is accountable to the state for such breach of responsibility. Since media circulates information for the consumption of members of the society, it is natural that they should be responsible in the dissemination of the information. With every increase in the power of media, this responsibility towards the society also increases.

Editors and others often say that they have a right to inform the public. These are self-imposed responsibilities. These arise from an unwritten understanding between the media and society. On the basis of the responsibility of the media to inform the public, media have fought for and gained the right to free speech and expression.

But state has also imposed some obligations on media like not to publish anything that leads to, or has a tendency to lead to, a breakdown of public order. These are responsibilities imposed in addition to, and sometimes in contrast to, self-imposed responsibilities.

***Role of Government*** : The First Press Commission was appointed in 1952, because after independence the role of the press was changing. It was fast turning from a mission to' business. The commissionfounded that there was a great deal of scurrilous writing often directed against communities or groups, of indecency and vulgarity and personal attacks on individuals. It felt that the best way of maintaining professional standards of journalism would be to bring into existence a body of people principally connected with the industry whose responsibility it would be to arbitrate on doubtful points and to ensure the punishment of anyone guilty of infraction of good journalistic behaviour.

Second Press Commission was appointed in 1978 and it wanted the press to be neither a mindless adversary nor an unquestioning ally. It wanted the press to play a responsible role in the development process. From the role that the two commissions recommended for the press, we can summarise the responsibilities of the Press thus-

— Help the country in its development process both by making constructive suggestions as well as criticism of delays and distortions in the development process.
— Give the widest possible access to people, reflecting the pluralistic composition of Indian society.
— Maintain internal stability and safeguard external security.
— Prevent and deflate social conflict.

Complaints are heard throughout the world that a section of the press functions without regard to its responsibilities to the society. There is a vast area not covered by any legal regime. Media ethics apply mostly to cases not specifically concerned by law.

The Second Press Commission observed that one of the functions entrusted to the Press council was the building up of a code of conduct for newspapers, news agencies and journalists in accordance with high standards of journalism.

The second Press Commission lists a number of codes drafted in India, the USA and Britain have through the years. The All-India Newspaper Editors' Conference formulated a Code of Ethics and a Charter for Editors in 1953.

The National Union of Journalists (1981), the All India Small and Medium Newspapers Association (1975) had all drafted similar codes. But the Editors Guild of India refused to draft any code arguing that responsible people do not need such a formal code. The second Press Commission said that it would not be desirable to draw up a Code of Ethics for newspapers.

The Code of Ethics (1953) of All India Newspaper Editors' Conference asks journalists to serve and guard public interest, to be alive to fundamental human and social rights, to observe restraint in reports dealing with tensions leading to or likely to lead to public disorder, to assume responsibility for all information published, to respect confidence, not to exploit their status for non-journalistic purposes, not to allow personal interest to influence professional conduct, to correct inaccurate information, not to demand or accept bribe. The National Union of Journalists' Declaration of 1981 is also largely on similar lines.

The idea of an Ombudsman is of Swedish origin. In Sweden the Press Ombudsman at the national level is appointed by all the newspaper organizations together. Ombudsman generally means an intermediary, investigating complaints by private citizens against government officials or agencies. However, at present private or voluntary organizations are also having Ombudsmen to decide public complaints made against themselves or their members. In India, the Lok Ayuktas in some states are Ombudsmen.

Although this concept first originated in Sweden, but it was first adopted by the Press in USA.

The world's first Press Council took its birth in Sweden in 1916. In USA, a Press Council (National News Council) worked for 11 years and today there are nearly 50 Press Councils all over the world. The Press Council of India was set up on July 4, 1966 and Justice J.R. Mudholkar, was its chairman. It consisted of 25 members who were editors, working journalists, proprietors etc. In 1970, news agencies were also put under its jurisdiction. The council has powers to levy a graded fee on newspapers and news agencies to meet its expenditure and to reduce its dependence on government's financial support.

The countries of North and South are separated by an enormous gap in their respective communication capacities. The developed countries continue to exercise considerable political, economic and technological control on information flows. Nearly 80 per cent of the information disseminated in the world originates from five largest transnational news agencies as told before.

About 15 great media corporations dominate the production of the radio sets, television sets and printing equipment, ten of these corporations belong to the U.S.A. Due to our dependence on the media delivery systems of the West, we also become dependent on the West.

Self-reliance in news and information distribution, both in disseminating news to the outside world or in getting news and information from various places in the world, for internal consumption, is essential for the following reasons-

(a) To provide the media a national identity and personality.

(b) To facilitate the analyses of the world events not from the perspective of the West but from the national perspective.

(c) To foster better understanding among the developing countries, which is far more essential now than ever before.

(d) To prevent the unwarranted entry of foreign and alien ideas, cultures and life-styles, that always tend to contribute to shaping public opinion in favour of foreign countries, particularly of the West.

(e) To provide an objective account of the news and developments that were considered newsworthy by the indigenous media.

As per the directives of the UNESCO to establish a news pool or consortium of news agencies, the 'pool' of news agencies of the non-aligned countries was formally launched in July, 1976 at the New Delhi Conference of Information Ministers and Representations of the news agencies of the non-aligned countries. The objective of the pool is to expand the mutual exchange of information among the non-aligned countries in a spirit of collective self-reliance.

The Non-Aligned News Pool is not a transnational news agency, but a system of exchange of agency information, based on co-operation and co-ordination among individual news agencies taking part in these activities. The Pool is not based on any formal membership. The Pool has no single directing centre, nor does it have its own budget.

Many of the developing countries do not have an extensive and elaborate telecommunication network. For some, high tariffs are major barriers. Optimum information exchange depend on the level of development of communication systems in the individual non-aligned countries.

A few year ago, about 85% of the news items received by PT1 from the Pool partners were spiked. The reasons for this were given as delay in news reception, poor quality, low news value, or propaganda material.

The lack of proper training among the non-aligned journalists and their inability to match the professional standards of the journalists of the transnational news-agencies, are the reasons for the poor quality of material put out by the Non-Aligned News Agencies Pool.

In many of the non-aligned countries, the news agencies

are under the strict control of the governments. The first casualty of such a solution is the objectivity of the news and information put out by their agencies.

The editors of private-owned newspapers in the democratic countries like India, either are not convinced of the need for such an inter-regional co-operation or they do not respect the news coverage of several agencies, which are participants of the pool.

While there has been a continuous effort to establish alternative news and information distribution systems in the world, the recent global changes have had a deep impact on the information scene.

The West has been for a long time using the concept of 'Freedom of Information' as an ideological weapon, and successfully deploying it to deflect the 3rd World from its pursuit of a new world information and communication order.

In the matter of broadcasting, the Western powers insist upon the 'open skies' policy, which they claim to be consistent with the principle of freedom of information. On the face of things, this seems a plausible argument. Open skies, seems to connote a situation of an unfettered information exchange of knowledge flowing freely across the national boundaries. On the contrary, the same western countries, show a complete disinclination towards free trade by imposing heavy tariffs to protect their own products.

These developments call for a greater unity among the 3rd World countries to come out of the dependence and dominance in the field of information, and promote self-reliance. The existing world information order provides an opportunity to the richer nations to use the scarce global natural resources, and exclude the poor nations from using the same. An attempt is made through the on going GATT talks to impose stronger forms of monopoly control over the content of information flows.

***World Standard :*** The developing nations campaigned for a 'new order' in the field of international information and communication, which would facilitate a 'free and balanced flow' of information capable of breaking through the stereotypes created and nurtured for over 50 years by the western media empires. The new order, they maintained, would create a new international information climate that would foster a closer and better understanding among nations and individuals. The most important step in this direction was the launching of the Non-Aligned News Agencies Pool, in 1975. The 'free flow' concept was amended to 'free-and balanced flow', when a declaration on the role of the media in the promotion of international understanding and peace was approved by the UNESCO in 1978. 'The right to know' was transformed into 'the right to communicate'.

The non-aligned nations coined the phrase, New International Information Order (NIIO). The MacBride Commission broadened the sphere by substituting the term 'world' for 'international' and incorporating 'communication' along with 'information'. Since then the phrase the 'New World Information and Communication Order (NWICO) has been widely used.

A major factor that helped the growth of US agencies was the wireless transmission technology, which reversed the world communication imbalance to the overall advantage of the American interest. Another factor was a general realization in the US of the advantages that world communication control bestowed on foreign trade and commerce. Following such realizations, ideas on unrestricted How of communication between nations began to crystallize in the US.

The following overlapping and mutually complementing factors are at the base of the demand for a new order in the field of information-

(1) The emergence of new nations following the dissolution of the colonial empires after World War II.

(2) The asymmetrical economic relationship between the new nations and the western industrialized nations which, while strengthening the latters' wealth and power, perpetuated the new nations' dependency, not merely economic but political and cultural as well.

(3) The coming together of the new nations under the umbrella of non-alignment in the wake of aggressive bloc-building by the US and the USSR.

(4) The new nation's realization that their under-development was related to their dependence on rich nations followed by a firm resolve to assertive actions to correct imbalances in world trade and commerce, and cultural exchanges.

(5) Their gaining in strength in international organization, such as the UN and the UNESCO. Four stages can easily be identified in the history of the NWICO. The first stage (1973-76) marked the evolution of a new order. The second stage (1976-79) saw the accumulation of data and empirical evidence to give credence to the new order demand. The third stage followed the publication of the MacBride report in 1980. The fourth stage is the period following the adoption of the NWICO Resolution in the UNESCO.

Generally, the evolution of the new order concept is credited to the NAM. Much of the credit for the enlarging communication agenda of the UNESCO in the 1970s goes to the Non-Aligned Movement, which saw communication, at least in the early 70s, as a means to an end, the end being economic development of the poor nations.

The Algiers Summit of the non-aligned countries, held in 1973, is a major landmark, in the history of NWICO, for it was here that communication concerns were addressed directly in more than one paper in the context of their economic development programmes.

The 19th UNESCO General Conference adopted a

resolution inviting the Director General to undertake a review of the problems of communication in modern society. Director General constituted a 16 member commission for the study of communication problems.

The 20th UNESCO general conference, held in 1978 was marked by a spirit of compromise. The new Mass Media Declaration (MMD) text now retitled as 'Declaration on Fundamental Principles Governing the contribution of the Mass Media in strengthening Peace and International Understanding and in combating was Propaganda, Racialism and Apartheid' was approved.

The 21st general conference of the UNESCO, held in 1980, accepted the MacBride report and unanimously adopted Resolution outlining the basic character and content of the NWICO. The establishment of the NWICO depended upon five major factors—(1) the will of the developed and developing countries to bring about changes in all areas of communication within their respective regions; (2) Co-operation between the developed and developing nations for removing all obstacles to a two-way and balanced flow of news and information among nations; (3) sharing of communication resources, including technologies, for countering monopoly of the international news flow by a few; (4) cooperation among the developing countries to correct imbalances with their own regions by increasing horizontal flows and (5) Co-operation between the media-rich and media-poor for mobilization of resources to strengthen communication infrastructure in the latter's region.

The 21st General Conference of the UNESCO approved the establishment of a news agency, the International Programme for the Development of Communication (IPDC) within the framework of the UNESCO to reduce the gap between the developed and developing countries by strengthening infrastructure and services through international cooperation and assistance. The objectives of the IPDC cover all facts of communication development.

The withdrawal of the US on December 31, 1984, and Britain and Singapore a year later, from the UNESCO, was not a deterrent to the objectives of the NWICO. Today, the evolving goals of the NWICO rest with not just the UNESCO, but a large number of international organizations such as the Organization for Economic Co-operation and Development (OECD), the International Telecommunications Union (ITU), the IPDC and the Third World and its organizations for moving the aim of the NWICO to a higher plain.

The IPDC has done its best to help develop communication capabilities of the media-poor regions. Between the second session in 1982 and the seventh session held in January 1986, it had allocated US$ 9.74 million for some communication projects in the developing countries. Those included 3 regional news agency projects Pan Africa News Agency (PANA), the Agencia Latino American De Servcios Especiales do Information (ALA SEI) and the Asia-Pacific News Network (ANN) and 14 national news agency projects in different 3rd World countries. These agencies and news exchange arrangements operating within the developing countries, no matter how inadequate they are, indicate that the NWICO has set itself on its evolutionary path. But there is more to be achieved.

Imbalances in the flow of news and information at international level have not ceased to exist. The one-way flow is still very much in evidence. Most of the news flowing through the transnational agencies into the developing regions concerns the developing world. The agencies continue to view the developing world's events and issues from their own perspectives. As a result, news everywhere is seen through the prisms of the West, the developed world. The Western media giants continue to set the world's news agenda.

The developed countries should be more open to redress the ever-increasing asymmetrical economic relations between them and the poor countries. This calls for hastening the pace for the establishment of the NIEO as it is linked with the NWICO. The developed world could make available resources for communication specific projects in the poor regions of the world. New technologies needed to be viewed as resources for the benefit of the mankind, and not as a new tool for exploitation of the disadvantaged.

Steps are needed to establish a balance in the information flow by devoting more space and lime to news and issues concerning the developing countries. The developed countries should join hands with the developing countries in making the telecommunications tariffs more suitable for a better use of existing systems.

The developing world, on the other hand, needs to formulate communication policies, without which the media development would get hampered. The press must make conscious efforts to free itself from the attitudes fostered by the Western news criteria.

The free flow of information is a Western concept, by which almost all western countries rationalise the operation of their media and information agencies. The term means that any person or persons and any organization or organisations can own and operate any media or information agency, gather any information, and disseminate the same, if they so desire, to any target audience, wherever and whenever they want. The concept is basic to the history, culture and life of the liberal capitalist western society. Any challenge to this concept is rejected on grounds that it is undemocratic, inhuman and even uncivilized.

The philosophy of free flow resulted in the consolidation of the centres of information gathering and dissemination in the western countries. The socialist and the 3rd World countries could see that they were not represented objectively in the western media. Significant happenings in their countries were paid scant attention and whatever done, those were only half truths coloured by the Western perceptions. Slowly, this situation got concretised, and the leaders of the 3rd World countries endured the situation as they were unable to take steps to change the situation. The 3rd World countries had no infrastructure or active network to make a difference.

There is imbalance in the flow of information between the developed West and the developing 3rd World countries, which can not have any say on the mechanism of gathering information as they do not own and control the technology of the giant information agencies of the West. Moreover, the 3rd World countries, knowing fully well that the information disseminated from these agencies doesn't represent all the truths about them. The imbalance is in terms of volume of information, flowing into the 3rd World countries, when compared to the volume of information flowing out from them.

The root of the problem goes back to the late 1950s and 1960s, when the concept of 'Development Communication' was born. The communication specialists thought that what the West achieved in centuries, the 3rd World could achieve the same in a matter of decades if aided by the mass media. Two eminent western scholars-Daniel Lerner and Wilbur Schramm-were in the forefront to suggest this theory. Their theories were tried in many 3rd World countries.

It was assumed that mass media used for creating a stable and sustainable democratic nation and implementing programmes to uplift the living conditions of the common man in society would transform the developing societies into modern, vibrant and stable societies. However, a decade later, it was found that most of the social problems remained unsolved. Instead more problems were created. The western media organizations focused the negative developments of the developing society.

In such a situation, an American author, Herbert Schiller articulated something very new. He said that the free flow of communication was essentially meant to safeguard the economical growth of the West. And any attempt to regulate the flow of information beyond borders is seen as a threat to the western economies. Thus, it is termed as interference with the basic human right. Hence, the concept of 'imbalance' is an economic issue, and the international flow of information is just another fact of this issue.

Although the flow is still imbalance, exchanges of TV programmes, specially educational programmes, are quite frequent. More western programmes are seen on the TV screens of the 3rd World countries. Despite the large scale changes brought about by technology, imbalance persists in the media and coverage of the development west vis-a-vis the developing countries of the 3rd World.

## Setting of Format

Although the government doesn't own a majority of the newspapers and magazines, yet it is the government that remains at the helm of affairs in matters such as newsprint allocation, Registration of newspapers and periodicals, conduct of research and collection and maintenance of exhaustive reference and archive material.

PIB is the central agency of the Government of India for the dissemination of information on government policies, decisions, programmes, initiatives and activities. It puts out this information to daily newspapers, periodicals, news agencies and All India Radio and Doordarshan. The PIB has its headquarters in Delhi. The Bureau in Delhi consists of information officers attached to different ministeries and departments of the Government of India. It also has the job of evaluating public reaction and accordingly renders advice to the Government of India on its information policy.

This is the largest publishing house in the public sector. It is the media unit of Ministry of Information and Broadcasting. Earlier it was known as Foreign Branch of the Bureau of Public Information and was renamed in December 1944. It has many wings to oversee the production of print material. These are Editorial Wing, Production and Art Wing, Business Wing, Administration Wing and Employment News Wing. Employment News Wing brings out the weekly Employment News and Rozgar Samachar. The Publication Division also publishes Kurukshetra, Aajkal, Bal Bharati, Yojana, Mass Media in India etc.

This is an agency that conducts research and provides reference information on a variety of subjects. Compilation work is carried out by the documentation and catalogue section of the library. There is a separate wing that specifically collects and maintains newspaper cuttings.

A Reference Annual is published every year by the division. The National Documentation centre on mass communication, set up as a part of the division in 1976, documents and indexes news items and information about the mass media.

The Photo Division comes under the administrative purview of the Ministry of Information and Broadcasting. It documents the socio-economic progress and cultural activities of the country through photographs. The photographic prints of major events in the news are distributed to the media through the Press Information Bureau. It has its head office in New Delhi, with regional offices at Mumbai, Kolkata, Chennai. It also has a photo unit at Guwahati.

The Press Council of India is a quasi-judicial body, constituted by an Act of Parliament. It has 28 members headed by a Chairman, who has traditionally been a sitting or retired judge of the Supreme Court. Twenty members are press personnel, five are members of parliament and one each nominated by the University Grants Commission, Sahitya Academy and Bar Council of India. It hears complaints by the Press and against the Press regarding freedom of the Press.

It was established in 1948 under the Imperial Library Act, 1948. It is situated in Kolkata and has more than 20 lakh volumes in its custody, excluding the maps, manuscripts, official documents and books received as gifts or in exchange schemes. It is a subordinate department under the Ministry of Human Resources Development, Department of Culture, Government of India. The special feature of this Library is that it organizes exhibitions, lectures and seminars at the national and international levels. It is headed by a Director in addition to a librarian.

We have already dealt with the growth and evolution of PCI. Here we will look into the principles, structure and function of the Press Council.

The guiding principle of the Press Council is that if any section of the Press violates the tenets of journalistic ethics, whether written or unwritten, the Press itself should take appropriate action against it rather than the authorities punishing newspapers. The PCI was first set up in 1966 under the Act of 1965, and was abolished after the proclamation of emergency in 1975. However it again came into being in 1979. The council comprises a chairman and 28 other members. Until now, only former Supreme Court judges have been selected for the chairmanship of the council. 13 members are nominated from among working journalists including six editors and seven other working journalists.

Not less than three editors and four other working journalists should be from newspapers in Indian languages. Out of the six owners or managers of newspapers, two each should be from small, medium and big categories of newspapers. One person is nominated from among the managers of news agencies.

The term of the chairman and of the council is three years. While the members retire on the expiry of the term of the council, the chairman may continue in office until a new incumbent is nominated, but not for more than six months beyond the three year term. A retiring member can be re-nominated for not more than one term. That is a person can be a member of the Press Council for maximum period of six years. Three person having special knowledge in respect of education and Science, law and literature and culture are nominated, one each by UGC, the Bar Council of India, and the Sahitya Academy. The PCI has very wide functions in furtherance of its dual objectives of preserving Press freedom and maintaining and improving standards of print journals. But it does not deal with the electronic media.

It has also been vested with powers of a civil court. It can summon and examine witness, require the discovery and inspect documents, receive evidence on affidavits, issue commissions for examining witnesses or documents, or any other matter which may be brescribed. The council holds open inquiries on complaints received both against newspapers and news agencies, journalists as well as authorities, individuals, associations or groups of people and on the basis of its inquiries the council declares its adjudications.

The Working Journalists and other Newspaper Employees and Miscellaneous Provisions Act. 1955, is a welfare measure meant to regulate conditions of service of the people employed in the newspaper industry.

Its provisions relate mainly to (a) special provisions in respect of certain cases of retrenchment, (b) payment of gratuity, (c) hours of work, (d) leave, (c) fixation of revision of rates of wages, (f) enforcement of the recommendations of the wage fixation machinery i.e. wage boards and wage tribunals, (g) employees' Provident fund and (h) recovery of money due from the employer.

A work of literature, drama, music or art is an intellectual property. It must be protected from illegal copying or reproducing. The Copyright Act 1957 accords this problem. Copyright has been held to be a right which a person acquires in a work which is the result of his intellectual labour. The primary function of the copyright law is to protect from annexation by other people the fruits of a man's work, labour or skill.

***Various News Agencies :*** It is an agency of the U.N. All UN Member states have a right to belong to it. UNESCO has been concerned both with the development of the media and also the problems such a development brings with it. It is always alert to find out how the media and development work in the 3rd World countries. For UNESCO, it is necessary to understand that the purpose of the organisation is to contribute to peace and security by promoting collaboration among nations through education, science and culture. It also realised that only a few of the developing countries had any newspapers and more so, news agencies, which could provide the media with news.

The role of UNESCO became more significant in the context of the demand by many developing countries for a better deal from the developed countries. The first step in this direction was a call for the establishment of a New International Economic Order (NIEO) and was realised that NIEO can not be independent from socio-cultural factors, apart from political and economic factors. The 5th conference of the Heads of State of the Non-Aligned Countries (1976) and the 19th General Conference of UNESCO crystallised the idea of a New International Information and Communication Order (NIICO).

ITU was founded in Paris in 1865, as the International Telegraphic Union to co-ordinate and monitor the development of the telegraph, which was a new invention. With the development of other systems, the name was changed to International Telecommunications Union.

In 1947 ITU entered into an agreement with the United Nations and thus became a specialised agency for telecommunications. The ITU secretariat is in Geneva and works at various levels. The main functions of ITU are to—

(a) allocate frequencies to avoid interference
(b) co-ordinate efforts to eliminate interference
(c) foster the creation of telecommunication in newly independent developing countries

(d) promote safety measures

(e) undertake studies in the area of telecommunications.

Although ITU performs a very technical function, it is an important agency that is central to communication development.

In addition to UNESCO and ITU, there are other UN organisations whose activities have a bearing on communications developments. Regional intergovernmental organisations, such as Council of Europe. European Economic Community, Organisation of American States, Organization for African Units, South Asian Association for

Regional Cooperation and Association of South East Asian Nations are active in the Communication field.

The essence of any interregional cooperation in the field of information is to bring about a new sense of common destiny, and unite news agencies operating under different levels of development.

The fundamental problem in the inter-regional news networks and co-operation is that the participating news agencies in the network being, essentially, domestic agencies are geared to serve purely national needs in their news coverage.

Another area is about the issue of relevance. Most of them are editorially ill-equipped to produce copy for the consumption of the other agencies in the region. They are mostly irrelevant to each others, needs.

In most of the networks, almost all agencies are in principle, committed to producing a regional file containing news reports and features, especially prepared for the consumption of the readers outside their national frontiers. However, the tendency that persists is to move copy originally written for domestic readership for the network transmission without necessary rewriting. A great deal of information may be missing in such reports for the readers abroad, or much more than necessary is included. But, criticism on several agencies, which are part of such networks are a large majority of reports transmitted in these networks are hard news, which rarely attract the attention of the editors in other countries.

Another criticism is that they do not make amendments and changes in the news reports, keeping in view the requirements of the readers abroad.

Information can be defined as facts about an event, a place, a person, or whatever is communicated, by a person or persons to another person or persons. Mere facts do not generate knowledge. The human minds in interaction with facts produce knowledge. This knowledge has helped and is helping the human race generation after generation. Knowledge is wealth and when this wealth is used properly, it brings power.

## Global Agencies

There are hundreds of agencies, which are in the business of supplying information to the mass media. These agencies are referred to as news agencies, feature services, and syndicates. The impact of these agencies on what we read and see is quite significant.

A news agency generally deals with news coverage. It combines spot coverage with interpretation of the important political and economic events. Although its emphasis is limited, the news agency plays a very important role in shaping public opinion on crucial national and international affairs. The news agency doesn't deal directly with the public. It works through the intermediary of the other means of mass communication, namely the press, radio and television. For a majority of the news media, the news agencies are a major source of news supply. The two leading news agencies in India are United News of India (UNI) and Press Trust of India (PTI), which have contractual agreements with these global news agencies. Certain studies reveal that there are about 1200 news agencies operating in the world.

However, the five transnational agencies, Reuters, Agence France Presse (AFP), Associated Press (AP), and United Press International (UPQ and Telegrafnoi Agentsvo Sovetskavo Soyusa (TASS) put out around 35 million words per day, and claim to provide nine-tenths of the total foreign news output of the World Media. Other major agencies are Deutsche Press Agenteur (DPA) of Germany, Kyodo of Japan and Xinhua of China.

**Different Agencies**

This news agency takes its name after its founder, Paul Julius Reuter. Around 1850, he set up a carrier pigeon service. Initially his services were confined to commercial information. His first major breakthrough came in 1859, when he sent a dispatch for shadowing a war in Italy. Since then the agency has expanded. Reuters supplies news to its media clients such as other news agencies, newspapers, the radio & television stations. Under its present form of ownership Reuters claim that it can ensure that no particular group or faction can have control. Consequently, it hopes to preserve its integrity and freedom from bias.

The impetus to provide speedy transmission of news was given by the telegraph invented by Samuel F.B. Morse, in 1844. The telegraph enables many small town newspapers in the US to get their news. The meeting of the leading New York publishers was held in this context in 1848. Although a decision was made to start a news agency, the name, Associated Press, was not used till about 1860. Associated Press took a concrete form in 1900 as a modern news gather association. The struggle by AP to establish its base and the restrictions the rivals placed on it is often cited as a case that is reflective of many 3rd World countries wanting to break the monopoly of the 'big five', which ironically includes AP.

AP with its wide communications network using advanced technology has bureaus in more than 100 countries. Its 5000 plus correspondents and a host of stringers cater to about 1300 newspapers, 3400 broadcasters in the US and 1000 private subscribers.

The growth of AP spurred the rise of competitors. Edward Willis Scripps formed the United Press Association in 1907. Scripps started two regional news services to cater to his own newspapers. At the same time, there was another association the Publisher's Press Association formed in 1898 by the Non-AP newspapers. In 1907. Scripps merged his United Press Association with the PPA to form United Press Association. A major set back occurred in 1918. It sent a report that the war had ended, and later it turned out to be false. Its credibility suffered. But slowly it recovered.

The backgrounds and personal accounts enabled UPA to score over AP. Parallel to these developments emerged a third press association, the International News Service (INS). It faced severe competition from AP. Although, it was emerging as a major service, by 1956, it decided to merge with AP in 1958 to form United Press International. UPI claims to have an overseas electronic strength of about 200 journalists overseas distributed in Europe, Latin America, Asia and Australia. Its broadcast related services are considered to be a specialisation.

AFP, founded in 1835, has the maximum representation on its board of directors. Although AFP is described as an unsubsidiscd autonomous organisation, in effect, the French government and various agencies under its control subscribed to AFP, and provided good support. AFP is regarded as one of the major global news agencies. It has more than 10,000 newspapers and 70 agencies as its subscribers. Its operations are in more than 150 countries with a network of 110 foreign bureaus.

Often it was customary to exclude TASS from the 'globals' as the transnational news agencies are called. However, in terms of influence, impact and coverage, TASS was in no way different from the other agencies.

TASS began on the foundation of what was known as the Petrograd Telegraph Agency, in 1917. It supplied news through a network of correspondents in all regional and territorial centres. TASS has approximately 20,000 subscribers both domestic and foreign.

The work of TASS was complemented by another information agency, Novosti Press Agency (APN), established in 1961 by the Union of Soviet Journalists, the Union of Soviet writers. TASS and APN merged to form anew Russian information agency called ITAR-Information Telegraph Agency of Russia.

The International broadcasting by different countries are aimed at serving their people settled in other countries, and also to propogate the policies of the respective countries.

BBC occupies a central place in terms of its international reach and influence. Now through satellites, millions have the benefit of watching the BBC-TV. BBC is a central institution in the broadcasting system of the United Kingdom. In 1922, several radio manufacturers established the BBC. In 1926 it became a public corporation. BBC draws international news from its correspondents. The operations are not commercial, and finance is provided in the form of a special grant approved by the British Parliament. Consequently, the Government is directly involved in the international broadcasting system. The External Services Department has responsibility for international broadcasting. The scape, nature and character of BBC External Services was affected during the Falkland crisis. It was also the target of criticism during the Iranian Revolution and the Gulf war. However, contemporary developments indicate that international broadcasting is here to stay.

Another country which has systematically used and realised the potential of the radio and television in international affairs is U.S.A. During the World War II, two government organisations, the Office of War Information and the Council of Inter-American Affairs were responsible for international broadcasts during the period. The programming titled Voice of America was done on a contractual basis by the private US broadcast corporations. And when US. Information Agency (USIA) was established in 1953, VOA became one of its divisions. Apart from VOA, there is a separate television service of the USIA. Through satellite networking, it also arranges for direct telecasts.

It is a London based international TV news film agency owned by a consortium of the BBC, Reuters, Canadian Broadcasting Corporation, Australian Broadcasting Corporation and New Zealand TV. It is related to the international broadcasting service in the supply of audio-visual material. The service has over 170 subscribers in 95 countries.

***Foundation Regarding to Structure*** : The degree of formal organization given to the media information service depends to some extent on the size of your organization or, for a consultancy, on the size of the fee paid by the client. Some large organizations have specially designated press officers working within a press office which, though coming under the surveillance of the public relations department, is separate from it. Other organizations designate a press officer within the PR office and others simply expect all the PR staff to act as press officers as the need arises.

It probably does not matter what title is held by the people who will be dealing with media enquiries, but what does matter is that they should be reasonably au fait with the company and its products. The lack of even basic knowledge is probably a fault encountered more when dealing with a consultancy than with in-house PROs. If the query is of a complicated or technical nature it is quite acceptable to pass it on to the expert. And you really should have price lists and stockists handy.

As well as having a good working knowledge of the subject with which you are dealing, you, as an efficient PRO, should also have at your fingertips the names and telephone numbers of people within the organization who are competent to speak to the media on specialist subjects, and this list should include others apart from the brand managers and marketing department personnel. It is annoying to a journalist who is working on a story to be told that the PRO will ring back with the relevant numbers and then not to get them for another two or three days.

If the queries coming into the public relations or press office are short questions they can usually be answered on the spot, but quite often they will be in the form of a general request for information on a specific topic and it could be that your organization has in its files material which could be sent out. Do make sure that all this material is filed in such a way that it is easy to find and is related to any photographic or other reference. Some information services are organized in such detail that they have a grandiose title such as 'The Barbed Wire Information Bureau', information sheets and a direct telephone line. However, such a detailed service is usually organized primarily for the consumer rather than for the media, though answering press queries will be part of its function.

If you do have a fairly sophisticated information service it is easy to think that you have all the answers to hand, but this may not be the case. So when taking down details of media enquiries don't just record them: listen, be constructive and ask questions. If you know what the story or feature is to be about and the angle from which the producer or journalist is approaching it you will be able to be more helpful. There may be a booklet on the subject, a special expert in the technical department who has sat on the relevant government fact-finding commission or a market research survey giving the latest market trends, any of which would help the journalists far more than the standard handouts.

## Factors at Work

Most journalists agree that the telephone manners of some PR departments leave much to be desired. Some of them leave the impression that they are really too busy to deal with media enquiries and unless the journalist can use the name of a welt-known programme or a national daily the service is grudging to say the least.

However, there are other PROs who are extremely friendly and helpful on the phone. This immediately puts their organization in a good light and the journalist is disposed to feel that this outfit may be a useful source of information in the future. If this friendly attitude is followed up with prompt service the good impression is stamped even deeper. Too often the executive forgets to phone back until the next day. Or even worse, the material promised does not arrive until the end of the following week. It has even been known for a company to respond to a request for information six weeks after the initial query and then to complain that their product had been left out! There also sometimes seems to be a feeling that the media could have got themselves better organized and asked for the material earlier. There is occasionally some truth in this, but very often the journalist's deadline is looming close, and the PRO is supposed to be providing a service not a favour.

***Checklist for an Efficient Enquiries Procedure***

1. Be friendly and helpful throughout; do not give the impression that it is all too much trouble.
2. Record the details of the request and ask for further details about the proposed story so that you can dig out the most useful in-depth material. Indicate that this is the reason for your questions.
3. Drop everything and treat the request as extremely urgent Even if you know that the answer can wait until the next day it is far better to deal with it at once. It may be forgotten later on.
4. If you need to phone back, do so as soon as possible. Phone back within hours to report progress even if you do not yet have the answer.

5. If you leave a message for someone else to phone the journalist back, check to see that they have not missed the message or forgotten to fulfil it.
6. If the request is for an expensive sample use tact in discovering whether it has a genuine background. You may not have heard of the journalist or author concerned but that does not mean that they are not engaged on a bona fide testing programme or working on a first-class magazine feature.
7. Where necessary send material by cab or messenger.
8 Check to see that both postal or hand-delivered material has arrived and whether the journalist needs any more material.

**Work Nature**

Getting the enquiries procedure right is only the first stage in setting up a good media relations programme. The second stage is the much more active one of going out and securing a steady stream of coverage for the company and its products or services. Start by making a list of the areas in which you think you might be able to generate coverage over a three-month period. Such a list of objectives for the PR department of a food manufacturer might look something like this:

1. Feature material on cooking with a variety of the products in women's magazines and in regional media.
2. A series of radio interviews on local radio.
3. A feature on the use of some of the products in pubs for a catering trade magazine.
4. An in-depth feature on the new soup production line in a leading food production magazine.
5. An in-depth feature on the work of the new product development team in a food technology publication.
6. A visit to the Peterborough factory-where new jobs are coming on-line-by the industrial editor of one of the national newspapers.

7. A feature on the activities of the Skelmersdale factory social club in the local media and a possible visit by the local radio station disc jockey to a social evening.

*A Similar List for a Heavy Goods Vehicle Manufacturer might Look Something Like This*

1. A release on the year's export success for both the heavy goods vehicle publications and all the publications covering the industries to which the goods were sold.
2. Local radio sponsorship of a motoring and good driving show.
3. An in-depth feature on the conversion of a stand ard line for use in a mountainous area for a leading magazine in the field of civil engineering and for publication in the country concerned.
4. An on-site demonstration of the current range of earth-diggers for publications covering public works and civil engineering generally.
5. A feature on the new managing director for the heavy freight publications.
6. A feature on safety aspects of carrying chemicals and other dangerous substances for a lorry drivers' magazine.

To achieve the list of objectives set you will need to be in constant contact with the leading media in your field and in occasional contact with all the other publications which might be useful. This contact may be by post, by telephone or by personal meetings. Some enterprising PRs have also used humorous tapes and promotional videos to put their ideas over. The choice will depend on how important you are to a magazine or radio and the magazine or radio to you and thus how often you are likely to be working with this particular publication, how physically near you are to each other and indeed how well you get on at a social level.

However, if you have creative ideas and good material, face-to-face contact is by no means necessary. Unfortunately many editors feel that this kind of creativity is absent from the activities of a number of PROs. The only material they receive is the syndicated material which is sent out to everyone on the mailing list, and there is little attempt at placing original and exclusive material.

Syndication of material can work quite well at a regional level, though even here blanket coverage can be a real waste. If for example, you are running a recipe or a beauty information service you will be able, over time, to build up a list of regional dailies and weeklies who use the material regularly. Some sophisticated services send out portfolios of material to selected users and these are updated from time to time. If the subject is one which is likely to be covered fairly regularly the expense of such an operation will be recouped.

But for most products and services this sort of exercise would be too expensive. Others run food and cookery programmes on their local radio stations or even sponsor national radio slots. The success rate for syndicated material can also be increased by sending out material with themes which are relevant to the local area or which are topical.

For national media the approach must be rather different. Monthly mailings are no use at all, and ideas are needed in the first instance rather than completed material. Once you have sold an idea to an editor you can then discuss how much material you will supply and how much the newspaper or magazine will want to write or photograph for itself. Some magazines are pleased if you can produce an illustrated feature to an agreed plan. Others have a large enough budget to be able to retain their independence, and these publications will probably ask for background material only or will send a journalist to cover the story on the spot.

However, if you are to write the feature remember to check on the editor's requirements as to length, the number of illustrations, the date of issue of the article and the copy deadline. Sometimes it is worth thinking about getting a well-known person in the field to write features for you or at least to suggest his or her name to the publication. This will be a more expensive way of producing feature material but it may also make it more acceptable.

If your work is mainly in the trade and industrial area it is even more important to keep in constant touch with the leading publications in the field. An editor will appreciate it if you supply him or her regularly with information about the company, giving advance warning of changes and additions to the product range, the factory or indeed any aspect of the company's activities. A good relationship in this area can mean extra coverage since the editor will be more inclined to ring your company for quotes or for filler items. Editors have also been known to remind PROs that their exhibition details have not yet been received. Nor should you forget the media local to your offices and factories. Community relations can be extremely important but they are often relegated to the bottom of the list of PR activities.

List areas which are likely to generate coverage during a set period. Look at this list in terms of the relevant media and make a list of objectives to achieve within the period.

Send out syndicated material to specially selected regionals and place specific features ideas with nationals and specialist magazines. Be as original and creative as possible by letter or phone.

Once features have been placed take care to fulfil the editor's requirements.

***Press Releases :*** Some PROs like to put together a newsletter to send to the media, outlining all the things that have happened to their company over the previous three or four months. These are often quite stylishly produced with a scanner and desk-top publishing packages. The idea is that journalists will pick up just those stories which are of particular interest to their publications.

The problem is that these newsletters are often so well produced that they look far too much like sales promotion material and they may indeed be of use in selling-in to the trade. Journalists are likely to bin this type of material before they even read it, assuming that it will be full of puffs and exaggerated claims.

Far better to forget the clever design and pretty colours and stick to the news. Write up the facts following the Who? What? Why? Where? When? If possible include some information on forthcoming events as well as past history and make sure that the latter is not too out of date. It is quite permissible to include ideas for features, but it is a waste of time to write the whole piece. It is better to negotiate the placing of the complete material into those sections of the media that are likely to use it.

***Various Angles :*** Though entertaining is not an essential part of the media relations programme it can help to smooth the way. Discriminate in your entertaining. If you are taking a journalist to lunch you should know exactly why you are doing it and what you expect to achieve from it. Even more important, you should know what you have to offer. Journalists will not appreciate your wasting their time, however good the lunch. Indeed 'launching' in the old-fashioned sense is on the decline. So do not be surprised if a journalist simply cannot find the time to join you.

Reasons for individual entertaining might include any of the following:

- Briefing editors or journalists on changes and developments within your organization which could affect the industry as a whole.
- Briefing a newly-appointed editor or specialist writer on your company and its activities and the service you have to offer.

- A 'thank you' for successful cooperation throughout the year, usually coupled with a briefing on the coming year.
- An introduction for yourself to editors or specialist writers in an area of the media which is new to you.
- A general briefing for editors or journalists with whom you are not often in contact, usually coupled withideas for specific features.
- To introduce new senior members of your organization to key journalists.

The question of where to entertain is a function both of your budget and the inclination of your guest. It might be a pleasant gesture to ask your guest where he or she would like to go. On the other hand, if you have reasonable in-house facilities this might be a better venue as it will be free from distraction.

It is sometimes even more valuable to entertain a group of journalists together. This can serve both as a briefing meeting and as a discussion group. It is a good idea, for example, to gather together representatives of your immediate trade or industrial publications, together with specialist writers from the national media, at a briefing lunch on the forthcoming year. Such an event enables the senior personnel within your company to meet the leading journalists in the field and to tell them first hand of the company's plans for the coming year. The journalists can ask their questions direct and can also air any grievances or problems in an informal atmosphere.

It is important that the senior management is briefed to be as open as possible at such meetings, otherwise the value of them tends to be diminished. The representatives of the media should see the meeting as a constructive activity and not just a propaganda exercise.

Another example of extremely useful group entertaining is illustrated by a luncheon arranged by an organization which was moving into sports sponsorship for the first time. Leading journalists covering the particular sport were invited to attend the lunch and to give their views on how the sponsorship could best benefit the sport and on how they would like to be kept in the picture. The lunch also served the purpose of introducing the company's executives to this particular section of the media, and much was learnt about how to get the most out of the sponsorship.

Some companies operating in the consumer field have also seen the value of group luncheons in generating special features around products which are not very exciting and which do not really merit a series of individual lunches. Journalists must be told that this is a speculative lunch with only a small information content and that the general intent is to discuss the subject in broad terms with the injection of a few ideas from the PROs. The discussion around the table often generates even better feature ideas which can be taken up by one of the journalists present. The trick is to ensure that there are no magazines represented which compete directly with each other. A luncheon to talk about nail care and nail care products might take in one representative of each of the following types of publication: general women's interest magazines, teenage publications magazines, holiday magazines, regional newspaper, London office women's editors, retirement publications and secretarial magazines. There is very little clash of interests here and it will be quite obvious which magazine will be interested in which idea.

### *Checklist for Informal Entertainment*

1. Entertain only if you have a good reason for doing so and only if you have something of value to impart to the guest.
2. Decide whether it will serve your purpose better to entertain individually or in a group.
3. Make sure that colleagues who are to be present from sections other than the PR department are fully briefed on their role and on what can and cannot be said.

4. Have a variety of ideas ready to throw into the conversation and listen carefully to the resulting discussion. Make a note of all requests made for further information and of any interest expressed in ideas for features.

Whatever the means of communication has been, it is important to follow up properly. If a specific idea has been discussed over the phone confirm the details in writing. If an outline idea has been discussed over the lunch table ring up to carry it further, and if you have floated an idea by post and heard nothing phone up to see if it has fallen on stony ground. And when an idea has been fully agreed make sure that you deliver on time. But whatever you do, do not send out a general mailing and then ring up and ask whether the recipient is going to use it or not. If they are, your phone call will merely be a slight irritant, but if there is no appropriate slot at that particular time your call could cause enough irritation to prevent the material ever seeing the light of day.

It is worth mentioning here that the PRO's job should be a two-way one. So far we have been talking about the flow of information from the company, but it can be equally important for management to receive information on how the world is thinking about the company and its activities, about rival companies and about the industry in which it operates. Thus a press monitoring service becomes even more important. If your organization is involved in foreign markets then reaction in these countries would also be important.

The Media Relations department may also be called upon to act as a general information service, in addition to media directories you may need to keep company and financial directories-*Who's Who* and the like. These may be physical or electronic.

The choice of electronic reference works includes CD-ROMs such as *Microsoft Encarta*. This is a kind of electronic encyclopaedia which you can use to find all kinds of facts and figures. Your electronic database might also include the *Oxford English Dictionary, Grolier's Academic Encyclopaedia* (US) or *Microsoft Bookshelf* (half a dozen standard US reference books).

Alternatively you can subscribe to a variety of services such as CompuServe which provides access to large commercial databases such as Reuters News, Associated Press On-Line and Dun and Bradstreet. Others include the Financial Times 'Profile', British Telecom's 'Gold', 'Prestel' (which will also get you into the French 'Mintel') or 'Gateway' the international airways guide, all of which offer a variety of services. 'Profile', for example, holds every word published since the early 1980s in every national newspaper save a couple of tabloids and a few of the more important regional newspapers. BBC Enterprises have also made their database available.

The Internet is another vast source of information and it is growing all the time. Whole newspapers and magazines, complete books, hotel and restaurant guides, tourist information, weather forecasts-the list is endless-can all be downloaded from the Internet. A useful book which will give you some idea of what is available on the Internet is *The New Rider's Official Internet Yellow Pages* published by New Riders Publishing.

The choice of which kind of electronic reference base to use will depend upon the time taken to access it and the cost. The Internet is often the cheaper option but it can take a long time to find the information you need.

***The Principalities :*** In essence, the mass media are the tools or technologies that facilitate dissemination of information and entertainment to a vast number of consumers. They are the tools of large-scale manufacture and distribution of information and related messages. These tools 'mediate' the messages; they are not the messages themselves. However, Marshall McLuhan, the media prophet, liked to proclaim that 'the medium is the message', though the title of one of his books suggests rather that 'the medium is the massage.' The media are technologies;

they are also messages and massages. They can also be looked at as industries, as cultural or entertainment industries. While cinema, radio, television, cable, and the press can easily be recognised as 'mass media', it requires some stretching of the established meaning of the term to include recent technologies (sometimes termed the 'new media') such as pagers, cellular phones, satellites, computers, electronic mail and the internet as 'mass media'. More correctly, these new media may be termed 'interactive media' for they are not as much transmission technologies from one source to many receivers, as interactive technologies, which involve feedback, exchange and participation.

'A mass medium' says Wilbur Schramm, 'is essentially a working group organised round some device for circulating the same message, at about the same time, to large numbers of people.' Such a definition excludes the folk media, group media, and interpersonal communication such as rumour, education and preaching, where communication is not 'mediated' by a 'device'. Further, the pejorative term 'mass' (a way of looking down at people as 'masses') suggests that the modern media are 'experienced' not by individuals and groups in terms of their own cultures but as part of the 'mass' and as 'mass culture.' The term 'mass' also suggests that people's interaction with media is homogeneous, inactive and unquestioning. In communication studies today, however, the term 'mass media' has come to be a useful collective phrase, though it slurs over the distinctions among the various media.

As generally interpreted the 'mass' media are the press, cinema, radio and television. But books, magazines, pamphlets and direct mail literature and posters also need to be included in the label. They are so termed because their reach extends to vast heterogeneous masses of the population living in a wide and extensive area of a country. The means they employ to communicate messages to the masses are technological—printing machines, records, cameras, cable, modems, computers and satellites. Their communications are thus interposed and mediated; they are not as direct or face-to-face as in interpersonal exchanges.

The organs of the mass media are technological means of transmitting messages to large numbers of people. Indeed, they are much more than that. As they are very expensive media, (particularly the cinema, radio, television, video, cable, computers, and satellites) they have to be run by institutions like the Government or well financed private commercial bodies. They require a group of people to organise and administer, to produce, distribute and constantly maintain in working order the whole set up of, say, a studio, a transmitting centre, or a publishing house.

Yet another feature of the mass media is that they are founded on the idea of mass production and mass distribution-the marks of an industrial society. Copies of newspapers and magazines, for instance, are printed in thousands (some national and regional dailies in India have a circulation of over half a million) and are circulated over a vast area. But to enjoy a mass audience, the media have to cater to a taste that is not very 'cultured' or sophisticated. What the mass media therefore reflect and propagate is a popular culture. The culture made popular by Hindi films in our cities is a case in point. With the rapid expansion of television and video in cities and towns, popular culture is likely to take on new forms; the 'myths' of our culture will find expression in ever-new ways.

But the mass media in India are in fact a minority media as access to them is still restricted because of poverty, low literacy levels, and familiarity with Hindi and English, the major languages used in the various media; moreover, reach is limited to populations living in metros and large cities. The folk media, in contrast, have a wide audience; they are media close to the hearts and minds of the people, suited to a poor country, and help facilitate identification and participation.

Modern mass media serve functions very similar to those fulfilled by traditional media in some ancient societies, and in some developing countries today. Western media theorists generally identify three major functions; surveillance of the environment, interpretation of the information and prescription for conduct, and the transmission of heritage. The developmental and liberation or empowerment functions, or even the ritualistic or celebratory functions of the media rarely find mention in Euro-American media theory. South American media theorists have contributed to our understanding of media for 'liberation' while African and Asian scholars have explored the relevance of media to 'national development.'

***Moral Principles :*** Surveillance of the environment relates to information or 'news' about happenings in society. The mass media carry out this function by keeping us posted about the latest news in our own region and around the world. In rural societies, however, the word-of-mouth method is still the most credible means of spreading news.

But the mass media cannot or should not stop at watching the horizon for us, through news bulletins or through advertisements of documentaries. They need, and often do help us to correlate our response to the challenges and opportunities which appear on the horizon and to reach consensus on social actions.

In rural India, the panchayat meetings help the village elders to decide on the challenges and the opportunities.

The mass media help us to keep the culture and heritage of our society alive, and to transmit it to others. This is what the media should ideally do, but often don't. Folk media serve a similar purpose in developing countries.

A fourth function is the vital function of entertainment. Entertainment has been a legitimate function of the traditional folk media, but the mass media provide it with a vengeance. They help to pass the time, and to relax with family and friends.

Anthropologists of culture and communication discern a

symbolic function of the media: the media provide a 'shared symbolic environment.' George Gerbner, for instance, sees television as the central symbol of American culture today. Horace Newcomb and other 'culturalists' (such as James Carey and Robert White) perceive the media as providing a ritualistic and 'liminal' experience.

An equally vital function is that of the mass media helping to sell goods and services through sponsorships and commercials. The commercial function has indeed been served well, perhaps too well, especially in the United States, where the networks would have to close down if the support from commercials were to dry up. At the same time, it would be suicidal to let this function dominate the mass media at the expense of the other four functions. India too promotes the commercial function, and though it has not allowed its representatives to take over the programming of radio and television, the influence is still strong. This is equally true of the press and its dependence on advertising.

In the developing countries of Asia, Africa and Latin America, the mass media, which include traditional media have a different function to perform. In a word, development communication i.e., communication that focuses on the information needs of the poor and the oppressed, and their socio-economic and cultural interests.

While these may be the five functions of the mass media, it does not necessarily follow that audiences go to them for the same reasons. In his book The Play Theory of Mass Communication, William Stephenson argues that fun is both the greatest impact and the greatest public service of the mass media. Audiences use them as a form of play, or lila. Victor Turner, the anthropologist, believes that the media provide a 'liminal' ritualistic experience. James Carey, Horace Newcomb and others of the 'culturalist' school have developed this approach further by analysing the television experience in terms of 'ritual.'

So, for a good number of the audience, the mass media may be marvellous time-fillers, like listening to the radio while cooking or while driving, or reading during a long train journey. Further, some people use the media to fulfil psychological and social needs. They perhaps get vicarious enjoyment out of sex and violence in the media, and use the media to get topics for conversation at work, or to solve their own problems.

Still others might seek information, merely to be well informed, or perhaps to learn how higher-status people dress and live. Or, they might watch advertisements on TV not so much to know more about a product as to assure themselves that they have bought the best product. These are the 'uses and gratifications' of the media.

So whatever functions the media pundits say the mass media have, the people will continue to use them in the way they (the people, not the pundits) like. It is in this sense that audiences are 'active' rather than 'passive' receivers.

***Ethics of Journalism :*** Western theories of the mass media (particularly of the news media) were first propounded by Fred Siebert, Theodore Peterson and Wilbur Schramm in their book Four Theories of the Press.

These theories have now come to be termed 'normative' in the sense that they 'mainly express ideas of how the media ought to, or can be expected to, operate under a prevailing set of conditions and values.' So, strictly speaking they are hypotheses rather than theories. These 'theories' were first enunciated in the United States during the height of the 'cold-war' against communism and the Soviet Union. They were thus part of American propaganda and only loosely based on actual practices in the media.

They idealise the American practices, which are touted as being democratic and socially responsible, and deride 'Soviet' and 'Communist', practices as being 'dictatorial' and 'authoritarian.' They do not take into account the 'public service' models of print and electronic media widely accepted in Western Europe, and in many countries of Asia and Africa.

The 'original' four theories of the press/media are authoritarian theory, libertarian theory, social responsibility theory, and Soviet media theory. Each of them suits particular political and economic circumstances, and focuses not so much on the relationship between the press and readers as on the relationships between the press and Government. The major concern is with ownership and control rather than with different perspectives of Journalism or the people's right to information. Siebert, Peterson and Schramm limit their analysis to 'four' theories; three more need to be added to the original four to take account of circumstances in the developing countries of Asia, Africa and Latin America. The last three could be termed 'Developmental or Alternative Theories' of the media.

According to this theory, the mass media, though not under the direct control of the State and the ruling classes, must do their bidding. The press and other media are expected to respect authority, to be always subordinate to established power and authority, and therefore should avoid offending the majority or dominant moral, political and economic values. Journalists lack independence and freedom; their reports have to be submitted for advance censorship. This censorship is justified on the ground that the State must always take precedence over an individual's right to freedom of expression. Such censorship is more rigidly enforced in times of war and during 'internal' and 'external' emergencies. It needs to be noted that both dictatorial and democratic regimes resort to such authoritarian control of the media. The strictness with which the Official Secrets Act is enforced in Britain and in India is a case in point.

The basis of this 'free press' theory goes back to 17th century England when the printing press made it possible to print several copies of a book or pamphlet at a comparatively low price. In contrast with the authoritarian theory, libertarianism is founded on the fundamental right of an individual to freedom of expression. Western liberal democracies swear by this belief. The First Amendment in the American constitution is an embodiment of this theory; it flows from the individual's right to life, liberty and the pursuit of happiness.

The individual, not the State or society, is supreme, and popular will (vox populi) is granted precedence over the power of the State. The argument is that 'truth' can be arrived at only through the free expression of diverse points of view, no matter how erroneous. The great apologists of this theory were John Milton, the epic poet (in his Aeropagitica) and John Stuart Mill (in his essay, On Liberty). A free press is seen as essential to a free society and the dignity of the individual. Moreover, the freedom to publish is often linked to the right to property, and the free market system.

In practice, however, the theory provides the prerogative of free speech only to the rich and the powerful elites of a society. The marginalized groups do not have access to, and indeed, cannot afford the means or the tools of free expression. What happens on the ground is that media merchants and media monopolies (e.g. the big newspaper chains, the television companies) exploit that freedom to expand their empires. Market forces rather than public good mould the kind of information to be purveyed. The theory thus protects media owners rather than the rights of editors and journalists, or of the public. What the theory offers, in sum, is 'power without social responsibility'.

This theory can be said to have been derived from the Hutchins Report (entitled 'A Free and Responsible Press: A General Report on Mass Communication: Newspapers, Radio, Motion Magazines and Books'). The Hutchins Commission on Freedom of the Press (1947) was established and financed by Henry Luce of Time Magazine at a time in the history of

American Journalism when press barons like Luce sensed that government regulations on 'yellow journalism' were round the corner. Moreover, the years following the Second World War witnessed the rise of the Democratic Party in the United States, the restraints on business under the New Deal, and the strengthening of the trade union movement. The American press (which was known to be largely pro-Republican) feared that the federal Government would issue legislation to regulate the 'freedom of the press', despite the First Amendment.

Robert Hutchins, the Chairman of the Commission, was the Chancellor of the Chicago University at the time, and he was assisted by twelve others who were experts in different fields. The Report appeared in two volumes: the first on newspapers, the second on the other media.

The Commission found that the free market approach to press freedom had not met the informational and social needs of the less well off classes; in fact, it had increased the power of a single class. There was little expression of diverse views; the emergence of radio, film and television also suggested that some public control and some means of accountability had become necessary.

Thus, the theory had its roots in the view that the media had certain obligations to society-to serve its needs, rather than that of the free market. Hence the need for high professional standards; of truth, accuracy, objectivity and balance. Self-regulation and also state regulations were imperative. Public interest was a greater value than unregulated freedom of expression. So news offensive to religious and ethnic minorities, or news likely to lead to social violence needed to be underplayed. The Hutchins Report led to the establishment of Press Councils, the drawing up of codes of ethics, anti-monopoly legislation, and to press subsidies to small newspapers. State and public intervention in the exercise of free expression was therefore considered legitimate under certain circumstances.

This theory is derived from Lenin's application of Marx and Engel's dictum in The German Ideology that, 'the ideas of the ruling class are in every epoch the ruling ideas.' The media are thus a means of 'mental production' of the ideology. Hence the need for their control by the working class, that is, through the Communist Party, so that the interests of the working class rather than those of the ruling or elite class are projected.

In a Socialist society, therefore, the media should be used as tools to 'socialize' the people; the primary functions of the media are to educate, inform, motivate and mobilize citizens, and to support 'progressive' movements everywhere. What is expected is 'objective' (or 'scientific') presentation of society. Censorship and restriction on the media are legitimate for the media are accountable to the State, to the public and to the Party. The public is encouraged to provide feedback, as it is only in this way that the media will be able to serve the public interest.

The 'four theories of the press' are not fully applicable to the experience of the non-aligned countries of Asia, Africa, and South America. While in most Asian and African countries, the media (especially the broadcast media) are owned and run by the State, in Latin American countries, commercial ownership of all the mass media is the norm. A common factor in the experience of the majority of the non-aligned countries is the dependence on industrialized countries for both hardware and software. Another common factor is the commitment of these nations to social and economic development on their own terms; they would like to employ the mass media as tools for 'development', for 'nation-building.'

The larger national interest and the public good are of paramount importance to them. So certain freedoms need to be curbed in the interest of say national integration, and economic and social development. Hence the stress on 'development communication' and 'development journalism'. According to development theorists, journalists have the responsibility to support national governments in their efforts at eradicating illiteracy, promoting family planning, promoting national integration, and increasing production and employment. The weakness in the theory is that 'development' is often equated with government propaganda.

Latin American critics (notably Paulo Freire, Reyes Matta, Luis Beltran, Diaz Bordenave and Valerio Fuenzalida) of commercialized ('commodotized') media have come out strongly against the top-down, one way and non-participative character of contemporary mass media. Like the development theorists, they lay stress on the positive uses of the media, on the need for 'access' and the 'right to communicate.' They insist on the need for local and community participation in media and news production. The people must speak for themselves, they argue, not through professional journalists and producers.

What is vehemently opposed also is commercial, political or bureaucratic control of the media, which exist to serve audiences, not the interests of government or commercial enterprises. The 'demassification' of the media, according to this theory, is as vital as 'democratization.' The ultimate purpose is to put the media in the hands of communities (as in people's radio) for their own 'liberation' through a process of 'conscientization.' Thus is created, in Reyes Malta's words, a 'critical national audience.'

***Mutual Relationship :*** Successful media relations involves understanding the media, how they work and what their requirements are. It also involves relating this knowledge to the needs of your own organization and the objectives of its media relations programme. It is important to work out the best strategy and to plan accordingly.

This book is essentially practical. It is concerned with the tools, the organization and the planning of the media relations programme. But it also seeks to show how a thorough knowledge and understanding of the media can make your efforts more effective.

There is, after all, no point in spending a fortune on trying to communicate an important story if you are telling the wrong people, in the wrong way, at the wrong time. Putting yourself in the recipient's place and deciding exactly what will be of interest and what will not will be much more useful from everyone's point of view.

This kind of practical knowledge of the media will put you in a better position to build up a harmonious and helpful relationship with those sections of the media which cover your organization's particular activities. And this relationship will in turn help you to establish a smooth communications channel between media and management.

Unfortunately, the senior managements of some organizations tend to view the press or media relations department as a buffer between the media and themselves. This can only lead to trouble. Very often the Public Relations Officer (PRO) is not qualified to answer detailed and possibly highly technical questions. Nor does he or she have the authority to answer for the company on important issues. Such an attitude inevitably leads to an unnecessarily bad press and a lack of cooperation by the media on future occasions.

Rather, the PRO should be the means by which the two sides can talk to each other more easily and with more understanding. You must stick to your professional guns in telling senior management what the consequences of their actions in the media relations field are likely to be. You must, however, also follow up such a stand with sensible advice on dealing with the media and be on hand to see fair play.

Of course, there are occasions when certain sections of the media behave with some dishonesty and as PRO you must watch out for signs of such a situation arising and warn your management in time. But the vast majority of dealings with the media will not be like this, and management must be encouraged to be as open as possible.

Building up a favourable relationship with the media often involves building up a good personal relationship with key journalists in your field. You cannot hope to achieve this if you are not convinced yourself. If you do not think you can be committed to an organization's activities, do not work for it. Honesty is as important at this level as it is on individual issues.

This applies equally whether you are planning to work directly for the organization or for its PR consultants. Indeed everything in the book applies to both situations, for they differ only in their organization and lines of control. To all intents and purposes a PR consultant must act as though he or she works directly for the client organization. 'Public Relations Officer' has also been taken to be synonymous with Press or Media Relations Officer' for the purposes of this book.

Of course a harmonious relationship with the media does not mean that everything will always go smoothly. Sometimes your objectives and those of your media friends will be in conflict and this is where your powers of diplomacy will be tested to the full. Competent journalists will be probing critically. That is their job. Yours is to present the facts in the most favourable light for your organization and, if the problems are severe, to ensure that ultimately your organization's worst story receives the best hearing.

A good example of successful media relations concerns a multinational oil company, one of whose oil tankers was wrecked, causing extensive spillage along the Californian holiday beaches. Sales at petrol stations immediately started to fall. The company instituted an expensive and wide-ranging mopping up programme including very quick cleaning of the popular beaches and a bird sanctuary, a marine life survey and a restocking operation. Full details of the disaster and the company's prompt action were relayed to the media at once and this, coupled with the previously good relationship between the oil company and the media, ensured that most of the coverage was concentrated on the mopping up operation. This resulted in the company being seen as a responsible, socially conscious organization rectifying an inevitable disaster, rather than as an irresponsible multinational with no concern for the environment. Sales not only recovered but exceeded the previous norm.

There are times when the disaster is less obvious to the public view and this is when there is a strong temptation to deny everything. The short answer is, don't allow your management to do so either. If you or any of the representatives of your organization do lie, your reputation in the media will be shattered and its loss will precede you into whatever industry you go. It is very rare for the truth not to emerge, given time, and once a journalist has been castigated by his or her editor for believing your lies the journalist will, understandably, never trust you again. In future, the journalist will be suspicious of everything you and your organization have to say and will tell associates to be wary too.

Successful media relations, then, means understanding the people with whom you want to communicate-producers, editors and journalists-appreciating their problems, needs and audiences and treating them with honesty, efficiency and common sense. It is this principle that underlies all the detailed information and advice.

The term 'media relations' refers to the communication Pattern between an organization and those sections of the media which are interested in its activities. Such communication may be concerned with anything and everything which happens within and around that organization. It may also be concerned with local and national issues, with finance and legislation and with public opinion.

Communication between organization and media may be initiated by either side, but from the organization's point of view media relations is concerned with achieving the most favourable coverage possible. This can sometimes be achieved by reacting to individual happenings or to media enquiries, but at best this approach is haphazard and at worst it is inefficient and potentially dangerous.

It is far better to plan a media relations programme within the framework of your organization's objectives as a whole. This not only helps to channel your efforts into the most effective areas, but also ensures that everyone who comes into contact with the media knows what their organization is trying to achieve.

***Real Situations :*** The first step is to define and analyse the problems in order of priority and then to set objectives to be achieved. The problems will, of course, vary according to the field in which your company or organization is operating and what it is trying to achieve. However, for a manufacturing company the problems might include any of the following:

- The product range is seen as too expensive.
- The proper use of a new product is not really understood.
- The company has a reputation for bad service.
- The company is moving into a new high technology field and needs to upgrade its scientific image.
- The company is not thought of as a good employer.
- The more expensive end of the product range is not being retailed through the right kind of outlets.
- There is an important technical development behind the introduction of a new product which is not fully appreciated.
- The company is thought of as being old-fashioned.

All these and other problems will come in as feedback from the marketing and other departments. Obviously they need to be countered and an objective must be set. Ideally objectives should be measurable and achievable. If you set unobtainable objectives you will be seen to have failed even if you do a wonderful job. To some extent this is also true if the objectives are not measurable.

Whatever you do, do not try to link your objectives to sales. There may be a great temptation to do this as part of a justification for the very existence of the media relations programme. But you are unlikely to be able to show a link which is directly attributable to your activities and you will be encouraging the view that media relations is simply a cheap form of advertising.

If an objective is to be measured effectively it needs to be defined clearly. There is no point in stating that the objective is 'to increase awareness' or 'to change an attitude'. This is not enough. You must include the answers to the questions 'of what?' and 'by whom?' which will lead you into defining your target audiences. The answer to 'who are you trying to influence?' will in turn lead you on to 'how are you going to reach them?', and once you have reached this stage the programme starts to become viable.

Here is a very simple example of the start of a media relations programme for a small company producing torches.

Market research has shown that the company's torches are seen as dependable but rather old-fashioned and there is little awareness of the newer products which have been introduced to fit the contemporary life-style.

***Objectives***

1. To increase awareness of the more recent products.
2. To show that these products are up to date and invalu able to the modern man or woman.
3. To give the company a more go-ahead image, while retaining the dependable aspect.

The torch-buying public includes the following markets:

- Women buying torches for domestic and car use.
- Men buying torches for similar uses.

- Industrial buyers, for security services.
- The police and the armed services.

The media reaching the ultimate target audience include the following groups:

- Women's interest programmes and publications.
- Men's and general interest programmes and publications.
- Motoring programmes and press, and the caravan and holiday press.
- Security and safety publications (both consumer and trade).
- Police and armed services press.

This sort of analysis makes the rest of the programme much easier to plan. Working against the background of known developments and plans for the torch company for the coming year a single idea for each area will start the programme off. There may, for example, be plans to launch a new pocket or handbag version of one of the company's torches; if it is sufficiently different from anything else on the market this could form the basis for an onslaught on the women's interest press.

The frustration of life without a torch, illustrated by either a feature or a demonstration, could interest the men's press, and special car fitments for fixing a torch inside the car would be of great interest to the motoring media. Similar ideas for features, visits and events could be thought up for the remaining areas.

A plan like this not only shows up the priority areas and assists a sensible organization to plan its workload; it also shows where effort should be concentrated and helps in the measurement of success.

Massive coverage may look good but it is less valuable if it appears in media which are not seen by your ultimate target audience. There could even be occasions when extended coverage in a large number of regional and provincial newspapers is much more useful than a short piece in *The Times*. The temptation is, of course, to impress management with national press coverage, but this may not always be the most effective approach. It may be good for your ego, but is it good for the company?

Once you have an outline of your media relations programme worked out, and preferably written down, you will be ready to start thinking about the detailed use of tools such as media lists, press releases, competitions, press receptions, workshops, visits and special events.

However, the media relations programme does not end here. It must be assessed. Is the right message reaching the right people in the right volume or are you wasting your efforts talking to the wrong audience or giving the wrong signals? There are various ways of evaluating a media relations programme.

# 4

# News Selection

Newspapers fascinate people from all walks of life, but very few have the time or the patience to study the organisation, production and presentation of news. Most people look upon the newspaper, as a comprehensive presentation of news. Most people look upon the newspaper as a comprehensive presentation of all the important events in the past twenty four hours. Some newspapers have mythologised this concept by claiming that they print 'all the news that's fit to print. Apart from the fact that no newspaper can print everything that is worthy of printing and people's attention, there is another implication in this claim: news judgement. The newspaper organisation decides what is fit and what is unfit to print. Selection is inevitable. According to Walter Lippmann.

Every newspaper when it reaches the reader is the result of a series of selections as to what items shall be printed, in what position they shall be printed, how much space each shall occupy, what emphasis each shall have.

Traditionally, the newspaper has been looked upon as a platform of public opinion, a vehicle for moulding public opinion and an instrument to fight oppression and tyranny of the rulers by bringing to light their misdeeds.

Historically, the press has played an adversary role vis-a-vis the government and championed the cause of the people, particularly the middle and upper classes. The role of the press in freedom movements in all countries has been a very significant one.

But the modern newspaper is a different product from a different organisational structure playing a totally different role. Ever since the business and commercial class began to extend its influence on government, the newspaper's attitude to its own role in society had to change. The new commercial newspaper had to depend on the support of the commercial class since it was the product of that class. Its adversary role against government took - a new turn.

The newspaper had to become a vehicle for the criticism of those actions of government which went against the interests of the commercial class. Any action by government which smacked of interference in the free trade philosophy of the merchants, industrialists and financiers was jealously watched by the press and criticised vehemently.

Somehow people's interests were taken by the new press as identical to those of the commercial class. This was a phenomenon that occurred in the early part of the 19th century not only in the economically advanced countries but also in their colonies. It is still continuing in both the 'developed' and the 'developing' sectors of the world. In erstwhile colonies, the bulk of the press is still in the hands of the entrepreneurial class that uses the newspaper as an instrument to safeguard its financial interests and to prevent or forestall movements, if any, to change the existing economic order.

In the advanced countries, the press is in the hands of powerful media conglomerates which have strong banking and financial ties with multinational corporations.

**Process of Selection**

No newspaper anywhere in the world can print all the news that comes to it from various sources. Severe selection processes are thus inevitable. This section discusses first, the selection of news in general, and then turns its attention to the selection of foreign news in the light of certain major concepts associated with the making of news.

Economic considerations of total space, size and advertisement content put constraints on the amount and types of news and feature materials that go into the newspaper. The dependence of the modern press on the business world can be seen from the heavy advertising content of the modern newspaper. Even the New York Times which is acclaimed by many as the best newspaper of the United States has a 60 to 75 per cent advertisement content on any given day. All the front-ranking newspapers of the world have similar quantities of advertising in them.'

Whether newspapers change their editorial policy or news content according to the dictates of industrial giants who are heavy advertisers is open to, dispute; but it is only logical to assume that advertisers as a group do exert an influence on the large circulation press because the press depends on their support to survive the mounting costs of high technology currently being used by it.

Another important factor is the crucial interlocking between the news and information industry and other unrelated industries. This is especially true of the big Indian newspapers such as the Times of India, Statesman, Hindustan Times and the Indian Express. These newspapers are connected with vast industrial and business empires such as the Tatas, Birlas, Goenkas, and others. Directors of huge cement, jute, steel and rubber companies guide the destinies of some of these newspapers. The giants among the American newspapers are also connected with giant industries, a fact well brought out by Dreier and Weinber.

In addition to economic considerations, technological imperatives affect the nature and quantity of news, particularly foreign news, in a modern newspaper. In their bid to bring the latest news in competition with the electronic media which are naturally much faster, the newspapers have spent huge sums of money to install the latest electronic machines and computerised systems of news and picture transmission. They also depend heavily on the satellites and the global wire services. This situation affects the content of newspapers to a great extent, because what is electronically transmitted gets priority. The newspaper editors listen to early morning news bulletins from the broadcast media and then follow up the leading stories-from the wire-services.

The wire services play an important role in the selection process in all news organisations that have installed teleprinters. Whatever comes off the wires is considered more urgent and important than reports coming through other sources. In fact, half a dozen major wire services in the world-Associated Press (AP), United Press International (UPI), Reuters, Agence France-Press (AFP) and TASS-determine the type and quantity of the news content in the newspapers of both rich and poor countries. This is particularly so in the case of foreign news. Since newspapers are in the business of producing under pressure, they find it very convenient to adapt readymade wire service reports and meet the deadline. Moreover, most newspapers cannot afford to station their correspondents in major cities that provide most of the news. Heavy dependence on the global wire services is the characteristic of all newspapers. Diversity in news is likely to suffer from the practice of all newspapers depending on the same wires.

## How to Present News?

The very nature of newspaper production imposes certain constraints on the product that reaches the audience. Lack of time and stall imposes restrictions on the selection process and hence on media content. Indepth reports have to wait; what is readily available will form the top story since immediacy is a primary consideration of news organisation and news workers. This will put severe constraints on completeness journalists are sometimes torn between two equally opposing forces: the desire for completeness which may delay the transmission of messages, and the desire for immediate release which may affect completeness.

If a large enough staff is not available for research, a story may be 'killed' or delayed indefinitely, or alternatively, the story may be reproduced verbatim from another source more readily available. Most of the time, the wire services determine what stories go into the day's newspapers. Since this is the age of computerisation in newspaper production, standardisation becomes inevitable.

But, are technological reasons the sole determining factors is selection? Are there sociological, organisational and hierarchical factors exerting a decisive influence on the selection process?

In order to understand the sociological, organisational and hierarchical factors exerting a decisive influence on the selection process?

In order to understand the sociological aspects of selection, some theoretical matters connected with the definition of news, function of news organisations in society, structure of news organisations and the decision-making process have to be examined.

First, a look at the process of communication itself. There are four components in the process: the communicator, the message, the channel and the audience. Theorists use four other equivalent terms: the encoder, the symbols, the media and the decoder. The communicators and the audience interpret the message properly only when they have the same frame of reference. Those who produce and present the messages and those who receive them should have the same symbolic frames of reference for proper understanding or communication to take place. Normally those messages which are out of the symbolic context or experience of the audience will be left out by the communicators.'

In his case study of selection and communication in a television production, Eliott identified seven distinct stages:

> Programme ideas and outlines; researching and collect on of programme material; programme material; selection of programme material; detailed outlines and scripts; cuts and adaptation; and programme recording-in that order.

If we transfer this model to a news report production, we can identify the following major steps:

1. Selection of an event to report, or an idea to convey. This may be done by the reporter or a source outside the news organisation. For example, a government or private source may contact the news agency or newspaper organisation, or its representatives with a ,story' for possible inclusion in the next issue of the paper.
2. The report prepared by the reporter or outside person.
3. The report goes to the receiver's desk for selection. It is here that the fate of the report is decided. The selector here is usually referred to as 'the gatekeeper'. From here the report may go in toto into the next issue of the paper or it may be totally rejected; sometimes it may be modified a little through further consultation with the reporter and the source, or without any such consultation. Cuts, additions and alterations are made here.
4. If the report goes into the paper in part or as a whole, it reaches the fourth selection stage, namely, that of the audience. The audience may or may not see it. It depends on the positioning of the report, the audience's interest in the subject matter, the size of the headline

used, and the relevance of the report to the conditions of the time.

In all the above stage, sociological factors affect the selection process.

A closer look at the four stages is important here.

The communicator is not just the sender of a message. Whether he be a reporter, special correspondent or an outside informant, the communication worker has grown up with certain impressions and value judgements about the socio-economic, cultural and political significance of an occurrence. His impressions are not substantially different from those of his compeers and colleagues the media organisation, and ultimately, they are the sa as those of the top management personnel who control the medium. There are some exceptions to this general rule.

Some newsmen have left their organisations precisely because of the incompatibility of their vie with those of their organisations. By and large, however the selectors in all stages have certain common bonds selection philosophy which is unwritten, yet visible actual operation. Communication is part of the to socio-economic and political structure prevailing in country. Culture is again manipulable by those who control the ingredients of its social structure: means production (technology), marketing, finance capital and employment capabilities.

In the first step of selection, therefore, the selector leaves out certain aspects of reality (which is one, holistic, and integrated, although consisting of several aspects). He does this either intentionally or unintentionally, probably because of a set pattern of selection in his mind conditioned by his past education, cultural upbringing, his country's national and foreign policies, his social class, or his corporation's economic objectives. The modern newspaper organisation being a huge, capital-intensive, highly centralised and high technology-oriented corporation, stays in business to make profits.

Therefore, those who work for it will have to select a story that will sell.

Is there any coercion on the selector at this stage? Perhaps not journalists are by nature free spirits who wish to do their job unhindered by their own bosses or by pressure groups or by government. However, as Gans says, journalists, despite their resentment of bureaucracy and toeing the hierarchical or organisational executive line, are in fact, part of a well-formed bureaucratic set-up that 'suggests' rather than 'orders' -specific tasks.

Senior executives in a news organisation exert a certain amount of pressure on the newsmen because like any other business or social organisation, the press is hierarchical in its structure. But the whole hierarchy is conditioned by the socio-economic and political climate prevailing in the country. It is I relevant to quote Gans again as he studied newsroom decisions by participant observation. He writes:

> Because news organisations are assembly lines on which people must work together to manufacture a product against a deadline, they almost always generate conformity. Few top editors are either sufficiently powerful or Machiavellian to manipulate the pressures for conformity ... [Yet] they resolve uncertainty, decide which selection considerations have priority, set tones and some precedents, which then require conformity. Senior editors do much the same in their sections (1979-98).

Informal methods failing, formal authority is used to bring the 'deviant' reporter back to the organisational policy track. In fact, 'deviations are discouraged or prevented by six factors', according to Warren Breed. They are:

> the use of formal authority and sanction, with the possibility of giving controversial stories to 'safe' men to handle' desire of newsmen to get on in their

careers, the lack of any alternative group allegiance to support deviance; the gratifications of remaining in the in-group and finally handling news according to policy becoming a value in itself.

The policy, according to Breed who studied the role of news selectors or 'gatekeeper' in detail, is usually to protect property and class interest.

**Taking a Start**

The communicator in the first step is, therefore, news organisation, he is still under the influence of the business or government organisation he works for, whether or not be admits it. This factor of corporate influence over selection is of vital significance in modern media organisations because of the trend towards concentration and centralisation of mass communication technology, production, and ownership; and the interlinkage between organisations and out side organisations including some government agencies. As mentioned earlier, communication industries in both rich and poor countries are under the tight control of either huge conglomerates which, have multinational connections or multinational corporations which have direct or indirect control over several media in many countries. This is the age of monopolistic communication practices.

In the second stage of selection, that is preparation of the report, words or pictures are selected in such a way that those aspects of reality selected in the first step are presented effectively. Again, the reporter's subjective decisions play a role at this stage.

In the third stage, when the message reaches the receiving end, that is, the media organisation, the decision-makers there begin their selection. The message goes through the 'gatekeeper'. Kurt Lewin was the first to introduce the term 'gatekeeper' in 1947 with reference to the people in a news organisation who watched the flow of news. David Manning White and Warren Breed popularised the idea. According to

Breed, the policy of a publisher gets translated into action by the 'gatekeepers'. McQuail found that the 'gatekeepers' had the power to decide if an item would have to be changed before it was transmitted. At this stage, major decisions are made regarding the selection of stories for the day's issue the decision-makers go through the stories selected by reporters and judge wire service news stories. The decisions are usually made at the afternoon editorial conference where each section editor brings in what he has chosen for inclusion in the next issue. As Lippmann observed, there are no written rules on decision-making, only conventions.

Some scholars have given more importance to the decision-making process at the first step, namely, the news gathering stage. For example, Bass considers the news gathers' decision more important than the news processors' decision. The news gathers, according to him, consist of the writers, reporters, bureau chiefs, and city editors; the news processors include editors, copy readers and translators. But this does not deal with the organisational and sociological imperatives exerting influence on the climate of the news gathering and selection process. For an understanding of this influence, we have to refer to some other studies based on the content of news media.

In their classic study of a demonstration against the Vietnam War, Halloran and others showed how events were selected for news reporting in terms of their fit or consonance with preexisting images. In other words, the news of the demonstration confirmed earlier ideas. Their conclusion was:

> The more nuclear the news item and the more uncertain or doubtful the newsman is how to report it, the more likely it is to be reported within a general framework that has already been established.

Four other factors were cited by Halloran based on the findings of Galtung and Ruge as vital components of news value: reference to elite persons; references to elite states; personalisation or personification; and negativism. Do media select top people and top nations more frequently than others? Is news reporting person centered? Are negative events preferred to positive ones?

Another important finding of Halloran and associates was that despite he outward differences among various newspapers, all of them showed a fundamental similarity in the presentation of factors which made events news. They found little variation in the approach of the various newspapers to the demonstration against the Vietnam War.

Viewers and readers were not presented with various interpretations focusing on different aspects of the same events, but basically the same interpretation which focused on the same limited aspects-the issue of violence.... Events were not so much deliberately distorted or otherwise falsified by presentation, as selected and interpreted for their relevance to the basic and predetermined news issue.... The simple negative image built up for the demonstration story was the only image made widely available to the public by press the television news.

It is in the function of selection and interpretation that the news producers exercise, their value judgements. This function is performed with reference to a framework of ideas and symbols considered important not only to the communicators but the 'communicatees'.

Stuart Hall's comment on the process of interpretation in broadcast media is relevant to that in the mass circulated press as well:

> Every news event is already, completely, assigned to a context which explains it. The broadcaster, or his reporter and camera-man in the field, must already have such a context in mind in order to know what to film, which to select and send back to the editor, which to include in the broadcast.

If we accept this premise, we have to concede that in the process of news selection. Agenda setting is unavoidable lit-cause the recipients of communication should be provided with certain stories presented in a certain way for contextualisation. For many years, researchers have been trying (and they are still trying) to find relationships between media usage and attitude change. Agenda setting is a trend discernible in the mass media and it is resorted to by the media owners to bring about a symbiotic relationship between their priorities and their audience's supposed priorities. The ultimate aim is to find that perfect fit or consonance between the communicators and the audience which is essential to maximise sales of media products and hence profits. Through agenda setting, the media fare will synchronise, it is hoped, with 'what the public wants'.

## Audience of News

We are now in the fourth selection stage, namely, the audience of media fare. There have been many studies of the audience of all types of news including foreign news; but most of the studies have concentrated on how to effect behaviour modification through appropriate messages to the audience. Since a study of the effects of messages on the audience is not our aim, it is enough to mention that members of the audience select messages depending on their particular needs and interests. Newspapers are aware of their audience's selection of messages, and they hope to reach messages they consider important for the readers by placing them in special positions or displaying them distinctly. The placement of messages and their display is allied to the concepts of selection and agenda setting. Since agenda setting is linked to the fourth selection stage in the communications model, some details of that concept are worth examining.

The press, as Walter Lippmann said in his classic work, Public Opinion, fills in our unseen environment, and helps us to form our mental picture of the world on a daily basis. People exposed to the mass media do learn from them and form opinions based on that learning. Can the press steer the course of their thinking or influence their thinking process? According to Shaw and McCombs, the two researchers who studied this issue empirically, the press presents to the people should be concerned about. It may be argued that enlightened people will have their own independent judgement on all such issues: but research has shown that the press through the agenda setting process provides issues and event to think about, if not opinions to hold.

The concept is defined as 'the ability of the media to influence the salience of events in the public mind. It has been derived from two important pronouncements made half a century apart-one by Walter Lippmann in 1922 and the other by Theodore White in 1972. Lippmann spoke about the power of the press in creating pictures of the world in the minds of the readers. White spoke about the press setting the agenda of public discussion.

Through the process of selection, as already explained, the media transit to the audience those national and international issues which they consider newsworthy and hence worthy of the audience's attention. Shaw and McCombs have shown that people form their individual political cognitions based on what the mass media present as salient. The agenda-setting function of the press is put into practice through the following steps:

1. daily selection of news events and issues by the wire service reporters and editors;
2. daily selection from the wire service news and issues by the newspapers' editors (gatekeepers); and
3. placement of the news and views in the newspaper by the new editor.

Placement in the broadcast media is achieved by the numerical order in which the news and views are presented. Whichever is announced first is the leading news story of the hour. In the newspaper, what the news editor considers to be more important news events will be placed on the front page. These -will not only be placed on the front page, but discussed in the editorial and opposite-editorial pages. Among the important stories on the front page, the most important will be presented in large size types, with bold letter synopsis, 'boxing', etc. Sometimes pictures are incorporated to heighten the importance of the event.

Items placed on the left hand corner catch the readers' attention first since people's eyes move linearly from left to right, except in those countries where they read from right to left. What the media emphasise through selection, placement and display go down in the audience's consciousness as salient. According to Shaw and McCombs.

The agenda setting power of the press may be thought of as a process of consensus building between those who have access to the press or whom the press regularly covers with news, the press itself, and the audience or society at large. Agenda setting represents social learning.

The above discussion shows that reporters and news editors or the maker of news have the power to select events and topics. They exercise this power on a daily basis and what the audience gets is the product of their selection. We move on now, to some more conceptual matters relating to news selection and newsmaking.

Access to the press is supposed to be the corner-stone of democracy since it ensures open debate on public issues. The freedom of the press is ultimately people's freedom to express their views even when those views are against the prevailing authoritarian forces. But, can every citizen be guaranteed access to the media? Is the modern, well-established, high technology press small enough to be accessible to the ordinary citizen?

## Technology and its Role

Technological progress has changed the structure of media organisations and the very nature of mass communication. The trend towards centralisation of the technology and ownership of the mass media has been referred to already. Big newspapers force the smaller ones out of business and multimedia conglomerates dominate the communication scene. The concentration of the media in the hands of a powerful elite minority is not conductive to citizens' access and to the freedom of the press. In the United States, newspaper monopoly exists in 95 per cent of the cities.

In India, there are thousands of small towns and villages which do not have any newspaper circulation at all. Lack of access leads not only to the loss of vital information but also to the stifling of dissenting views and to a lack of diversity. Despite the argument that it is impossible for any newspaper to publish everything that comes to it, it should be recognised that the only way to ensure access is to multiply media voices through alternative media, if necessary. If the media of communication continue to depend on centralised, capital-intensive, high technology, they will remain inaccessible to the average citizen's points of view.

This is a quality often stressed by newsmen. It is closely linked to completeness, but since newspapers are mainly in the business of bringing the latest news, and not that of completing an already broached story with additional facts and figures for the edification and education of the readers, continuity is not often adhered to as an inviolable news principle. A big story of yesterday will be discontinued or inadequately treated today in order to play up today's big story which in turn will be replaced by another story tomorrow.

Do various newspapers follow a pattern of omission or inadequate treatment of an already broken-in story? Are there reasons for this other than the desire to bring the latest 'big story and action news' to the readers? Are there organisational pressures or governmental pressures? By discontinuing stories or reporting incompletely, especially news about other countries and cultures and national minorities, will not distortion occur in news treatment? These are questions that have been answered to some extent by Gans and Tuchman who, like Gans, Audied the newsmaking process as a participant observer.

Tuchman gathered, over a period of ten years, relevant data on the process of newsmaking in two television stations and three newspapers. She also interviewed several news-related organisations and workers. Her main theme is that:

> act of making news is the act of constructing reality itself rather than a picture of reality.... Newswork transforms occurrences into news events. It draws on aspects of everyday life to tell stories, and it presents us to ourselves. By accomplishing this second task, it serves us as a basis for social action. But the process of making news is not accomplished in a void, and so a second theme is that professionalism serves organisational interests by reaffirming the institutional processes in which newswork is embedded.

**Proper Order**

According to Tuchman, bureaucratic chains of command are developed in the newspaper organisation to keep p track of daily occurrences out of which particular stories are woven into news and in this process, /news worthiness' is bestowed on selected occurrences. Reporters and editors create a 'web of facticity' for the sake of news credibility, and this web legitimates the status quo.

Newsmen identify some sources and institutions as the appropriate location of facts and dismisses others. When legitimate leaders are unavailable, new's organisations bestow authenticity to news into hard news, soft news, spot news and developing news. They also call some news items 'continuing news'.

But in their pursuit of more important news every day, they leave out the concept of continuity, although they may claim that a 'fair amount of coverage' is given to all stories. Perhaps certain news events are covered more frequently than certain others depending upon the importance the news organisation bestows on them.

Connected with selection, continuity and access, is the idea of objectivity. Some newsmen consider their papers to present 'objective news' and take great pride in it. Objectivity is, no doubt, an ideal worth striving for. In it are included other ideals such as impartiality, fairness, truthfulness, reality, and total detachment of the newsmen from their sources and their news. Objectivity is not an ideal that can be achieved easily or frequently. In practice, subjectivity is involved in the selection and presentation of news.

Even definitions of news are subjectively derived and not scientifically or objectively tenable. At any given moment, what is newsworthy depends on the decision-makers' socio-economic and cultural background, and the political climate that prevails in his country. As members of a social group, newsmen have certain symbols embedded in their consciousness which they use to interpret reality. Very often these symbols help in the perpetuation of the existing order and systems rather than in replacing them with something different or hitherto untried.

Objectivity is usually considered attainable by reporting opposing points of view. In fact, searching for the opposite side has almost become a ritual with newsmen. But there are a thousand shades of opinion between the two sides. On specific issues, many hundreds of people do not take any rigid view based on party affiliations. Since the newsmen's objectivity is limited in scope, the differences they try to bring out from opposing camps are not real differences but artificial ones couched in terms used by opposing camps. This, can create a semblance of objectivity.

The average citizens are sometimes misled by the artificial objectivity in news reports. Even in the first selection stage itself, subjectivity determines what news items and which news sources should be let into the news framework. Once newsmen realise and recognise the process of selection that goes on in their day-to-day work, they will not be as vehement in their protestations of objectivity.

An argument put forward by Tuchman is particularly relevant here. She believes that although it is wrong to accuse news workers of bias, and though it is difficult to define objective truth, it is valuable to identify news as an artificial accomplishment attuned to specific understanding of social reality. Those understandings, constituted in specific work processes and practices, legitimate the status quo.

A newspaper does not hold up a mirror to nature or to events because its reflecting scope is limited. News cannot be comprehensive because of the very nature of newsmaking. The 'reality' constructed by newsmen is not, or need not be, the actual reality or the whole reality. It is only aspects of reality which they produce and present to the public. Berger and Luckmann have discussed the concept of 'construct reality' elaborately in their work. That concept is applicable to the newspaper because, irrespective of the nature of external reality, journalists see it only through their own constructs. As far back as 1953, Kuart and Gladys Lang had shown that events covered were themselves journalistic constructs of related phenomena.

The 'medium is not the message', since the message depends on the men who utilise the medium. Communicators work in a national culture constructed out for several sub-cultures but very much under the powerful influence of the dominant group that holds economic, political and military power. This is why Gans calls news among other things, the exercise of power over the interpretation of reality'.

Similar views are expressed by Tuchman who believes that the work of the media should be evaluated in terms of the sociology of knowledge. Since knowledge is power and communication is part of the knowledge industry, those who run the media are doubly capable of strengthening their network of power over society. They, in fact, start from an already powerful position for reasons of conglomeration with other forms of production. Readers and viewers are not totally helpless if alternative media choices are possible, and if journalists try to maintain news credibility and reliability; but as McQuail has said, the media's views ultimately prevail because they have the final say on what gets into the channels and hence on access and availability.

In the interpretation of reality, the news media use certain techniques for attracting the audience, the most important of which is the technique of dramatisation. This is especially true of television news as confirmed by Epstein who studied the news manufacturing process in the three major networks of the United States. There is no doubt that the newspapers are now compelled to imitate television practices to survive the fierce competition from the electronic industry in technologically advanced countries and also in some developing countries where television is gaining strength. Most news stories open with a dramatic lead.

The element of fiction in news stories is also not negligible. These news practices will continue because newsmen in the print media listen to the radio and television news bulletins broadcast early morning for lead stories in their afternoon editions, and the bulletins of the evening broadcast for their morning editions.

## Some Compulsions

Newsmen's preoccupation with personalities and their tendency to personalise news are also allied to the technique of dramatisation. It is easier to dramatise an event if colourful and controversial personalities are involved in the news story. Pictures will heighten the dramatic aspects of a news event. Selection of news is influenced by picture possibility as well as opportunity to dramatise the event through well-known personalities. But who are the personalities who usually appear in the news? After studying a six-month sample of stories appearing in alternate months during 1967, 1971 and 1975, Gans found that most of the news was about affluent people; the main actors in most stories were people in the top 1-5 per cent income bracket, although most were distinguished by their geographical, racial, ethnic and religious background far more often than by their economic background. The magazines were found to universalise upper middle class practices as if they were shared by all Americans. Gans concluded that news story selection was based on availability and suitability of news and that it was the economically and politically powerful people whom journalists sought out for news stories. But drama and colour may not be the only considerations by newsmen since most often, those dramatic events and colourful personalities are chosen, who fit the socio-economic and political environment in which the media operate.

Under the influence of the electronic media, newspapers have changed the format of their pages, increasing the picture content and visual appeal of every page. One of the editors interviewed by this researcher said that he had standing instructions to use at least three pictures on the front page-one big and two small, and one picture on each inside page besides advertisement pictures. News items with picture possibilities and readily available pictures naturally find a place on the front or inside page much more easily than those without a picture. Thus, questions of immediacy, objectivity, completeness, continuity, and other values usually held in high esteem by news workers, are affected by the actual process of newsmaking.

The foregoing discussion should convince us that it is essential to look at the newspaper as a product of the, efforts of a professional group of people who have identical interests and who belong to more or less the same socio-economic, political, and cultural systems. The newspaper is not just a picture of constructed reality, but constructed reality itself to those who produce it. It serves socio-economic, political, surveillance, cultural and entertainment functions news does not simply happen. There are occurrences in everyday life in every part of the world out of which news events are woven with due attention to factual correctness, balanced judgement as far as the selected facts are concerned, relevance to the audience, clarity, contextuality, completeness as far as the chosen facts are concerned, authentic references to news sources specially selected for the purpose, the reliability of the facts selected and presented.

One of the substantive considerations among newsmen and newspaper organisations is that domestic news is more important than foreign news; however, when national interests abroad are threatened, foreign news relating to those interests becomes as important as, if not more important than, domestic news. In the study planned here, foreign news presentation occupies the major position and hence a detailed discussion of foreign news selection is necessary.

Newspapers and all mass media disseminate information not only about events happening in their own countries but in other countries as well. The selection of foreign news is stricter for several reasons, some of which are discussed here.

## Fulfilment of the Task

Normally, only about one-third of the total space in a commercially successful and profitable newspaper is devoted to news. The rest of the paper is taken up by advertisement matter of one kind or another. And the bulk of the area devoted to news (called newshole) goes for metropolitan, state capital, large town or newspaper town and suburban news. A sizeable portion is cut out for regional and national news. It is the remaining space that is devoted to events occurring in other countries. Completeness, continuity, objectivity, access, authenticity, and other qualities expected in domestic news presentation will suffer heavily in the case of foreign news because of the pressure on space.

In an investigation of the reasons why newspapers rejected most of the foreign news that flowed into them through the wire services, Casey and Copeland found that 20 per cent of foreign news copies were rejected by American newspapers for 'lack of space', 35 per cent for lack of appeal or interest to readers, lack of news value and significance; 16 per cent because of loss of timeliness and 27 per cent for various technical reasons. They also found that large metropolitan papers allotted proportionately more space to foreign news than did non-metropolitan papers. The International Press Institute study of 93 US newspapers during four separate weeks between October 1952 and January 1953 during the Korean war concluded that the average proportion of foreign news material to text space was little more than 8 per cent.

Sunwoo Nam hypothesised that the flow of news reflected the power configuration of world politics and depended on the political alliance and functional proximity of the reported country, rather than on geographical proximity or any other factor. He also expressed the view that the bulk of foreign news is not meant for the general public, but to help specialised audiences, decision-makers and foreign affairs experts in the functions of surveillance. According to his argument, the press in developing countries reports more foreign news because the press in these countries is elitist. Markham and Hart expressed similar views in their studies of the South American press.

Smith indicated that the growth of a country's interest in international communications is directly proportional to its military, economic and political interests in international areas. Gerbner has indicated that the modern mass media are the cultural arm of modern industry and business. A study by Onyisi under Gerbner's supervision concluded that the southern part of the African continent received the most attention in the United States media because the multinational corporations with headquarters in the country had strong economic interests concentrated in that region of Africa. This relationship had already been studied more elaborately by Schiller in the case of the United States and he concluded that the American mass media were part of an American industrial and military complex. Abu-Lughod found that the degree of international coverage in a country's media depended on that country's dependence on other countries. He also hypothesised that the

United States received a disproportionate amount of 'big power' coverage because several countries depended on it.

Lent has pointed out that 'national interests, crisis reporting, foreign censors, and a shrinking corp. of correspondents' constrain international coverage in the US media. Gerbner and Marvanyi have graphically represented the many worlds of the world's press after making a multinational comparative study of foreign news coverage, confirming that coverage depends on the big power configuration that dominates the modern world.

But Elliott and Golding have pointed out that foreign news like domestic news is developed by the media organisers as a marketable commodity throughout the world. According to them, the culture to which news, and other aspects of the international system contribute, is not related to any single society or social structure so much as to that network of economic interests and organisations that is international corporate capitalism. Increasingly the growth of the international media system enables the news media to play broadly the same ideological role at an international level as is already apparent nationally in particular developed countries. The international media system is one mechanism by which developing countries are brought within the common cultural hegemony of western capitalism.

## Working Bodies

Heavy dependence on the global wire services has been cited by some as a determining factor in the selection and quantity of news from other countries. The IPI study, already referred to, found that the news agencies were the paramount source of international news and that the coverage by the news agencies centered heavily on the major countries of the world. To Hachten, the flow of news concerning less developed countries seemed to be more, closely related to the use of a world news agency than to geographical proximities or language similarities.

Most newspapers of the developing countries do not have the economic capability of stationing their own correspondents in foreign countries. In developing as well as developed countries, it is the big chains and conglomerates that have their own wire services staff and special correspondents in other countries. All the rest depend on the big news agencies of the world. This leads to verbatim reproduction of news agency reports, sometimes including spelling and other errors.

Foreign news in most countries' newspapers is likely to have more or less the same content as far as a particular news story is concerned. There may be differences in the stories selected, but not much variety in the presentation of individual stories.

The history of the development of the news agencies have a great impact on the process of foreign news selection and reporting.

The history of colonialism had an equal impact on the growth of the international news media. Towards the end of the nineteenth century, the newly established European news agencies concluded a series of cartel agreements by means of which they divided the world between the, according to the prevailing imperial spheres of influence. These first links in the international media system set a precedent for much that was to follow as the media in developed and developing societies alike became progressively more involved in corporate capitalist economy.

Colonial news-agencies are still strong in erstwhile colonies, and several of their reports could reflect the national interests of the countries in which those agencies originated. They reflect their national ethnocentrism which paves the way toward cultural imperialism. They reporting of an event in a developing country may be influenced by the world's leading wire services, all of which are headquartered in the developed countries. The wire services' reports, thus, could lead to distortion and omission of vital aspects of the events, since they tend to interpret the event from their own national and global economic interests.

This leads us to the fourth factor that influences the selection, presentation and quantity of foreign news.

**Abroad-oriented News**

As mentioned earlier, domestic news becomes foreign news depending on the foreign policy actions of a country. When millions of refugees from East Pakistan fled to West Bengal, and Bihar their plight was first considered a foreign problem, but the stern action taken by India against Pakistan made it domestic news in India. Similarly, news about a country's nationals in other countries, although strictly news of foreign origin, becomes domestic news because of special domestic links with the nationals residing abroad. With the deep involvement of the United States in Vietnam, the latter country became domestic news in the US media.

Afghanistan has now become well-known in the US and the USSR, after the latter's troops marched into that country. The conflict in the Falkland Islands became national news in the British news media. Thus, foreign news is not wholly foreign; it is in a way domestic news extended to a foreign country.

Several researchers have found that three types of countries dominate foreign news in a country's newspapers: its closest or most powerful allies; its chief foes and their allies; and the rest of the world when something extraordinary occurs there. Gans, for example, fund that most foreign news in newspapers in the USA was about England, France, West Germany, Italy, Japan, Israel, Egypt, the Soviet Union and mainland China. He observed that:

> Foreign news deals either with stories thought relevant to Americans or American interests; with the same themes and topics as domestic news; or when the topics are distinctive, with interpretations that apply American values... often limit themselves

> only to the most dramatic overseas events. In addition, they tend to follow American foreign policy, even if not slavishly.... Foreign news adheres less strictly to objectivity than domestic news; but... the values it applies are not very different from those that appear, less explicably, in domestic news.

This observation is not only applicable to the US, but to India and other countries as well. In fact, major newspapers of all countries toe the official foreign policy line most of the time.

Issues of nationalism and patriotism might motivate the media to conform to their national government's foreign policy. It is difficult to find consistently favourable reports about socialist countries in capitalist countries' newspapers (unless there is a very special relationship between them) and vice versa. Similarly, it is difficult to find reports, not to mention favourable reports, about enemy countries in a nation's news media unless the government itself wants certain information to be passed on to the people in order to alert them.

Since foreign policy is a major determinant of foreign news selection, most economic and political developments are seen in terms of the East-West ideological conflict or of the Cold War. Smaller countries are usually ignored unless news about them has some relevance to the newspaper's country. Some major countries are seen as allies or foes. Favourable reports about allies appear in the country's newspapers despite the existence of some very grave threats to human rights in those allied countries. Reports about Latin American countries in newspapers of the US are examples of this.

Every foreign news event is likely to be interpreted in relation to either the US or the Soviet Union by most newspapers of the world. 'The daily task of constructing the segment of international reality takes place in a particular kind of setting, both institutional and social', says Cohen. His views about the selection of foreign news are relevant to our discussion:

> Effective decisions are made... at a number of different points, although the general news editor and the telegraph editor, who preside over the bank of news tickers, together with whatever assistants they might have, make the major decisions involving selection and layout. These men do not, of course, start the editorial process de novo each day; they approach the task with an experience and a perspective that have both long and short term components. Over the long term, particular classes of stories preempt the leading news spaces-economic reform, war, international political competition... In the short run, the editors carry in their heads the knowledge of what the news has been over recent days and weeks. Hence, they come to their tasks every day with half-formed and unarticulated notions of what the news is apt to be like.

Cohen agrees that no newspaper can 'shovel out to its readers as news the total stock of information and stories that it receives/ but he points out that :

> Priorities and not absolutes determine the amount of... foreign affairs news. Foreign news has to compete with other types of news for getting into the paper. Space allocations are not made every day, but as part of a long term policy, which will be changed only by the top personnel. The selection of all types of news is done by editors on the basis of prior decisions on what the readers will buy.

However, it is not always the sales angle that determines the selection and presentation of foreign news. Political or ideological considerations, global economic interests, military strategies, patriotism, national security interests all these exert a decisive influence on the selection of foreign countries and themes for presentation to the newspaper readers. Journalists often willingly cooperate with government when national security is threatened. As Cohen observes, 'personal friendships between government officials and newsmen are common, extending right up to the Presidential level'.

**Disputing Points**

There may arise an occasional conflict between senior government officials in charge of foreign policy and some journalists who go wrong in their facts. But by and large, there develops a symbiotic relationship between the foreign news correspondent and his country's local embassy officials and this leads to reporting of events from the official point of view. Sometimes, conditions ripe for revolution in a far-off country, or the true facts of a revolutionary movement may miss the attention of the correspondent who hastily accepts embassy hand-outs for transmission to the newspaper's headquarters.

The newspaper organisations are willing to cooperate with the government by resorting to self-censorship on matters of national security or safety of citizens abroad. Several instances can be cited from the reporting of the Vietnam war or the Indo-Pakistan war where , journalists as citizens cooperated with the government. Gans even goes to the extent of saying that journalists occasionally report news from distant countries based on slender evidence.

The intimate cooperation between journalists and government has been discussed by Cohen:

> Stories about foreign aid, Christmas food packages, disaster relief packages, etc., illustrate how the press as a system of communication has become an integral part of the battery of instruments by means of which American foreign policy makers try to influence the expectations and the behaviors of other peoples and governments-friends and allies as well as potential enemies and countries with wandering affections.

The mass media's supply of international news is an important factor in everyone's picture of the world. But foreign policy influence on the press affects the public's attitude towards, and image of, the people in other nations. According to Petersons, there is a correspondence between public opinion and official attitudes with regard to foreign policy.

In the formation of national images of international events and personalities, the transnational news agencies play a dominant role. They also play a role in educating the people of poor countries about rich life-styles. There is a view among researchers that after constant exposure to media fare from rich, technologically advanced countries with multinational economic interests, people of the poor, developing countries learn to identify whatever news they receive over the international news agency channels as relevant to their own circumstances. Himmelstrand and Hedman believe that 'in the long run, people's definition of news will become the same as the supply of news, as they will demand the information they are used to receiving from the news agencies. One might say the news agencies create their own demand'.

It must be stressed that the multinational agencies are under the strong influence of their own national government's foreign policy when they report foreign countries.

How newspapers change their attitudes to countries on the basis of changes in their own countries foreign policy has been documented by Sahin, Kreisberg, and by Lynch and Effendi. These three studies were based on the pattern of reporting in the New York Times over long periods of time. Very little news, for example, appeared about China in the US papers during the two decades following the Chinese revolution. But once President Richard Nixon broke the ice, the newspapers began to turn more frequently to China for news.

There is some merit in the argument that foreign news is meant primarily for the benefit of foreign policy formulators and top echelons of government, and that the average citizen is not deeply interested in foreign affairs. Much of the foreign news published may not be read by ordinary citizens. Some theoretical support to this view has been derived from the oft-quoted 'nature of news' theory of Schramm. Schramm's assumption is that by its very nature, foreign news cannot occupy any significant proportion of the newshole since it may not given immediate reward to the average news consumers. For immediate reward, the average reader turns to soft news: sports, crime, disasters, adventures, comics, movies, other entertainment, society, human interest, scandal, gossip, sex, psychological questions and answers and the like.

They also turn to personalities, especially colourful personalities, such as kings, queens, dictators, ruthless tyrants, movie stars, mavericks, controversial figures such as racists, atheists, sex therapists and others, who generate more heat than light for the average reader. Then why does foreign news appear regularly in all newspapers? How much foreign news does appear? What countries and themes are more frequently reported?

Past research has indicated that 'prestige' or 'quality' newspapers devote somewhere between 10 and 30 per cent of their newsholes to foreign affairs. The 'popular' newspapers do not report as much foreign news as do the 'quality' ones. Do newspapers of different press systems have different approaches and attitudes to foreign news reporting? A comparison of two press systems operating in widely different environments may yield answers to the above questions, and clarify some of the conceptual matters discussed in this chapter.

While the lead should arouse the reader's interest, the body should sustain it. The body should flow-smoothly and logically from the lead. It should expand each of the points mentioned in the lead and, as far as possible, in the same order. The body should be as complete and as tight as possible. It should provide all the relevant information within the shortest space possible. The essence of good journalistic writing is brevity and simplicity. Do not use two words where one word would do. And do not use a complex or long word where a short word would do. Eventually, you should reach the point at which, choosing the story structure becomes second nature to you. This will, of course, come with experience and practice. You will then begin concentrating on the more creative and experimental aspects of writing.

A good reporter will spend a great deal of his time not sitting in the office but visiting places and meeting people who are potential sources of news. He should always keep his ears and eyes open. He should know where to go for the facts he needs for the story, recognise news when he encounters it, select the vital points for inclusion in his story and discard the inconsequential details.

**Distinguishing Strata**

Let us now turn to different types of reporting such as objective, interpretative investigative and crime reporting.

Reporting of news, unlike editorial writing, is often described as a coldly impersonal job. A reporter is essentially a story teller and he should tell the story in an objective and truthful manner, without lacing it with personal opinions or subjective comments. He should be fair and impartial and present both sides of the story. Complete objectivity is a mere concept. The reporter is a human being, not a robot, and he has certain ideas, feelings, attitudes, opinions and prejudices. However, a good reporter should try to rise above them and tell the facts as he has collected them in his search for truth.

No responsible reporter would behave like the notorious American journalist, Janet Cooke, who won the prestigious Pulitzer prize in 1980 for a story about drugs which was later proved to be fictional and fictitious. The journalist committed a deliberate fraud by dramatising a fake scene in which an eight year-old boy is injected with heroin supplied by the lover of the boy's mother.

Nearer home, the story of "mass rape" at a students function in a Madhya Pradesh town, published in a national newspaper was found to be baseless. When the report appeared on the front page of the newspaper it caused a sensation.

The Editor asked a reporter to investigate. On arriving in the town the reporter first questioned the reporter of the news item, who insisted that the mass rape did take place. By , way of corroboration he produced a number of eye-witnesses. However when they were cross-examined and asked specifically to reveal only what they had seen, and not what they had heard, the investigator soon realised that the reporter had written the story on the basis of a bazar gossip and field it without verifying the facts. All that had happened was that during a function to celebrate the annual day of a local college, a portion of the shamiana came down, the electricity got cut off and a few students entered the women's enclosure and molested some of the girls.

There is this apocryphal story of a cub reporter, who, on his, first day at work wrote a piece with a cocksureness which was misplaced. On reading the piece, the editor advised him to be cautious and a little circumspect when writing about sensitive issues. The press, the editor reminded him, must not ordinarily violate the various laws on the statute book concerning libel, national security and parliamentary privileges.

The next day the cub reporter submitted a story which ran as follows:

> "Mrs. Gulab Paniwala alleged wife of Mr. Rakesh Paniwala, who claims to be the mayor of Shangrila, gave a cocktail party at her house in Model Town on Monday to bid farewell to Mrs. Jyoti Jariwala, reported to be the wife of the well-known industrialist, Samar Jariwala. Among those present at the party were Mrs. Romi Puriwala, said to be the widow of the late Hansraj Puriwala, a former cabinet minister, along with her alleged offspring, Jani Puriwala..." and so it went on.

The reporter had quite clearly gone to the other extreme in writing this report which was quickly consigned to the waste paper basket.

In reporting news, you must remember that facts are sacred. You must check and cross-check the facts from different sources until you are absolutely sure of them. Only then should you write your story. The golden rule is: tell the truth.

Objective reporting is, of course, not synonymous with dullness. It means fair and impartial reporting that is free from personal bias or prejudice.

***Reporting in Depth :*** It is difficult to define the term "investigative" journalism. Some newspapers scoff at the very idea of an investigative journalist. In one way, of course, "investigative" journalism is a redundant concept, since all stories require some kind of investigation on the part of the reporter. However, the investigative reporter is expected to dig deeply beyond the facts stated in the hard news. Though we may face difficulty in defining the term, we cannot ignore the concept of investigative journalism.

Many journalism students have an ambition to become "investigative" reporters. An "investigative" journalist sees himself as the conscience of society, pursuing corruption in high places without fear or favour. In his book Press and Law (Vikas, New Delhi 1990), justice A.N. Grover has quoted from the forward of Investigative reporting by Clark R. Mollevhogg. According to the Foreword, investigative reporting has three elements: It has to be the own work of the reporter. Under no circumstance should it be of others. The subject of the reporting should be such that it is of importance for the readers to know; and There must not be any attempt made to hide the truth from the people.

Investigative reporting has made great leaps in western countries. In India, it is still in its infancy. Most Indian newspapers do not have, or do not allocate, the manpower and funds necessary for a first-rate investigative job.

Attempts at investigative reporting, to quote one eminent Indian editor, are like drilling for oil. A fair amount of wastage of effort has to be taken for granted. But when the oil is discovered and becomes marketable, the sense of achievement is usually more than in any other sector of journalistic enterprise.

The best example of investigative reporting in our times, was the Watergate story which led to the disgrace and downfall of U.S. President Richard Nixon. When the two young reporters of The Washington Post, Bob Woodward and Carl Bernstein, started investigating the arrest of four men for a burglary at Watergate, the Democratic Party's national headquarters on June 17, 1972, they had no idea that their inquiry would culminate in the resignation of the President.

The remarkable thing about their investigation was that it kept to the highest standards of professional journalism. The reporters did not start gunning for Nixon from the beginning. They merely pursued the burglary attempt and only later came up with startling facts linking the White House with it. "We did not go after the President, we went after the story", they explained.

Though the Washington Post stories led to the downfall of President Nixon, the same paper, later in 1980, got involved in the most celebrated case of journalist fraud in modern times- the case of Janet Cooke, already described in this unit. Janet Cooke's case gives a clear warning that every story whether "investigative" or not, should be handled by editors with great care and caution, otherwise, it will bring the newspaper to disrepute. N.J. Herbert Altsehull in his book from Milton to McLuhan (Longman, New York, 1990) states how the Janet Cooke story got into the Washington Post. An internal investigation by the newspaper's Ombudsman, Bill Green, blamed "failure of a system" for not checking up thoroughly on Cook's story.

The failure to check was in part, Green said, the result of the fact that Cooke was black and that white editors did not want to be seen as racist. The Cooke's story appeared in the Post on 28 September 1980 and the edition featuring 8 Green's report appeared on 19 April 1981. Cooke was fired from the Post and was forced to return the Pulitzer Prize.

In our country, investigative reporters have brought to high a number of scandals-the Bhagalpur blindings incidents by the police, Kuo oil deal, A.R. Antulay's Private trusts, the securities scam involving Indian and foreign banks and stock brokers, etc. An enterprising reporter once got himself arrested so that he could give a first-hand account of life in Delhi's Tihar jail.

With governments becoming increasingly secretive and corruption spreading its tentacles far and wide, the need for investigative reporting cannot be over emphasized. Yet we must remember that investigative reporting is not everybody's cup of tea. It requires hard and sustained work. The investigative reporter should be combination of a crusader, super detective and blood hound and he should have the necessary time and finance to carry out his work.

In the pursuit of his quarry, the investigative reporter must draw a line between candid reporting and muck-raking, mud-slinging, character assassination or blackmail. He should base his report on incontrovertible facts, not on half-truths and lies. He should be wary of lobbies and lobbyists-political or commercial-trying to misguide him, and he should not behave like a peeping Tom or a prosecutor.

The best king of investigative reporting is that which keeps the public interest in mind. It may highlight an injustice, expose corrupt practices or unmask dishonest politicians and bureaucrats.

Experience has been that unless an investigative reporter or a crusading reporter gets the support of the Judiciary, the executive or the legislative, cannot bring his reports to logical ends. The Bhagalpur blinding report would have ended like any other report if a public interest litigation would not have been filed against the police. In the USA the Watergate stories would not have produced any result if they did not get the support of the legislative which threatened the impeachment of President Richard Nixon.

**Crime and Reporting**

Crime reporting is not separate from the objective, interpretative an investigative form of reporting. Here it is separately dealt with because it is a separate and important beat in all big and medium level daily newspapers.

There is a tremendous public interest in crime stores and no newspaper can afford to ignore them without damage to its circulation and credibility. Attempts made by some newspapers to keep crime out of their columns, proved to be counterproductive and were soon abandoned.

Crime is a part of life and it is a newspaper's duty to inform the readers of what crimes are going on in their city, state or country. However, crime reporting should not aim at satisfying morbid curiosity or sensation mongering.

Although crime reporting is usually assigned to one of the junior reporters in a newspaper, it is a highly responsible and specialised job. The reporter should not only have the ability to shift the grain from the chaff, and the truth from lies, he should also have good contacts in the police and other departments of the administration as well as a working knowledge of the penal codes and law on libel and other relevant matters.

Besides, he must observe a code of honour. He should be as objective as is humanly possible and avoid resorting to sensationalism or cheap gimmicks to catch the attention of the readers. He should not suppress news of public interest. Nor should he seek to settle personal scores with police officers or lawyers or judges. And he must be careful that in the course of this work, he does not unnecessarily, invade a citizen's privacy. There has been much criticism of press reporting of crime and not all of it is baseless. Some reporters have been found quality of unethical standards, thus causing much pain and sorrow to their victims or their families and friends. In the case of the brutal murder of two Bombay nuns, some newspapers published totally baseless allegations conveyed to them by irresponsible police officials that the nuns were in the habit of receiving male visitors. The reports offended all decent citizens, particularly the members of the Christian Community.

A leading newspaper once published a fictitious report about a couple having been waylaid by a gang on the national highway. The report said that the husband was beaten up and the women was molested. The story was subsequently found to be incorrect, the product of the imagination of a reporter anxious his by-line in the paper. Reports glorifying the activities of criminals or making heroes of them should be discouraged as much as a resort to sensationalism. The crime reporter must never violate standards of decency and good taste.

*Crime as News :* There are several types of crime news-murders, fires, accidents, robberies, burglaries, fraud, blackmail, kidnaping, rape, etc.

*Fires :* The reporter must get his facts correct about the essential elements of a fire story-the number of persons killed or injured, the extent of damage to property, the loss of valuables, etc. He must also find out if the fire brigade responded in time or was guilty of delaying the fire fighting operations through sheer lethargy or incompetence or a lack of water supply. He should question eye-witnesses about any acts of bravery or cowardice. All these are essential ingredients of a fire story.

The lead in a fire story would normally suggest itself. It, for instance, lives have been lost, it needs highlighting in the lead. Where possible, list the names of the dead and the injured.

A major fire caused extensive damage to New Delhi's Vigyan Bhavan, the premier venue of international and national conferences, on Monday night, a chowkidar on duty received minor burns. According to preliminary investigations, the fire broke out in the kitchen and soon spread to other rooms on the ground floor. The chowkidar raised an alarm which alerted the head clerk on duty who informed the fire brigade and the police. Ten fire tenders soon arrived on the scene. However, their fire fighting operations were hampered by lack of water in the hydrants. By the time water tankers rushed to the site, the fire had engulfed a large area and damaged files, furniture, curtains and ceilings.

The police suspect electric short-circuit as the cause of the fire.

***Homicides :*** In cases of a major murder, the reporter should rush to the scene as soon as possible after receiving a tip and gather all the relevant facts. In nine cases out of ten, crime reporters in, say, Delhi, depend on police information about murders and there is a time lapse before they can begin their investigations.

This often hampers their search for the truth. The reporter must, in any case, exercise great care in how he handles the story. Otherwise he runs the risk of causing offense.

In reporting dowry deaths or alleged dowry deaths, for instance, the reporter should refrain from levelling uncorroborated statements by one party or the other. He must therefore get his facts correct-by talking to the investigating police officer, the girl's in-laws and her parents, and, if possible, the neighbours.

A 25 year old housewife, Renu, died in NN Memorial Hospital on Monday morning from burns received in a kitchen fire. The housewife's parents allege that she was murdered by her in-laws who had been dissatisfied with the dowry she brought at the time of her wedding a year ago.

However, the husband, Kishore, a garment merchant in Chandni Chowk, and his father who were in the house at the time of the accident maintain, that Sushmita's sari caught fire when she was lighting a stove in the kitchen. Since the kitchen door was closed, they did not hear her cries for help.

The police are questioning the women's relatives as well as neighbours and are reluctant to offer an opinion until the investigations are complete. At the insistence of Renu's parents, however, they have registered a case against her in-laws.

***Accidents*** : Most accidents are reported on the basis of police bulletins or information supplied by police spokesmen. However wherever possible the crime reporter must rush to the scene of a major accident to give authenticity to his story.

Three members of a family-husband, wife and daughter-were killed on the spot when a speeding truck rammed into their car on the road to Indira Gandhi International Airport on Sunday morning. A fourth member of the family had a providential escape. According to the police, the truck driver lost control of the vehicle and swerved sharply to the right and hit the car coming from the opposite direction.

Those killed are Ram, a businessman of Agra, his wife, Janki and their daughter, Aasha. The second daughter, Geeta, had a miraculous escape and suffered only minor bruises on her arms and legs. She was treated at the Safdarjung Hospital and allowed to go home.

The truck has been seized by the police but the truck driver, Sasi Singh is absconding.

## Formation of News

All copy reaching a newspaper office from different sources is processed at the news desk. The desk is manned by sub-editors and usually a chief sub-editor leads the team and works as copy taster and also as revise editor or slotman. He sits in the very useful slot of the horse shot shaped copy desk facing other sub-editors on the rim. After distributing copy to other subs he also checks their work for any mistakes and passes to on to the composing room.

The sub-editor does some or all these to every story:

- Reads the story for clarity of language and meaning and rewrites where necessary.
- Shortens the story while retaining the essentials and maintaining coherence.
- Combines one story with another, or perhaps combines running reports from several news agencies, correspondents and reporters to produce a single intelligible report from different and sometimes contradictory messages.
- Saves space when verbosity creeps in.
- Corrects the grammar and checks for house style.
- Checks for apparent errors of fact.
- Checks for taste.
- Adds important background facts and provides answers for any implied questions.
- Writes headlines which attract the attention of the reader and also writes sub-headings if necessary.

The chief-sub of revise editor checks the work of sub-editors ensuring accuracy of details. He also becomes the fist reader of the story and sees whether the headline and copy make sense.

Another senior sub-editor or chief sub looks after the work at 'the stone'. He is called 'stone editor' also. Though with change in technology the stone has vanished but the term persists. The job of the composing room where the pages are made up with metal types and picture blocks or with strips of film or bromide.

The stone sub can also be called production editor or make up editor. He deals with minor disharmonies. If the text is too long, he cuts it. If the page plan does not work, he changes it. If there is late news, he makes room for it. He checks the galley proofs and page proofs and finally sends them to the press.

Thus a sub-editor has to know all about news writing and how a reporter should write news copy. He is supposed to improve upon the work of the reporter. He should not change something for the sake of change but he must make sure that every correction or change the makes improves the copy.

**News Procurement**

The bulk of copy which comes to the news desk is from wire agencies. The teleprinter keeps on creeding information almost all the time during peak news hours of the afternoon and evening. This copy comes in takes the unit of news agency transmission or unit of newswriting.

Foreign news items have their own serial numbers, FG, FS, FES, FTF, PAS and POOL. Whereas FG, FS and FES files carry news items received from Reuter, AFP and UPI and are credited to those agencies, the PTF file is made up of reports received from PTI's own correspondents and stringers abroad. Items taken from the services of agencies like TASS. Xinhua, Antra Bernama, Tangug and other agencies with which PTI has exchange arrangements go under the PAS series. The POOL file is devoted to agencies participating with PTI in the Press Agencies Pool of Non-aligned countries.

Sobhraj-style is slug-an identification tag. Every story even a story consisting of only one take, must carry at the top a suitable slug. Generally the slug is one word which is often the key work in the story. Thus a story about rain would which is often the key work in the story. Thus a story about rain would be slugged "rain" and one about the police firing, "firing". Slugs are nouns and not adjectives pour in from various points, a master slug should be used with sub-slugs for individual story. In the above example Sobhraj is master slug while style is sub-slug.

Play boy of prisons once more outwitted is the headline. This is a new development. Agencies normally are not supported to give headlines but now to lighten the burden of newspaper sub-editors they have also started putting headlines.

If the sub-editor. At the newspaper desk likes it he can indicate the type size for the headline.

New Delhi Apr. 7 is dateline and PTI is credit line. It appears just after date line in the fist take of the story and again at the end of each take. All the takes of the story except the last end with More-PTI as in the above example. The last take of the story is closed with PTI. For Spl of Espl services or sometimes for all stories the story can be reopened. In re-opening an item, reference is given to the previous take by its number for instant, "Sobhraj five-New Delhi-re-open Del 33".

RR RT BDS are initials of the reporter, the deskman or deskman processing it and the teleprinter operator punching it on the tape. Each take also carries at the end ,that time at which it is transmitted in the services.

*The Lead :* In news agency lead is used in the case of developing stories for updating the top, as necessary, in the light of fresh facts as they become available. Examples of such stories could be train or air mishap, a conference or meeting, an election, a state visit by a VIP. Such stories may require one or more leads as the story advances with the day. A lead can also be used to tie up loose ends of dispersed story, or to provide combined top for two or three different items about a single subject or related development.

There can be one or more leads to a story. For example, the leads on an air crash story, slugged "Crash" could be "Lead Crash", "Second Lead Crash", and so on. The final wrap-up story would be "Lead all Crash".

A lead often overhauls a substantial part of a story or even the entire story. Such lead is also called a "round up". Close to deadlines of newspapers roundups are not useful and therefore the lead is in the form of a brief one or two para top, that is, just the new intro. This intro introduces the new element that has emerged in situation. In such cases an appropriate pick-up line is given linking with the part of earlier story specifying the item by number, slug and dateline and giving the location of the point of pick-up.

If an agency wants to withdraw or kill a story which has come on the ticker, it puts out a kill note. The kill note has priority marking 'Kill' and is without a dateline. It gives the number, slug, dateline and subject of the story which it kills and also indicates whether a substitute follows.

Similarly, corrections are also issued specifying the take line and words of the earlier story and then the whole take is re-issued with corrections.

Sometimes service messages which are meant for internal use also reach newspapers. Such messages have the word "service" at the top. Ordinarily a service is addressed to the editor at a particular place. These messages should not be confused with messages and stories sent for use in newspapers.

In order to prevent mistakes the words not, now and nor are repeated in news agency copy. While editing the copy a sub-editor should delete one of these words.

News agencies keep on creeding takes of different stories one after the other, while reporters and correspondents also continue filing copy so that subjects covered by news agencies are also covered by the members of newspaper staff.

If the same story is covered by a member of newspaper staff his copy should get priority over the news agency copy. Additional information given by the news agencies can be added to his copy giving credit to the agency.

News copy coming from different sources is sorted out at the desk and all copy relating to a particular story is kept separate. This helps the sub-editor doing that story to read the whole-copy, analyse it and do justice with it. This sorting helps also in knowing whether the news agency has completed the story or some more takes are likely to follow.

Judging the importance of the story the chief-sub decides the space to be given to it. This has to be in relation to total news fall. The relative importance of the story also determines the page where the story would go. Except developing or running stories, all other stories are edited as soon as it is decided that they are to be used. For running stories the deskmen wait for more information. When they come close to the deadline of the edition they proceed with what they have. When additional information comes, the story is changed again for the next edition.

A word about copy. Good copy, also called clean copy, has the name of the reporter and the date on the top of the first page. At least a third of this page is left blank to allow room for instructions to sub-editor and the printer. Sufficient margin should be left on both sides of the copy-say one and a half inch on the left hand side and one inch on the right hand side of all pages of the copy. At least a two inch space should be left at the top and the bottom of each page. News copy should be typed double space.

Every page of the copy should start and end with a paragraph. I there is a mistake in typing a word, it should be typed again. Corrections should be made above the line.

A reporter should leave underscoring paragraph, indents and all other typographical markings to the sub-editor. Wrong under-scoring and paragraph marks make a mess of copy. At the end of each page before the last 'more follows' or MF is essential and the end of the last page should be marked 'End'.

On the copy the sub-editor crosses out certain things and circles others. Neither will be set in type but the distinction is that what nobody needs to see any more is crossed out, but essential service messages are circled. The page and edition where the story will go are written on the top of the story and encircled. For example, P 1/2 would mean page one of the second edition. Sub-editor's name or initials are also written and encircled, if there is a printer's or proof reader's query it can be referred to the sub-editor who has edited the copy. Type size and columns are also indicated and encircled. For example,

8 x 1 would mean that the copy is to be set in 8 point type of the newspaper text print across one column. There is no need to specify the face or to say that it is in roman. The rule in newspaper setting is to specify the unusual and otherwise to keep the copy clean. The fewer the marks the better it is.

Catch line or slug is also essential on edited text takes and headline folio, the operator setting the text sets the catch line and it can be married, with the other folios of the same story. Thus a story may have 'Rajiv' as slug or catchline. Its headline folio will carry 'Rajiv I' and its first text take would have 'Rajiv 2', and so on.

Every headline is written on a separate folio. The headline should be written clearly-in capitals if necessary. The letter which need capitalisation should be double ticked. Edition and page mark go on the top left hand corner and the catchline on top right had corner. It also carries instructions regarding type and the columns over which the headline will be spread and the headline style. For example, '14 CBLCX1 set left' would mean that the headline has to be set left over single column in 14 point century bold type in lower case. If the normal headline style is set left in that case it need not be specified in the instructions. However, it is essential that the style breaking headlines should be marked with words and symbols.

The first headlines were single column. Now they can be spread over all the columns in the newspaper. Newspapers today use the opportunities for display by mixing single column and multi-column headlines depending on the importance of the news.

Banner headline should not be in lower case because lower case letters across such a wide measure look straggly. Moreover, headlines should be crisp and lower case headline will be unduly wordy.

There is a wide range of possibilities regarding arrangements of headline. A newspaper may standardise on one form, such as the centered head, or it can mix them between headlines. But much depends on the skill of the page planners and the ideas they try to communicate.

The basic typographic arrangements are flush left, centered, stepped, flush right and hanging indention.

Many newspapers have switched to this style. The flush left heading has one or more lines which are set flush to the left. This should not touch the column rule. The flush left headlines look better when each line is indented on the column rule leaving 6 points or half an em space on an 11 cm column. In this type of arrangement each line of headline type is centered on the white of the column. The well-constructed, centered heading, whether of a multiline or a multi-deck has its own symmetry and it is neatly framed in white.

The patterns created by this need slightly more attention than the patterns the flush left heading creates, but neither needs as much attention as some other patterns.

If one is writing a multi-deck headlines they should be centered where they look best. The common double column headline is a single deck of two lines with centered headings. The second line should always be shorter than the first at least by two units. One should never try to write headlines in tight caps. They need more white around themselves for legibility.

In this arrangement the first line is set flush left and the last flush right and the middle lines centered. Each line has to be about the same length, and they look like steps. To achieve a smooth step requires great care in headline writing. This style is discouraged by modern experts of readability. However, the greatest difficulty is that the stepped style depends too much on a precise count and any failure can lead to ugly results.

Each line is pushed against the right-hand margin to create a stepped effect on the left. It has even more limited application than the stepped headline. It may be occasional variant in a paper but it cannot be recommended as a regular style. It is slow to set and difficult to read.

The first line is set full out and the others indented, usually to the left. It cannot be a regular style but can be used as an occasional variant.

Old school considered that quotes and dashes were full letters. New school thinks it is an ugly habit. No headline should need double quotes: Only simple quotes should do. With flush left headings the flush line should be, the initial letter of each line-not the quote. The quote should be left to hang in the white.

Writing headline involves half the skill of a good deskman. The difficulty in writing headlines is in conveying in a few attractive words the essence of a complicated set of facts. In half a dozen words the headline has to inform the reader what the story contains.

The headline gives emphasis to a few words in bold types. Hence every word should be weighed. Accuracy, intelligibility and vigour are the requirements and any newspaper which is careless with its headlines is careless about its own purpose and vitality. Wordy and vague headlines leave a newspaper reader confused and irritate him. Where every headline goes to the print with precision or wit, the whole newspaper comes alive.

Headline writing is art and craft at the same time. The art is in imagination and vocabulary and the craft lies in accuracy of content, attractiveness of appearance and practicality.

A headline must fit in the space available to it. A headline with too many letters to be accommodated in the width and type required is called a "bouncer". It bounces back to the desk from the printer's room and wastes time at various levels. The deskman should always write a headline which should fit. But if there is a superb headline which will not fit in the heading scheme, the scheme can be changed to fit it. A chief-sub may consider this if the merit of the headline so demands.

A sub-editor counts the units in the words he writes for

a headline. These units must not exceed the number of units allowed by the size of the type, its style and the number of columns the headline is being allowed to run.

The unit count system begins by giving a unit value to every letter and figure in the alphabet. It is based on a count of one for most letters with adjustments for thinner or fatter letters, and for capitals when they are mixed with lower-case letters. While m and w are counted as 1½ units; i, .1, f and t are counted 1h unit. Other letters are counted as one unit. Where capitals and numerals occur in a headline which is otherwise in lower case, allowance must be made for the extra space the capital letter or numerals will take compared with the lower-case letter. In a headline set u/lc (upper and lower case), count any ordinary capital letter or numeral as an extra 1/2 unit, that is, 1½ units. Exceptions are: M and W which should be counted as two units when in caps and I and J and numeral I should be counted as one unit.

If the headline is in all caps the letters M and W should be counted as 1½ unit while I and numeral 1 should be counted as 1/2 unit. Other letters and numerals will be one unit. The space between the words is counted by some experienced sub-editors as 1/2 unit, while others insist that the space should be counted as full unit. It is better to count it as full unit as if it is in excess it is on the right side and it also simplifies the count.

How does one know the number of units available? In newspapers there is always a list of headline types composed and pasted somewhere for ready reference. It may be available in the style sheet or style book.

If it is not available then the sub-editor should prepare a unit count card which gives the various counts at a glance. Unit count card can be prepared from the type schedule or by counting headlines as published in the newspaper for each style, size and spread. Count a dozen representatives of each headline and average the unit count obtained. Working in this way from published examples the deskman can write headings that fit without the need to count them. Experienced sub-editors resort to a unit count only in case of doubt.

But the real art in headline writing is in using the language to sum up the news item and attract the attention of the reader. Before writing the headline the sub-editor must read the copy carefully and decide on the basic news point. The sub-editor must think hard about the single element in the story which makes it worth its space in the paper. When he finds one or more such points he should write them on a piece of paper.

Some sub-editors prepare to write a headline first and sub the copy later. Their argument is that it concentrates the mind on the subject of they copy and becomes the test for intro. If the basic news point is not in the intro it has to be re-written. So, while the sub-editor tries to look for basic news point for headline he is also evaluating the work of the reporter. However, in many cases headline has to be given later, after a first few takes are composed. But even in such a situation the sub-editor must write down the basic news sentence. Often when edited this basic news sentence yields a good headline.

However, the headline writer should always be cautious about the meaning of the words when they are written in different lines of the same headline. There are a few rules. Never split a hyphenated word, look for another way of saying the same thing without using a hyphen at all; never split compound verbs or compound nouns between lines.

A sub-editor must pretest the headline on himself. He must read it to himself and at the end of each line think if t means what he wants to say. If there is any doubt or awkwardness he must re-write the headline.

When multi-deck headlines are used, there is no point in repeating the same information in several decks. Only the first deck should be completely self-contained. Once the first deck has declared the subject area, other decks can take it for granted and use the space to supplement and elaborate.

The first deck should have the most important news point. The second deck may elaborate this with a significant detail without repeating any word or -it may add a further newsprint. Repetition of a word should be avoided but in no case should it be replaced by a difficult or confusing word. In that case the general rule is to repeat rather than to confuse. Overline, if it is there, should elaborate or supplement the main deck.

Accuracy and impartiality are the basic requirements of a good headline. A news headline expressed the news and not the views of the sub-editor who is writing it. Care should be taken to write headlines of political stories. They should not look as if the paper is supporting some political party's view point while in fact it is just reporting the view point. To avoid such a situation one may use quotes on name the person or, party in the main deck. The headline writer must put his personal views aside. He must remember that his job is to reflect as accurately as possible the content of the story.

Quotes are one of the devices for dealing with strong opinions in headlining speeches or political party resolutions. One may put the name of the speaker or party in the headline. Headlines entirely in quotes are usually weak and should always be avoided. It is better to use single quotes for the part of headline which really needs them. When headline is in decks often the attribution is, given in the second deck, it is a bad practice. A headline with opinion and without quotes cannot be made acceptable by putting an attribution in the second deck. Attributions must be contained in the same deck as assertions, otherwise the statement in the first deck seems to have the authority of the newspaper for it.

But there should be no quotes when the opinion is obviously of the paper or the critic or columnist. It is unnecessary and may mean- that the critic or columnist has relayed gossip. Another word of caution is that the people in the ,news, particularly in crime stories should not be identified by race, colour, religion or nationality unless such identifications are pertinent in the news context. It is wrong to indulge in puns when the subject is death, injury or religion. Funny headlines should not be given for serious events. The sub-editor should always check whether the meaning of the headline is the same as the content of the story. Normally it is the duty of the chief-sub to check the work of subs as far as copy editing and headlining is concerned. He must also keep all these considerations in the mind, for he is again a person on whom the headline and the copy is pretested for clarity of language and meaning.

There should always be a verb in the headline. News is activity and verbs bring activity and life to` headline. In a normal headline there should be no room for adjectives. Its colour and spice must come from a rich verb. One should avoid using parts of weak verb 'to be' or 'to have' as the main verb in headline. The verbs 'to be' or 'to have' are not needed even as auxiliaries. For example "Sobhraj arrested" is better than "sobhraj is arrested". There are occasions when the very 'to be' should be omitted even though this seems to leave the headline without a very. This verb is better when implied. Its physical presence in the headline makes it weak.

Passive voice has been major culprit in headline writing. A verb should be used in active voice as far as possible. At least before using the passive voice the sub-editor should himself try the active voice and should explain to himself the reason for not using active voice Passive voice normally breeds extra words and burdens a headline. Usually, rejecting a passive voice construction can lead to a more vivid headline. However, care should be taken to see that the main news point is as close to the beginning of headline as possible.

The headlines have been using the present tense to describe events that have already happened. The arguments in support of this phenomenon is that the present tense is active, it puts the reader in the middle of the action and gives him a feeling of participation. The event described in present tense in the headline may be past, but it is recent past and the reader is learning about it now. He also understands the convention and will imply that in the present tense his morning newspaper's headline is giving the news of yesterday. 'Yesterday' is almost never justified in a morning newspaper headline because in that case almost all items could have yesterday in the headline. The reader takes for granted that it was yesterday unless it is otherwise specified.

There is an added advantage in using present tense. It is invariable shorter. It gives the feel of recency to the news below the headline.

Subject is an essential part of a sentence like verb and headline is really a truncated but still meaningful sentence that the reader understands. It should be in the headline either as such or as understood. It may be possible to write a headline without a subject in many circumstances but one should remember a headline with a subject tells more about the story than one without it.

The rule regarding the use of subject in a headline is to give the name if it is well known or the title if he is not well known. One must headline a name in case of obituary even if a person is not so well known.

The weakest form of subject in a headline is 'he' or 'she.'. It is not an identification. But it will be at times good to use 'he' or 'she' headline on a human interest story with a picture of the subject.

'Man' or 'woman' are weak identifications of subject but at times they are unevitable. 'Wife, husband, father, mother's are better because they narrow the field. But they should not be taken as another name for man or woman. 'Husband banned at club' will suggest that he cannot go while wife is allowed. Thus it is better to be more specific about the subject but it should be ensured that there is no distortion. Don't say "child" in headline if the child is not yet two. Better use 'baby' or say boy or girl and give age.

Headlines should be as specific as possible not only in identification of the subject but also in other matters as well. One should be specific about the main newsprint and a headline should tell as much as possible. It does not however I mean that 'where' of the story should always be included. One should test by examining the headline whether the addition of a place name adds significance. It is sufficient to say 'Barnala condemned terrorism at a Chandigarh press conference.' Further place name comes the first thing after the headline as a part of dateline. But in stories where place is important it must be there in a headline. For example, 'Earthquake rocks Simla'.

The language of headline should be positive. Some stories must be negative but the headline writer should avoid using 'no' or 'not' and try to express the same thing in different words. Short and simple words should be used for longer ones. For example, talks can be used for 'negotiations' and 'goods' for 'commodities'.

Headline should express a single thought to ensure clarity. It is difficult to communicate, a single idea in limited space; if more than one idea is involved it becomes almost impossible. Therefore the most important idea or thought or event should be identified to be put in headline. The deskman has to decide what the news really is and then he should express it with verbs and nouns using positive, simple and short words. This is the rule If the circumstances need the rule can be broken but the sub-editor should know that he is breaking a rule and should be careful about clarity and content of the headline.

# 5

# Team at Work

A newspaper office or news agency receives a large assortment of news items. These originate from different sources. The news copy is written by experienced and inexperienced people and hence lack uniformity. In any newspapers, there is always a shortage of space for all news items, which are received in the office. A newspaper's success largely depends on the space and its most efficient, judicious and economic use. Hence, within the space set aside for news, as much news as possible needs to be packed to serve a divergent readership. Considering these factors, editing of the news copy becomes essential.

All incoming news items, collectively called copy, is sifted, before being possessed, to achieve a balance of news between that originating within the organisation and that pouring in from outside. The unwanted matter gets weeded out and only the newsworthy stories are finally selected.

The news room is headed by an editor or a chief editor or an editor-in-chief or a chief news editor. He plans and directs the day's news operations. He is supported by a team consisting of the news editors, chief sub-editors, senior sub-editors. In a news agency, news editors and chief subs looks after the smooth functioning of the news desk. They plan and write 'leads'.

News has a number of characteristic elements:

> The nearer the origin of news, i.e., the closer it is to home, the more is its impact. For example, on a particular day, there may be 45 deaths in a boat tragedy in Bangladesh. But, on the same day, a local bomb blast that kills five people is sure to have more impact on the readers.

News grows old quickly. It decays and perishes fast. The more recent its occurrence, the more worthy it is. On the contrary, an event that happened six months back, but is discovered and reported now could grab the front page. For e.g. the bank securities scam including Ketan Parekh.

Names make news and the newspapers like to use as many local names as possible. For example, if the vice-chancellor of a university gets hurt while playing cricket, few people will take note of the incident. But, if a public figure like a minister is injured in a game, we have a more interesting story.

A reader's interest is aroused in a large measure if an event or occurrence affects him, and more so, if he participates in the event. He is eager to know what will this mean to him in the long run. How will it affect him and his family. A steep hike in the prices of petrol, cooking gas, milk or an increase in water and electricity tariffs will have widespread consequences.

Any interesting story about people and their peculiarities, and their infinite variety, make for wider readership. The human interest stories are pure identification. These are the little things that have happened, or could happen to yourself or to your neighbours or friends. These stories are worth little or nothing as news in any strict sense. Yet these are worth telling.

Ideally read a story, preferably thrice-once for familiarisation, once while you edit and third time to check your work. If the story has no glaring problems and if you fully understand it, you would be ready to edit it.

A news story is divided into two parts-the lead and the body. The lead describes, simply and briefly, what happened and the body documents and elaborates the lead. Adequate attention should be paid to the lead. The intro should be concise and crisp. Details should be dispersed and blended in the subsequent paragraphs.

The most significant information is placed at the top and other details follow in their order of importance. Each succeeding para should add an essential detail without being dependent in content or style on what follows. Next, see if the second para supports the lead. The third para should continue the development implicit in the lead and in the second para. While editing a story, the subeditor should look for errors in spelling, grammar and correct these. But an instant second look might sometimes compel him to rewrite it. Highlight the news point, taking care to avoid distortion and respect the facts produced by the reporter.

When a reader looks for something interesting in a newspaper, it is the heading which catches, his eyes. A story, howsoever well-edited, would not attract him unless it is given a headline. The headline attracts the reader to go through the story. A headline sells the story. Writing a headline is like applying the finishing polish on a well-crafted piece of furniture.

Kicker is another conventional headline, usually a one-line heading with a second line (kicker) above it in a different style and half the type size. It extends no more than midway above the main line.

Hammer is the reverse of kicker, but, usually, in all capital letters. The big type is the kicker and the smaller type the main headline. One word, or two at the most, will suffice of the hammer. By virtue of their size, hammers impress the readers with their importance. But too many hammers on one page may dilute that significance, and destroy the look of the page.

This lead is different from the one already talked about. Suppose there is a train accident at a place 60 km from Punjab. Just an hour before the first edition of a newspaper goes to the press. But we cannot wait till the reporter telephones from the spot or comes back to file the story. We can give a short news about it and wait for further details. Many news items are bound to flow in on the same event, details will pour in once the reporter reaches the site, there shall also be eyewitness accounts. All these are tied together, highlighting the major facts and the lead is written for the newspaper's city edition.

A lead is a device, used mostly in the case of developing stories, for changing the story's emphasis in the light of new information of facts as these unfold.

**Editorial Desk**

A copy editor is a bridge between a reporter and the reader. He has divergent roles to perform and docs one or more of these tasks while editing a copy. He need not execute all these functions simultaneously. A copy editor is a gatekeeper and image builder who protects a newspaper's reputation.

***Duties of a Copy Editor :*** A Copy Editor :

(a) Removes rough edges from the copy and polishes it to make it presentable.

(b) Adjusts the copy to the style of his newspaper.

(c) Should carve out each story in a familiar language so that it runs smoothly through the average reader's mind. Smooth writing ensures smooth reading.

(d) Tailors story length to space requirements.

(e) Detects and corrects errors of fact.

(f) Simplifies, clarifies and verifies meanings.

(g) Adjusts stories to make them objective and fair.

(h) Adjusts stories to make these legally safe.

(i) Rewrites and restructures stories extensively, where necessary.

(j) Follow the policy of the newspaper.

(k) Corrects copy in the interest of good taste.

(l) Avoids sensation.

(m) Removes those points that could be called undue publicity.

(n) Deletes doubtful words and sentences.

The production of a newspaper is a delicate and complex process. There is tension since a deadline is to be met. Amidst this tense atmosphere, the sub-editor has to perform his job meticulously. He should possess certain qualities to discharge his functions efficiently.

***Calmness :*** Be calm and composed. You should not get excited when a big story breaks.

***Decisive :*** Take quick and correct decisions. The editorial department has no place for indecisives.

***Non-partisan :*** Never take sides.

***Memory :*** Have a sharp memory for counter-checking facts.

***Grasp :*** Size up the situation as it unfolds, and estimate its relevance.

Know your reader.

***Self Confidence :*** Have confidence enough to correct a bad copy written by anyone.

***Mature :*** Be mature enough to correct only bad copy, and not just make changes for the sake of changing.

***Sceptical :*** Do not accept anything at face value. You should approach everything as a source of potential error.

***Knowledge :*** Be a jack of all trades. A good editor should store most of the information as it comes across, and search for more.

***Stability :*** Have enough stability to work under pressure.

***Tools :*** The copy editor will require a set to tools, the lack of which may lead to loss of valuable time. These aids are indispensable. Often you may come across problems of spellings and facts. You should focus on the errors, and correct the name.

***Language :*** The basic building blocks of journalism are words. You should respect the words, and follow the way these are arranged and strung together. Any misplacement of words could twist the meaning. Hence, you should pay attention to punctuation marks, grammar and syntax. All these are important in the sentence construction.

***Punctuation Marks :*** Punctuation problems start and almost end with a comma. This little mark causes more trouble than the rest put together.

Punctuation marks brings in clarity and better readability. At the same time, too many of these clutter a story. There should be no comma after a verb unless it is immediately followed by a parenthesis.

## Work Skill

A news item or story may run into several paras, and also exceed one page. If running into pages, a news story has to be kept track of from amongst various stories, and chronologically arranged. Hence, these paras, in a page, are divided into two of three parts. Then, these parts are 'slugged' and numbered, i.e., given a label, which identifies that story for that particular day, and helps the editor on duty to bring different parts together. Related stories are slugged to make the relationship clear. Slug is an identification mark or tag. It is often the key word in a story and written on top left or right of a page.

As soon as you start editing a copy, the first symbol you use is for paragraph indentation. Even if your para is indented, you should mark this symbol on every para. This would help the typesetter in knowing that you want paragraph to begin at that spot. Always note that editing marks are large and clear.

Pictures submitted for publication in the newspapers and magazines have to be edited to fit into the layout of the page, and also the unnecessary portions cut off, which the photographer might have added in the actual composition. The competent photo editor's job is to see to it that he does not waste space, and trims a picture keeping the main essence of the subject intact. This reduction process is called 'chopping'.

It is the job of the photo editor to select the best photograph which tells the story on its own. The photo editor edits it to suit the space in the page without destroying or distorting the essence of the picture, and gives it a good display. It is the photo editor's duty to give the photographer ideas about the picture possibilities.

A good photographer must be able to handle every assignment the editor gives him to his own satisfaction. One has to work with a great speed on a location. You should actually shoot a news event from several different angles, and let your photo editor decide which picture to use.

The newspaper photographs are based on factual situation. The photographs illustrates an event, bring depth into it, and probably comment on it. Usually, the photographer is given only an idea to work with, and is expected to create an appropriate photograph to illustrate it. This is where a good memory or a notebook will come in handy. The photographic techniques involved in shooting for magazines are not much different from those in newspapers. The technical skill is again taken for granted, and your primary concern is to illustrate the story clearly and completely.

The intelligent photo editors adopt different creative cropping techniques to bring out the exact point of emphasis a 'pix'. They try to enlarge the main image, which will have a better visual impact. A photo editor studies the picture carefully, and decides about the cropping. First, he crops the picture mentally and then decides on the final edited photograph. A badly cropped pix can not be repaired. A good photo editor is one who can visualise how the picture will look like when it is cropped and printed in different sizes and shapes.

In a professional organization, the photographers leave contact sheets with the photo editors to enable them to choose the right frame, and mark the composition. Sometimes, the photographers send the exposed rolls, and leave the rest of the job to the photo editors. In most countries, where there is competition amongst the leading newspapers, the photo editor looks for pictures from the freelancers as well. He chooses the best picture, and places it in the newspaper. It leaves no bad feelings amongst the staffers, because they also know that their newspapers should have the best coverage. This system makes every photographer work very hard on the assignments, and be alert with the competitive spirit.

Even though the news picture is supposed to tell a story on its own, one should say where and when the incident took place. Caption writing is an art by itself, which conies with experience and aptitude. The picture and its caption are complementary to each other, and it is very essential to mention when and where the picture was taken, and who the persons seen in the picture are.

If the photograph is described in the body of the story, then there is no need for a separate caption and the pix could hang in between the paragraphs. Sometimes to box a powerful picture with just a detailed caption brightens the page.

In most coverages, photographer reaches the spot only after the incident takes place, and is able to take only the result of what had already happened. In such special cases the newspaper or magazine might have to depend upon graphic illustrations to detail the activities that had taken place on a particular spot earlier.

However, with the advancement of technology, photo editing is done by the computer, which eliminates all the unessential elements, and gives out only the section as per the commands. Photos can be stored and recalled on the computer as and when required.

The newspaper composing and printing methods have gone through major changes during the past few decades. However, the basic function remains the same, to convert the printing matter into printable format. The composing methods used by newspaper industry range from hand composing to computer-guided operations. The major composing processes are:

> Hand setting is the original method of setting movable type. In this the compositor works with a composing stick, a type case and the metal type itself: letters, punctuation marks, figures, and spaces. The compositor adjusts the composing stick to the desired pica measure or line length. After taking out proofs and carrying out the necessary corrections, the next step is to make up the page. Since the composed matter consists of hundreds of individual pieces, it is essential that it is locked up, may be directly on the bed of the press.

This method involves casting type from molten metal. There are four popular type casting machines:

These are mechanical methods of composing and casting type in the piece lines called 'slugs'. The name Linotype is derived from casting a line-of-type. In both systems, the operator sits at a keyboard. The machine is adjusted to set type to the desired pica measure and leading. The upper front section of the machine carries a slotted metal container, which holds the matrices and when the operator strikes the keys, the matrices fall into positions to form a line-of-type. After the matter is composed the type is locked up. Any change within a line means that the entire line, or even all the succeeding lines in a paragraph have to be reset.

The basic difference between linotype and intertype is of the intertype of matrices. They can be used for casting headlines as well as body matter.

As the name suggests 'monotype' casts the characters one by one rather than as a complete line. It is a combination of two machines, a keyboard and a typecaster. It is a two-machine method of casting individual type characters, mechanically.

To set type the machine is adjusted to the required pica measure and leading. As the copy is typed, it produces a perforated paper roll, which is used to drive the typecaster. A combination of holes dictates the letters, spaces and punctuation marks to be set.

To set type, the perforated roll is fitted on the typecaster, where it directs the casting mechanism by means of compressed air. The air passing through the perforations brings the matrix holder and the specific matrix ready to be filled with molten metal into proper position. Once the type has been cast, it is ejected onto a galley, one character at a time.

This is a combination of handsetting and machine casting operations. The operator sets the type matrices and leading in a composing stick by hand. The composed matrices are then locked up into a casting machine, where they are filled with molten lead to produce the slug.

It is also known as cold type-setting, as it does not involve metal casting. Its first phase resembles that of monotype setting. Unless the perforator or keyboard is attached to a video display unit, the operation is limited to conversion of copy matter into a coded perforated tape. This perforated tape is then fed into a programmed computerised unit, which projects the desired images of type characters onto photosensitive film. This film is then made up in mechanicals from which printing plates can be produced. Photo-composing provides a fast, flexible and reasonable economical method of setting type.

Newspapers come in different shapes and sizes. There are newspapers that provide general public interest news to the readers, there are other which cater to the needs of the specialists. Every newspaper has its own way of presenting news, views and features.

The front page of a newspaper should be attractive, which will hold the attention of the readers. The front page is the "face" of a newspaper.

Newspapers have a name and each newspaper tries to acquire a unique identity by observing different ways.

On the front page, the masthead of a newspaper is much more than just the name of the newspaper. Some of its characteristics are-

— it is in distinctive bold print,

— it is in a big type size,

— it has a fixed place on the front page,

— it remains in the same form for years.

Headlines are a means to attract the readers towards the news items. It is the responsibility of the page-designer to make each headline as distinctive as possible. Headlines are given generally by the sub-editors/copy editors.

Picture is worth a thousand words. On the same basis, it can be extrapolated that a good cartoon is worth at least two thousand words. From a page designer's point of view, it is important to realise that photographs, cartoons and graphic have a special significance. Placing a picture or cartoon at wrong place may not only reduce its utility, but also reduce the design appeal of the total page. A page designer has to examine whether the picture, cartoon, graphic, chart, has an independent value or it has to be juxtaposed with a particular news story. The size may have to be adjusted due to placement or space considerations.

There is a design in the page, a form and a structure. Each page designer has his own concept of beauty and page structure. To bring it out, he uses different type sizes, white spaces, placement of pictures, graphs, charts, cartoons etc.

Inside pages of a daily newspaper differ from the front page in their format, structure and presentation of contents. By grouping news items on specific pages we are able to give the newspaper a structure. The inside pages under one group often tend to cover as many news items as possible. Hence, often these pages may seem cluttered.

The format of this page looks similar in many newspapers in India and abroad. There is a section, on this page, where the editor(s) write their analysis of the major national and international news items. Along with that, there may be one or two articles written by prominent people on current topics.

The design of the inside pages of a newspaper is relatively much more structured than the front page, which is dependent on the major happenings during the past few hours.

Advertisements have special significance for commercial publications. The very existence of newspapers and magazines depends on the revenue from advertisements. Hence, special care must be taken with regard to placement of advertisements along with the news stories on the pages. Advertisements are placed on these pages according to the product or service to be advertised. Large colour advertisements have special significance in page design.

Newspapers are meant to be read. As far as possible the news item should be contained in a neatly defined area. Each letter, each word and each story has special significance. Readability for a page-designer has a different meaning than that for a reporter, sub-editor or proof-reader. Readability from a page designer's point of view depends on placement of the news stories, typography and the overall page layout.

Today with the help of computers one can develop new type faces by incorporating variations in size, form and shape of each letter. It is the size, form and shape that determine and distinguish the type face of a letter. As page designers, we must select type by analysing its visual appearance as well as readability of its type face. While the choices may be many, editors of daily newspapers for the sake of economy, workability and convenience to its readers, make deliberate attempt to limit the variations of type faces used in their page make-up. Many newspapers adopt just one type face in different sizes throughout the newspaper.

Each letter or alphabet has immense potential to be used as a piece of art.

Because of economic and managerial reasons, newspapers use very limited type faces. Some newspapers may use only one. The only variation being the size. However, with the popularity of phototypesetting and offset printing, newspapers have a wider choice in matching and contrasting of type faces.

In page layout, when we want to emphasize or highlight a word, an expression, a sentence, a paragraph or even a portion of the news item, we have many options before us. Some of them are-

— Use of different type form of the letters such as italics.

— Use of bolder type face for the word or portion of the news item to be emphasized.

— Underlining the word or sentence.

The portion to be emphasized may be displayed with the wider margin, different colour or a combination of above alternatives.

***Recent Growth*** : Speedy transmission of news is as important as the actual news gathering. It has been made possible by the advanced electronic equipment. News is a perishable commodity. The newspaper staff have to be on their toes to ensure that important news items are processed quickly, to meet the deadlines of publication.

But rapid transmission of news becomes meaningless if information being imparted is inaccurate. In this context, the accuracy of the data and apparently minor details of spellings and language, assume importance. Such correction work is done with the help of the computers and 'fax' machines.

The computer are an ideal system for storing data in their memory and this data could be retained at a later stage. The computers act as the data banks, and are very useful sources of reference for the newspapers.

A computer is an automatic electronic apparatus for making calculations, besides storing and processing information. For this data along with instructions on how to process the same have to be fed into the computer. That is called the 'input'. The result obtained from the computer after processing of the data is called the 'output'.

The hardware components of the computers refer to all the physical parts viz. electronic and mechanical parts.

The software components of a computer refer to the set of instructions given to it to perform a specified task. These are fed to the computer in a language understood by it called a 'program'.

The arrangement of captions, photographs and graphic on a page would have to facilitate easy reading, besides being visually appealing. Certain parameters of format are fixed for any newspaper, such as those of the page size, print area, number of columns, positions of masthead, allotment of articles according to their categories and page titles.

**Computers' Use**

The Desktop Publishing, the DTP for short, refers to both hardware and software that are involved in preparing high quality prints of pages, once these are composed satisfactorily. The prints are used as artwork, and the actual duplication is done by offset printing, owing to the high costs involved in the DTP operations. The hardware of a DTP includes a large-sized colour monitor of the VDU (Visual Display Unit) and a laser printer apart from the CPU, which is programmed to suit the DTP software. The laser printer involves a high-speed, high-quality printer technology.

The DTP software consist of programmes to compose pages and their layout. These perform the function of the word-processing and automatic margin alignment, providing a variety of type-faces, page-numbering, etc.

Although DTP is considered incomparable when it comes to composing a page according to specifications. It handles the entire process with ease, completing the tasks at a rapid pace. But a few limitations persist in the new DTP packages too, like-

(a) It is not possible to obtain on the VDU an exact copy of the colours, as they would appear in the final print.

(b) The monitor is capable of showing the character in white against a background, whereas the actual product is black & white.

(c) The monitor shows only a restricted areas of each page. Such fragmented views make it difficult for an entire page to be visualised.

(d) A change once made in the typography might not eventually be printed as the package would not be programmed for it.

The appearance of a newspaper contributes to its having greater or lesser readership. There are number of readers who get addicted to their daily papers just because they take a liking to its layout and design. Each publication has a tradition which is flexible enough to accommodate innovative changes in the design layout with the passage of time. However, the readers might welcome such change only to a certain point. Both content and style of presentation matter in attracting readership.

### Heads of Sections

Every journalist unless he is happy to remain a worker for the rest of his life-carries the dream of being an editor. Who is a newspaper editor?

### Authority in Charge

He is not, as is commonly believed the man who writes the editorials. He is the man, who conducts a newspaper. Usually at the bottom of the last page of every paper, is what is known as the Imprint Line. The Imprint Line is mandatory and pins responsibility on what goes into print on the men who bring out a daily. Consider this Imprint Line.

Printed and published for the Proprietors, Bennett, Coleman & Co. Ltd., by *T.P. Pithavala* at *the Times of India Press,* Dr. D.N. Road, Bombay 400 001. Editor: Girilal Jain. Resident Editor: K.C. Khanna. General Manager: Dr. Ram S. Tarneja.... Everything is clearly stated.

If a newspaper in any way contravenes the law, the men responsible-the editor and the printer and publisher-can easily be identified and located and will have to obey the court's summons. The editor's chair in the circumstances, is not necessarily a comfortable one. The man who occupies it does not have an easy job. He bears a heavy responsibility and often has been called upon to pay a heavy price in the discharge of that responsiblity.

There is no one way applicable to all aspirants. Anyone who has the money to set up shop as an editor can become one. There are no rules and regulations, no memberships to be filled, no examination to pass. A mere declaration suffices.

Editors in the formative stage of the Indian Press were men imbued with a sense of mission. Robert Knight who made *The Times of India* into a great institution early in its career came to his job with experience in civil life and the running of public institutions. *The Pioneer* was started by Sir George Allen, a businessman of Kanpur and his son C.T. Allen. Of the three enterprising brothers Hemanta Kumar Ghosh, Sisir Kumar Ghosh and Motilal Ghosh who started the *Amrita Bazar Patrika,* the first two were working as employees in the Income Tax Department. S. Kasturi Ranga Iyengar who bought *The Hindu* in 1905 was a lawyer.

But there were others, men like Arthur Moore, Kalinath Ray, A.D. Mani, Benjamin Horniman, S. Sadanand and Prank Moraes who came to their jobs the hard way. Devdas Gandhi got his experience assisting his father in the running of *Young India.* Sadanand also had his apprenticeship with the same paper. Prank Moraes first worked as-an assistant editor with *The Times of India* from 1938 to 1946 during which, for a three-year period he also doubled as a war correspondent. He became deputy editor in1949 and a full editor only in 1950. Kotamaraju Rama Rao, who became the crusading editor of *National Herald,* had his apprenticeship as a reporter under T.L. Vaswani of the *New Times* of Hyderabad, Sind. M. Chalapathi Rao worked as an assistant editor first at the *National Herald* and later at *The Hindustan Times* before he became editor of *Herald.*

Pothan Joseph worked for a string of papers like the *Voice of India,* the *Indian Daily Mail* and *The Hindustan Times* interspersing his editorial career with a few executive assignments such as that of the Principal Information Officer of the Government of India. These distinguished men give the lie to the belief that editors are born and not made.

An editorship is not a bed of roses and has never been. Easy as his life may seem he works under all manner of pressuresland not all-necessarily coming from the management. Because his is the final responsibility in bringing out the paper he has to bear the brunt of the wrath whether of advertisers or of existing governments', During the Emergency (1975-77) in India, it was the editor who had to shoulder the burden of official wrath. Editors in India have been under pressure for decades, in fact from the very beginning of the British rule in the country. The Vernacular Press Act was passed in 1878 in order to control the *Amrita Bazar Patrika,* then published in Bengali as well as in English-the *Patrika* being bilingual. To get out of the clutches of the Act, its publishers changed over completely to English beginning 21 March 1878.

The *Patrika* has a long history of editorial daring and competence. At one time, the Government of Bengal recommended the deportation of one of the paper's earliest editors, Motilal Ghosh. On another occasion, the paper had to face prosecution in connection with the famous Barisal Conspiracy Case. Ghosh fought the charges and succeeded in getting the case dismissed. In 1932, the *Patrika* was penalized and a security of Rs 6,000 was demanded from it.

Another paper to fall foul of the government was the *Free Press Journal.* So powerful were the writings of its editor-publisher S. Sadanand that he had to forfeit the then phenomenal figure or Rs 70,000 as security. Indian editors were not the only ones to face the British government's wrath. E.G. Horniman of the *Bombay Chronicle* frequently clashed with officialdom and, at one time, the paper's printer and publisher were asked to deposit Rs 3,000 as security which was later forfeited. The history of Indian journalism is full of such instance of editors, fighting valiantly to protect the honour and integrity of the free press.

Many editors have also fallen foul of the owners of newspapers, though, in one instance, when C.Y. Chintamani differed from hispaper's Board of Directors and offered to resign, it was the offending member of the Board, Pandit Madan Mohan Malaviya who decided to quit instead.

No two editors are alike. The only common denominator that can be ascribed to them is their humanity, their concern for people, their interest in new. A delicate problem for every editor is the extent to which he can, and should, delegate authority. In a large paper an editor would have from two to six, sometimes as many as eight assistant editors. Each would have specialized in a particular field of activity such as foreign affairs, national affairs, law, finance, defence, agriculture or whatever. No editor can possibly be an expert in all fields and even if he happens to be an immensely knowledgeable man, he just would not have the time to keep up with new developments.

It is amazing how much a writer has to put in by way of reading. It could be new books on the subject, documents pertaining to it or upcoming literature dealing with the issue. No editor is expected to be a know-all. It is an editor's task to know who, among his colleagues, is best equipped to write on an event and to assign the task to him. By this the editor is not surrendering his responsibility, he is exercising it wisely. A good editor should know how best to tap the available talent in his office.

It is common in most editorial offices for the editor to have a morning conference with his staff. Often it-is done around the coffee table where assistant editors can sit informally and not only discuss the day's newspaper but engage in a post-mortem of the news. Depending on what the day's most important issues are, there will be a discussion of some of them at the end of which the editor would lay down his own views and give guidelines. If the editorial staff is fairly homogenous there would be no difficulty in arriving at a consensus as to what editorial line should be taken on any given subject.

Often, if the assistant editors have worked over a long period with the editor, they would know instinctively as to what angle would be projected. In any event it is the editor who lays down the policy and the subject of the editorials. Who will write what is also discussed and decided on at this conference.

An editor of a party paper will have no difficulty in the matter of policy as it would have been laid down for him. It would be his task to argue the party case as well as he can; he has a brief. An ideal paper, of course, would be one where its owners would let the editor make his own decisions and argue on the merits of a subject. In that event he would have to be as honest and objective as he can possibly be, placing, as he should, the public interest before anything else. He will know that life is not a bed orroses. He must expect to be subjected to all forms of persuasion, not all of them scrupulous, including flattery, bribery, even physical threats, not to mention behind-the-scene wire-pulling.

Though an editor is once removed from the actual production of a paper, it is in his power to decide what should be published and what shouldn't. In a sense he has to play God. This is a tremendous responsibility and cannot be ducked. It is an insensitive man and consequently a poor editor who has on occasion tortured himself over taking a decision that could possibly have harmed many people. The editors of *The New York Times* have admitted publicly their regret that they did not publish information about the US government's plans to abet the invasion of Cuba. If the paper had published the news, they have argued, the country may well have been saved the embarrassment of the Bay of Pigs fiasco.

Most editors may not be called upon to take momentous decisions, yet editing a paper is one long struggle against time, during: which decisions, one way or the other have to be taken. This is both the charm and frustration of being an editor Responsibility ends with him.

Editors have different methods of dealing with the problem of leader writing. Some dictate and then make the final corrections. Some do their own typing. Some others write laboriously in long hand. Some finish their writing by the end of the evening and place a phone call before retiring to bed to see that events have not-overtaken the editorial. Some others refuse to put down a word on paper until midnight.

**Social Awakening Effort**

The important thing for an editor is always to be keenly aware of the needs of the public and to be able to feel its pulse. It is to him that the reader will look to, interpret yesterday's news. An editor-and certainly a good editor-will offer leadership to the country as only he can. But for that, he will have to offer leadership to his staff, in the first instance. What often makes a news paper great is the right combination of inspiration, emphasis design, control, tone and selectivity. It is the editor who will have to see that through his personal leadership, this combination is,achieved. It is not-and cannot be-an easy task.

An editor will soon learn-if he has not by the time-he has become one-that his time is not always his own. In the office he will have to be in constant, if not continuous, touch with his colleagues. Outside the office he will be in demand as a public speaker,-as a guest at dinners and parties. These are chores that may not always be pleasant for him and more often than not are tiring and time consuming. And yet only by listening to friends and foes in various situations can an editor come to know what the public thinks. Dinners may be hard on the waistline but it is during the after-dinner coffee that an important politician may want to unburden himself to an editor to seek his reaction. An editor must make himself available to those who have something important and worthwhile to say.

This may not be very conducive to a settled married life, but it is an occupational hazard that editors have to face. A major problem confronting the "ideal" editor-the editor who 'puts public' interest before everything else is the extent to which he should extend cooperation to the government. It is not the job of the editor to give uncritical support to whatever administration is in power. Neither can it be said that his should be an unrestrained attack. Some journalists pretend that no one but the editor and proof reader read editorials. Such a view is extremely misleading. Whatever the situation be elsewhere in the world, in India there is ample evidence to show that editorials are read with interest. Editors often are more influential than they are prone to tell themselves. It may be that editorial influence is more over policy makers than over the public at large. The fact remains that editorials ("leaders") cannot be dismissed out of hand as mere space fillers.

An interesting comment has been made on the subject by James Reston of the *New York Times*. Speaking about the influence or the American Press on the American foreign policy, Mr. Reston pointed out that in his view this is usually exaggerated. "Its influence" he said, "is exercised primarily through the Congress, which confuses press opinion with public opinon. No doubt the press has great influence on American foreign policy when things are *obviously* going badly. It has very little influence, however, when things are going badly but the impending disaster is not obvious and the government is saying, as it usually does, that all is well or soon will be if everybody only has faith and confidence."

This is largely true. When things are going reasonably well, the tendency for the public is to accept government statements; the public frequently wants to be assured and is willing to believe or, at the very least, to suspend judgement. The crunch comes when things go badly and then it is to the critical editor that the public will turn. This was amply shown when, soon after the Emergency in India was lifted, the sales of newspapers suddenly soared to phenomenal heights. The public was turning to the editors to tell it the whole story unvarnished. The circulation of *The Indian Express,* for instance, showed a remarkable rise in the immediate post-Emergency months.

The important thing for an editor is, to be intellectually honest. He does not always have to be right; in the nature of things he cannot be so. But as long as he is honest and is seen to be honest, his responsibility to his profession ceases there. Nothing more can be expected of an editor and nothing more should.

The problem of honesty is more complicated than one thinks. What, for instance, should an editor's attitude be towards Mrs. Indira Gandhi at a time when the Janata Government is at sixes and sevens? Should the editor refuse to support her as a possible leader of an alternate government on the grounds that her role during the Emergency disqualifies her to receive any support any time or should he take the stand that as a leader of proven stature and stamina, Mrs. Gandhi deserves support at a time of national instability? It is here that an editor whose credibility is beyond challenge can get respectful attention from his reading public. In other words, for an editor, credibility is all.

## The Communication

It is important for an editor to be in constant touch with government officials from ministers downward. Senior editors get easy audience with ministers, since it pays the ministers themselves to nave their policies and views understood in the right perspective by the opinion-makers. The editor who lives in an ivory tower is becoming increasingly rare, if ever such a species existed. He cannot afford to be too far from the madding crowd. The crowd is and should be his business.

Almost all editors to a person, complain of the heavy schedule that they have to put up with. Consider this average day put in by one editor who usually is up around 6.30 in the morning and, goes for a half hour early morning walk. Then as he has his tea, he reads the morning papers, especially his competitors. If, as frequently happens, an item of interest has been missed by his paper, he will make a note of it for later discussion with his staff. He is in his office by 10 a.m.

10.00-10.45 a.m.: Staff meeting. This is the time devoted to dissecting the day's performance with assistant editors and assigning writing work to them.

10.45-11.30 a.m.: The editor meets the News Editor, the Chief Reporter and the Chief of his News Bureau. The discussion will relate to why some stories were missed, or why some were not adequately displayed or why some others should not have been displayed. The *post mortem* over, the discussion will deal with upcoming stories and how to cover them.

11.30-12 noon: Individual assistant editors will stray in to discuss specific ideas and to get editorial approval for them.

12 noon-2.00 p.m.: The editor will do whatever writing he plans to do for the next day's paper, taking a 15-minute break for a quick lunch.

2.00-4.00 p.m.: This is the time to look into copy submitted to him by his assistant editors, to select articles and special features to go for the next day's editorial page.

4.00-5.00 p.m.: This is Visitor's Hour when public citizens, usually those who have previously made appointments call on the Editor with complaints, suggestions or plain gossip.

5.00-6.00 p.m.: Time to look quickly into New Delhi and provincial papers and also at foreign papers and dispose off work with-the Bureau.

At 6.00 p.m. the editor leaves for his home where he will wash, change and relax.

8.30 p.m.: Dinner engagement. This is not an everyday affair but is sufficiently frequent to be taken as part of the day's work. Before going out, however, the editor usually calls the office and tell where he may be found in an emergency. Usually he himself calls the news-editor to check on late news breaks.

11.00 p.m.: Back home and one more late night call to the

office to check certain details. Mostly arrangements are made to send him the final proofs of the editorial page so that should last minute changes become necessary they can be quickly incorporated.

This does not permit much time to engage in sports or hobbies. A major complaint of editors is that they do not get the time needed to refurbish their minds. "I am living on my capital" is how Mr. Girilal Jain expressed his frustration. According to him, in 15 months he had taken only four days off and had seen only two films, which is probably a good average for most editors.

There are editors and editors. What makes for a truly great editor? According to Mr. M. Chalapathi Rau, C.Y. Chintamani was one. The following article written by Mr. Rau for *Swarajya* gives us a clear picture of why he thought so.

"Chintamani was a journalist, mostly an editor, with a pontiff's air but without pontiff's pomp. An editor of his period, enjoying considerable reputation, a legislator and political leader, possessing a muscular, vigourous style, he had a right to pontificate, and he pontificated giving a further lease of life to the leading article, before journalism made news techniques dominate the newspaper.

My acquaintance with Chintamani was brief but interesting my irreverence about eminence coinciding with the climax of career. It was my ambition not to be a journalist and neither the Spenders, nor the Chintamanis attracted me much. But style did, style as an extension of personality and not merely as an assembly of words, even if it was proper words in proper places or the best words in the best order.

With my interest in politics, I was reading in Madras with great interest the leading articles in a weekly edition of the *Leader* published from Allahabad. By then, I was forgetting Mill on Liberty and Morley on Compromise and was a convert to the Congress. So I could not but read the *Leader* critically. But an admiration for the argumentativeness, the consistency of outlook and the vigourous syntax of the main leading articles developed.

As an admirer of the orators who could rouse emotions one could not admire Chintamani, a speaker of cold logic, though with warm interjections, when I first heard him in Bombay. Then I heard him in Waltair in 1936 or so when he delivered his lectures which later became his book *Politics Since the Indian Mutiny,* abroad survey with many personalities, sketches and amusing anecdotes. Dr. S.Radhakrishnan presided. I rememher Radhakrishnan making caustic references to the Liberals and Chintamani reacting to them vigorously. I was among the few who listened to his Table-Talk as he sat at his brother's place in an easy chair-and pontificated off the record. He had no doubt about anything.

Sastri had intellectual honesty but no intellectual courage. Sapru had intellectual courage but no intellectual honesty. Sivaswamy Iyer, who had both intellectual honesty and intellectual courage was India's most accurate thinker, and came only after Gandhi and Malaviya as a great man. Gandhi, of course, was one of the greatest men the world had known but he had done immense mischief in politics....

I had no prejudice against Chintamani but my irreverence extended to him. There was much talk of what people called his phenomenal memory. I held even then that memory was selective. If one remembered certain things, one did not remember other things. Chintamani was reputed to remember all the Congress Presidential addresses, the list of all the Popes, the birthdays of famous Indians, when and where he had met Gokhale or Malaviya first and so on. He also remembered British constitutional debates on India or the debates in Indian legislatures. And many other things.

But I was afraid he did not remember many other things because he did not care for them or did not care to remember them. He did not seem to care much for foreign affairs though India had no foreign policy of its own then as an appendage of an empire. He could elaborate some historical parallels and narrrate vividly some historical anecdotes. But in general he showed no sense of history. My point is not that he was not sufficiently educated but that he concentrated on a few things and did not care for much else.

*The Leader* was read mainly for its leading articles and Chintamani was admired, even adored, for most of them. He wrote on all important Indian political subjects, leaving South Africa and other matters to his assistants and whenever he wrote, the world knew that he wrote. There was first his vast knowledge of Indian political subjects, there was then no mistaking the conviction with which he wrote, there was finally the force and vigour with which he wrote. To the Liberals, his was the voice of the Mesosiah.... He had read all the best biographies and auto biographies in the English language and remembered them. He did not forget what this Secretary of State or that had said or what this Viceroy had done. The unflagging energy with which he wrote sustained the readers' interest, even when he wrote two columns. My irreverence disappeared whenever I read leading articles written by him.

Above all there was character in whatever he wrote or did. This enhanced his intellectual and moral stature. He would be no turncoat, no Titus Oates. Chintamani had resigned his ministership on a matter of principle, somewhat rare in our history before Independence, and after Independence. The people in D.P. could not forget it. He enjoyed life. He was kind to young people. He was a fine conversationalist.... I found he did not know enough of economics, did not understand what the Gold Standard was. Chintamani had his personal predilections believed in the other world and spirits and while I was hearing, it, he surprised me by saying that Gokhale's spirit had dictated an editorial to him. He wrote even on the transfer of Superintendents of Police and his obituary editorials ended with 'May his soul rest in peace'. When Chief Justice Thorn died, he wrote that 'the summons had come to his Lordship from above' which roused my amusement.

The more I have known of Indian journalism, however, the more reverent I have become about him. As a leader-writer, he was a rare type. Other leader-writers who have given me equal pleasure were Kalinath Ray of the *Tribune* with his logic chopping and N. Raghunathan of *The Hindu,* who at his best reminded me of the leading articles of the old *Times Literary Supplement*. Chin tam ani was a personality; he had character. He was a great editor".

Consider here the qualities that Chalapathi Rau admired in Chintamani: knowledge, ability, good memory, vast knowledge of Indian politics, adherance to principles at any cost, unflagging energy, courage of convictions; style, character. And an overriding ego.

Editors, to be sure, have egos that seem to go with the job. An ideal editor, of course, will have opinions (or what is an editor for?) but will not be opinionated. Some of the great editors of our times have been men with strong opinions, men like Sadanand, "Stalin" Srinivasan, S. Natarajan, Frank Moraes or C. Narasimhan. They lent to the papers they edited their strength of conviction. An editor without an opinion is like a river without water. He will go nowhere.

Chintamani confessed a lack of expertise in economics. No editor, it is fair to say, can possibly be knowledgeable in all subjects but it is expected of him to have a lively curiosity and an abiding interest in what makes the world go. Today's editor, besides, must be more than a leader-writer; to be an effective editor he will have to know something of making layouts, or cropping a picture or reviewing a film; in other words, it would not hurt to be a jack-of-all-trades while being master of a few.

In the twenties, thirties and well into the forties and fifties, a paper could still sell on the personality of the editor, though it is pertinent to remember that newspaper circulation was in the mid 50,000s for most papers and a circulation figure of 100,000 was considered something of a distant dream. But editors of that era were well-known to their readers and they carried something of an aura about them. Editors today are less well-known; editorials are read but they are disembodied views rather than the live thoughts of a man passionately committed to truth. Newspapers no more sell on the strength of editorials no matter how well they are written or argued or presented. There was a time when writing in the *Indian Express* Frank Moraes placed his views on the front page. That did not perceptibly increase the circulation of the *Express*. If a paper is to sell it must take into account popular tastes whether in politics, economics, sports or films. That this is increasingly being recognized can be noticed from the fact that the *Express,* again, is devoting a page for features, an innovation in Indian journalism.

**Mass Taste**

We may take a brief *detour* to examine a subject that editors are continuously called upon to face, the public mind.

As all editors know, the public is not as well informed as it should be and it often does not even care. Editors are seldom known.

M.V. Kamath who has edited *The Illustrated Weekly of India* has had letters addressed to him in the name of H.V. Kamath, an older man and distinguished Member of Parliament whose name has long registered in the reader's sub-conscience. A Carnegie Endowment survey once established that many Americans believed and this in a country with a powerful communication media-erroneously that the NATO Treaty was negotiated through the United Nations. And the *New York Times* disclosed that nearly one third of the Americans surveyed by its reporters did not know that Berlin was located in communist East Germany. Social scientists can document such findings also in India at all levels of public intelligence.

If this be the case what is the public that the editor is addressing himself to? If public knowledge is limited should he, as one writer has facetiously suggested, put out papers that look like Mother Goose rhyme-books and write for readers with an intelligence,quotient just slightly above that of a moron? The fact of the matter is that in India, at least, there is a substantial section of the public that is highly sophisticated. This is borne out by the letters that editors get every day, some of which are witty, provocative and often throwing new light on old problems.

**Editor's Job**

An editor enjoys immense powers such as are not often realized even in editorial sanctum sanctora. He can make or mar reputations. This is difficult to prove statistically. It has been said that even if the average mind could be plumbed for its reaction to any given editorial, no standard could be devised to project its long-term effect. The effect of the written word, by its nature, is incalculable. We know, for example, that newspapers down the years have been suppressed and the only conclusion that we can draw from that fact is that governments have always been conscious of the power of the press. Obviously not every editor is powerful. And the size of a paper's circulation is no guidepost to an editor's influence.

The circulation of *Harijan* that Mahatma Gandhi edited was not much to speak about. It never really ever touched even the 50,000 mark. And yet, in terms of moving the governments, it was probably the most powerful paper in its time, certainly as long as Mahatma Gandhi was actively engaged in editing it. But it was the Mahatma who made the *Harijan*. These days, too often, it is the newspapers who make the editors.

Nevertheless, editors have certain responsibilities commensurate with their powers. These are *(a)* to the state, *(b)* to their proprietors, *(c)* to their readers, and *(d)* to their own conscience, and not necessarily in that order. An editor without a conscience needs to be watched. He could be an enemy of the people. Unscrupulous editors may one day get their due, but they can do irritrievable damage to a nation's psyche, while they are in circulation.

The problem of an editor's responsibility to the state has never quite been defined though, when efforts have been made by governments to muzzle the press, it has been loudly articulated. During the Second World War, Arthur Moore of *The Statesman* was sought to be muzzled and the Viceroy even suggested that he be repatriated to England, on security grounds. In times of war, of course, governments will clamp down censorship on the press, but it is the peace-time relationship between the government and the press that call for examination. When senior correspondents asked Mr. V.K. Krishna Menon-after the Goa take-over was completed-why they had not been given prior intimation of the "invasion," Mr. Menon blandly replied. "How was I to know that you would not leak the information to foreign embassies?" Mr. Menon is not alone in the kind of thinking that goes into government press relations.

On 2 October 1962, toward the end of the Cuban crisis week, Arthur Sylvester, Assistant Secretary of Defence for Public Affairs (and a former Washington correspondent of the *Newyork News)* called a press conference. It was a tense session. Newspapermen charged the US government with withholding the facts regarding the Cuban crisis and giving out misleading and even untruthful information. Sylvester responded:

I can't think of a comparable situation, but in the kind of world we live in, the generation of news by actions taken by the government becomes one weapon in a strained situation. The results, in my opinion, justify the methods we use. News generated by actions of the government as to content and timing are part of the arsenal of weaponry that a President has in application of military force and related forces to the solution of political problems, or to the applications of international political pressures.

Sylvester and his State Department counterpart, Robert

Manning (who was later to become editor of the *Atlantic Monthly),* signed orders requiring the military and civilian officers talking to the press report to whom they talked and what was discussed. (The State Department order was rescinded a month later but the Defence Department order was in force for full five years). The memorandum for Defence personnel said:

> Procedures for handling media representatives.
>
> The subject of each interview and telephone conversation with a media representative will be reported to the appropriate public information office before the close of business that day. A report need to be made if a representative of the public information office is present at the interview.

In such a situation how should an editor handle his job? Sylvester had suggested, by way of justification of the government's handling of information that there is a need to "speak in one voice to your adversary." Commenting on that- and laying down what an ideal editor should do in the circumstances, the *New York Times* said in an editorial on 31 October 1962: "To attempt to manage the news so that a free press should speak 'in one voice to your adversary' could be for more dangerous to the cause of freedom than the free play of dissent, than the fullest possible publication of the facts."

Another and a yet more fitting answer was given by the chairman of the House subcommittee on Information of the Committee on Government Operations, John E Moss. He said: "Government pronouncements during a conflict of wills obviously have an effect upon the outcome of the conflict, but to imply that the entire government information process is part of the manouvers in international relations is to ignore the working of our democratic system."

That, of course, is not how the US Administration saw it. President Kennedy, for example, thought that by not using the information about the presence of Russian missiles in Cuba which the *New York Times* possessed, the paper had made "far-more effective our later actions and thereby contributed greatly to our national security."

There will always be two opinions as to what the true relationship between the government and the press should be and it will be argued that the circumstances in the end will dictate what such a relation should be. By and large it has been suggested that relationship is best which is adversary in nature. The press which means the editor-is better off to be on guard where the government is concerned than to work in cahoots with any administration.

***Information Network :*** The relationship between an editor and the proprietor is an even thornier one than that between an editor and the government. Where the proprietor is himself the editor-as it used to be in the *Free Press Journal* when Sadanand was alive-the problem obviously does not arise. But there were times when Sadanand employed separate editors and with his kind of temperament, conflicts between him and them were routine. On one occasion Sadanand without so much as consulting his then editor S. Natarajan, changed editorial policy overnight. Natarajan thereupon did what any self-respecting editor should do, resigned on the spot.

Pothan Joseph who, in his time, had served many masters and was willing to argue any case has been reported to have said that, an editor, like a lawyer, should have no compunction to posit the owner's point of view. Joseph himself at different times edited *The Hindustan Times* (a paper that strongly supported the Congress) and the *Dawn* (mouthpiece of the Muslim League). Pothan Joseph found nothing wrong in this.

Some old-fashioned editors have held the view that an editor is responsible solely to his conscience and to his readers and that any proprietorial interference in the discharge of his duties is an assault on the freedom of the press that should be resisted. Theoretically such a position is unassailable. In practice, however, many editors have learned that he who pays the piper calls the tune. An editor is well advised prior to his accepting his appointment to see that he is on the same wave-length as that of his employer. That is the best way to save later embarrassment and agony. Most editors are hired on contract and an editor who claims special privileges for himself on grounds of editorial independence may soon find that editorial independence and job security do not always go hand in hand.

***Job of News Editor :*** The news editor is a very important functionary in the organisation of a newspaper. He is the real backbone of the newspaper. The news editor is responsible for doing the most important work in the publication of a newspaper. In certain ways, he can be called the number two man in a newspaper organisation. He is solely responsible for the news coverage activities of the newspaper. It is his duty to see that the news service of his paper is always up to the mark and ahead of its rivals.

The news editor deputes the reporting staff for news collecting activities. He also directs the work of the sub-editors. He is the final arbiter to whom all questions affecting the news columns are referred, and ultimately he decides the fate of every report and paragraph. However, much of this responsibility in actual working may be delegated to his subordinates. In the western countries, sometimes, the news-editor performs the functions of a general supervisor, because his work is divided among other employees of the newspaper like copy testers, planners etc. Generally, his time is occupied with administrative work.

He merely controls the activities of his assistants and makes the most important decisions. The rest of the work he leaves to his subordinates. But in India the position is quite different. In our country, the news editor has to deal with many aspects of collecting the news and making use of it. He is responsible for all the news stories that appear in a newspaper. In fact, he performs many functions which were previously performed by a district editor, copy tester and a planner of news coverage.

The news editor not only acts as a senior journalist guiding other journalists, but he also has to deal with the administration of the staff under his control. He is responsible for alloting duties, giving assignments and making leave arrangements for them. The news editor is generally a very experienced person. He knows all the ins and outs of his job.

In a newspaper the news is received from various sources like reporters, correspondents, national and international news services etc. The news is continuously received on the teleprinter which is installed in the newspaper office. It is the news editor who plans how to use the news which is continuously arriving in the newspaper's office from various sources. He prepares the dummy for the next day's paper in which the space to be occupied by advertisements appearing in the newspaper is indicated. In fact, on the basis of this dummy, the next day's newspaper is planned by the news editor. For special reports he obtains photographs to be published in the paper. He tries to be in touch with all the events and news which are taking place or the reports which are trickling in.

He also discusses the coverage of news and events with the chief reporter as well as the editor of the newspaper. The timings of the city edition and dak edition are also decided by him. He tries to coordinate with the printer and the production side for bringing out the newspaper in time. He gives instructions to the chief sub-editor regarding the use of important reports and news items. Although the chief sub-editor is the ultimate incharge of the actual shape the edition will take, yet the news editor always tries to know as to what is happening.

It is the duty of news editor to build up the news service of the paper on a sound footing. No doubt, in the fast moving world of today this is not an easy task. He has to keep in touch with his paper's local reporters, correspondents, foreign as well as the numerous national and international news agencies for collecting the latest news regarding the important happenings. He may have to meet many callers as well as attend to immense correspondence reaching his office.

The news editor has also to make arrangements to cover the unexpected occurrences hurriedly. To meet the rush of work and unexpected situations, things may have to be done in a hurry, yet in a systematic and proper manner. The unexpected is always happening in a newspaper office. It may be report regarding a big air crash or a railway accident, a mining disaster or a huge fire, a gruesome murder or a cyclone involving loss of many lives. Whichever of these occurences it may be, the same has to be dealt with promptly and appropriately, no matter what hour of the night or day the news arrives in the newspaper office. A good news editor evolves cohesion and order, even out of a chaotic situation due to his cool direction.

The successful news editor possesses a highly trained news sense. He has the knack of anticipating events intelligently. A good news editor is a man of tireless and boundless energy. He should have a lot of driving force to direct his staff, sparing neither them nor himself, when a big story is about to break, or when the reputation of his paper is at stake. Above all, he should be able to make quick and accurate decisions in a crisis and remain cool and calm under all circumstances.

***Job of Sub-editor :*** The sub-editor plays a very important role in the publication of a newspaper. He is a very important member of the newspaper's staff. The quality and style of a newspaper greatly depend on the good work done by the sub-editor. It is the sub-editor who prepares the copy for the printer.

Although the editor of the newspaper exercises the supreme direction and legal responsibility, yet it is the sub-editor who performs most of the functions of the editor, as far as the production of a paper is concerned. In a way, we can say that if the editor is the top stone, then the sub-editor is the key stone of the arch. In ordinary matters the sub-editor has undisputed control over every article and paragraph that reaches the newspaper's office. As far as the difficult and important articles of news publicity are concerned, he may be guided by the editor.

The functions of an editor have become very vague now-a-days. His control is now merged into the managenial side of the paper from which side he may exercise both a journalistic and commercial influence. An editor may hardly write much for the newspaper. In fact, it is the sub-editor who does most of the editing work in a newspaper. If the functions of the editor have now become a little less, as far as the production of a paper is concerned, then the functions of the sub-editor have definitely increased greatly.

The sub-editor is mainly responsible for the manner in which a journal or a newspaper is made-up, sent for printing and offered to the public. There is no doubt that the sub-editor must be a man of high ability and judgement. He must know thoroughly the news value of every matter which comes into his notice. He should have the ability to see the importance of even a small paragraph and the competence to reduce a lengthy paragraph to its deserving size. A sub-editor may not generally do much of original writing like an editor, but he should be an expert in revising the news articles as well as supervising the work of those who do the writing work. Thus, a sub-editor must possess the capability either to reduce or to expand a subject matter as per the needs of his paper.

All sorts of news go on trickling into the sub-editorial department all the time. It is just like a raw material out of which a sub-editor produces a finished product (the news to be published in the newspaper).

The sub-editor has the power of life or death over all the newspaper's material that reaches him. Thus, the responsibility of the sub-editor is really enormous. A newspaper receives its copy from a variety of sources like reporters, correspondents, telephones, news agency reports and verbal communications. All this information is filtered by the sub-editor. The sub-editor is actually responsible, more than any other person for what the paper looks like and stands for, to the readers.

There are many ways in which a sub-editor can leave the impression of his personality on the newspaper. The format of a paper is in reality determined by the sub-editor. The sub-editor has the nose for selecting the right type of news. It is the task of the sub-editor to decide as to what is going in for tomorrows's newspaper and in what form. In fact, the sub-editor with a wide experience in his work, is the most suitable person to become the editor in due course of time.

There is always a big pile of news reports and other communications lying on the table of the sub-editor. He is also pressurised by the printing department for the copy. He has to attend to his functions in a very quick manner, using his best judgement as to the relative urgency, importance and the desirability of printing a particular news or article.

The sub-editor has to separate the grain from the chaff out of the great number of news material lying on his table. He should have an eye for accuracy. He must check the facts of a story and look out for the errors, if any. If there are certain facts which are missing, he must ask these from the reporters. The sub-editor has to read every story and sometimes contrive to make it interesting and news-worthy.

Mainly, we can say that a newspaper receives the news from two sources, one from the paper's own correspondents and the other from the various news agencies. Generally, out of these two sources preference is always given to the news brought by the paper's own correspondents, because a good report under the headline 'from our special correspondent' indicates the initiative and enterprise and adds to the prestige of a newspaper.

Sometimes, a newspaper may receive a number of versions of a particular story from different sources. The paper's correspondent may give a different story where as the news agencies may give their own accounts. The sub-editor has to put all these conflicting accounts into one coherent and wholesome story. If the reports contradict or conflict with each other, then he has to believe the story put in by the newspaper's own correspondent. It is thus the responsibility of the sub-editor to make the story clear. He should see to it that the news story is based upon facts, it is as complete as possible and is clear from every angle for easy understanding.

A sub-editor checks the news stories one by one. He goes through every single piece of the copy. Then he adds a catch-line, if the reporter has not already provided a suitable one. He also writes a suitable headline for the story. This is a very important and difficult duty of the sub-editor. After this, he edits the story, cutting the unnecessary matter and trimming the length to the right size according to the space where it has to be printed. He checks the spellings of names and places so that these are not printed wrongly. A sub-editor also has to correct errors of grammar, capitalization, punctuation and abbreviations. He cannot afford to allow even the most minor error in the newspaper.

If a sub-editor feels that the intention of the writer of a story is not clear or the message of the story is very vague, then he can refer the copy back to the reporter and ask him to rewrite the story. Sometimes, he may have to refer to books like 'who's who', encyclopaedias, telephone and civic directories, almanacs etc., to confirm the facts of a story. He may even have to telephone the source of the news item to seek any clarification regarding which a doubt creeps up in his mind.

The sub-editor has to take into consideration the policy of his paper before allowing a news item to be published. He has to breathe life into some dead matter lying before him so that the story is made lively. Sometimes, he tones down a story which is too lively. He may also trim down a story, if it is too dangerous, to make it safe. He has also to decide the suitability of the news stories and articles on the merits of their news value to the particular paper. He has to reject a superfluous article and prune another to its justified size. He is always on the look out to print a news story which is a scoop, well ahead of his rivals.

After deciding the main contents of his newspaper, he has to use his utmost skill in their make-up and display. This is just like the window dressing of a shop which is fully stocked. And it is a very important function of the sub-editor. He has to be careful that in the final rush no mistake creeps into the print and no paragraph gets mixed up or overlooked. The maximum attention a sub-editor has to pay is to the layout of captions and the main news page. Balance and proportion are the qualities which should be aimed at before anything else.

The principal test of sub-editorial capacity in the art of make up is, of course, the appearance of the main news page. It is the page which the majority of the readers read first of all. Some very busy readers only read this page and no more—they simply turn the other pages. Although the eye may be arrested by the heading of the principal news, yet the total effect of the whole page should not be crudely sensational. In fact, the make-up of the first page should be in such a way that a reader is helped to find at a glance how the world has behaved during the last twenty-four hours.

There is no doubt that the make-up of a newspaper is the reflection of the sub-editor's appreciation of news value. Sometimes, the value and significance of a news feature is largely neutralised by an ineffective handling of make-up.

Side by side with the presentation of the news, a sub-editor should also know something about the gathering of news and arrangement of regular features. He should be fully acquainted with the reporters and correspondents employed by his newspaper as well as with the regular contributors who write special features from time to time, which are published in his newspaper. The sub-editor should also know the principal news-agencies which supply news stories to his paper. In fact, now-a-days more and more news is supplied to the newspapers by one or the other national or international news agencies.

The sub-editor should also be acquainted with the important photographers and photographic agencies which supply photographs of important events and news items to his newspaper. In fact, now-a-days every big newspaper has its own staff photographers, who cover the special functions and events for their newspaper. By knowing these sources of news as photographs, a sub-editor can contact them in case of any contingency without any difficulty.

Of course, many of the troubles of the sub-editor will be lessened, if the correspondents and other contributors take a little more pain to make their copy readable. If the reporters and writers try to follow the style in which their writings are presented finally in the newspaper, then they can greatly save a good deal of unnecessary work and worry on the part of the sub-editorial department. Sometimes, a contributor or a correspondent may even have a complaint against the sub-editor for the way in which his article has been cut down by the sub-editor, who may not be sufficiently acquainted with the importance of the material. Every sub-editor should be careful in the use of scissors and the blue pencils, so as not to give any cause for complaint later on to the conscientious writers.

There is no doubt that ultimately the public is the best judge of the work of a sub-editor. The good work done by him in the selection of the news and views will be much liked by the readers of his newspaper, whereas any fall in its standard may result in a reduction in its circulation. It is, therefore, the duty of every good sub-editor to do his best to put as much exclusive news in his newspaper as possible and as early as possible.

# 6

# System at Work

To the outsider, journalism and ethics are about as incongruous a mixture as you can get. Even to put the two words in the same sentence is to risk reducing the listener to helpless laughter.

To the insider on a mass-market tabloid, ethics are largely an irrelevance. Editors, pressured by intense competition for readers, demand that staff cut ethical corners; and competition among staff encourages some to respond. Lecturing these journalists about ethics is as pointless as advocating celibacy to sailors arriving in port after six months at sea.

To the insider working on a quality paper, where there is virtually unanimous agreement about basic professional morality, ethics are a code of principles to which all journalists should adhere, or at least feel guilty about if they do not. They are rarely, if ever, required to step outside this code.

Ethics, more than any other aspect of the job, are where personal circumstance produces experiences so that the different ethics employed are barely recognisable as the same thing. The reason is that ethics, as actually practised, are conditioned less by morals than by what is rewarded or punished in any given newspaper. On a British mass market tabloid (or agency serving one) journalists may be regarded, paid and promoted according to how many dramatic, possibly invasive, stories they produce. Not too many questions are asked about how they obtained them or what degree of exaggeration is involved.

Indeed the news desk, or higher executives, often tell reporters what line they want, regardless of any reservations reporters have. Not much scope for Mr. or Ms. Proper here. At the other extreme - on a US paper enjoying a monopoly and sharing the same city as its sources and readers-reporters are judged and rewarded differently, with ethics playing a far greater part in their lives.

Ultimately the main factor in deciding what ethics are actually practised is competition. In monopoly situations, papers know that there is no rival paper to scoop them, and readers have no alternative to turn to-save for giving up papers altogether. This lack of competition gives the journalists the moral luxury of generally being able to apply far more idealised standards of professional ethics. In a mass market, highly competitive and with a macho culture, almost the only sanction on what papers will do to get a story, or publish once they have got it, is the prospect of upsetting readers, especially to the point where they will not buy the paper.

Only then will word go out to the staff, and the little news agencies that feed them, that it is time to call a halt (perhaps only temporarily) to stealing pictures from the bereaved, invading hospitals where sick celebrities are being treated, publishing pictures of royal children in private moments, condemning a community for violence without sufficient evidence, or whatever. On tabloids especially, the periodic little eruptions of ethics that are sometimes seen nearly always come from proprietors acutely aware that readers can always, and maybe are about to, buy another paper. Or that the government is about to legislate.

But journalists have a sanction, too. We do not have to be mere creatures of the papers we work for; we have a choice. Just as readers can stop buying, so journalists can change jobs. We can decide that there are some things we will not do and leave the paper - either discreetly after having found another post, or publicly, in a blaze of righteous indignation. If more of us did that, and made clear our reasons for doing so, journalism would be better for it.

This element of moral choice, the distinction between how papers acting under commercial pressures expect us to be have and how we can choose to behave, explains why ethics have a daily purpose - or rather, two purposes. The first is to provide some kind of moral compass, telling us how far we are diverging from a desired route. So far as I know, the magnetic north in our trade is found in the clauses of an unwritten contract which should exist between all newspapers and their readers:

- Every story in the paper is a result of decisions made free of political, commercial or non-commercial pressure.
- None are there because of any favours or money exchanged.
- All stories are written and edited in a spirit of free enquiry, and chosen for publication entirely on their own merits, be they real or imagined.

Second, ethics provides a practical guide to the production of safe and credible journalism. Honestly, with plain dealing and with the removal of conflicts of interest are the best ways to do this job because they are the safest ways to do it. At the most base level, they keep you out of the courts and help you to sleep at nights. And, at the risk of shocking some of the more raunchy reporters, ethics are the most decent way to do the job, too, giving us attitudes to readers (and sources) that are based on some sensitivity, rather than mere sly commercial calculation.

## Fundamentals and Guidelines

Viewed like this, ethics are not some optional extra but are integral to every aspect of the job. This book therefore deals with them as they occur - in handling sources, asking questions, writing, etc. - and not in some moral parking lot tucked away from the main action. There are, however, some general principles and these have been gathered here.

If you want to be a propagandist, then go and work in public relations, or politics. Journalists should owe no loyalty to anyone or anything else; not a political party, source, commercial interest, non-commercial interest or particular cause, however worthy. Balanced journalism is difficult enough to achieve without such conflicts of interest. The Washington Post newspaper has a rule that its journalists cannot take part in any political activity. That includes marching on demonstrations. So when several Post reporters were spotted on an abortion rights demonstration, they were told they would not be allowed to cover anything touching on the abortion issue.

The dangers of allowing a missionary zeal for some cause to infect reporting are even more obvious. One of the more notorious examples is Walter Duranty, the New York Times correspondent in Moscow in the 1920s and 1930s. So taken was he by the ideology of the new Soviet Union that his reporting was often little more than propaganda. At the height of the famine in the Ukraine, for instance, largely engineered by Stalin to break local resistance to Soviet control, Duranty wrote of 'village markets overflowing with eggs, fruit, poultry, vegetables, milk and butter' at prices far lower than in Moscow. 'Anyone can see this is not famine, but abundance', he added; and a Pulitzer committee, knowing no better, gave him a prize. In fact, millions died, and Duranty knew this full well, telling colleagues in private that he thought the death toll was around ten million. Malcolm Muggeridge, the Manchester Guardian's reporter in Moscow at the time, called him 'the biggest liar of any journalist I have ever met.'

Each story should be an open-minded attempt to find out what really happened, accompanied by a willingness to print that truth, however uncomfortable it may be to our own, or the paper's, cherished beliefs. Thus, journalists should not accept work which seeks to bolster a point of view in the face of evidence, or undertake reporting which aims to support a preconceived theory.

You would think this so self-evident that it would not need stating. But every day you can read reporting which stretches and strains the facts to fit a particular thesis. One of the worst examples in recent memory was committed by the Sun, Britain's biggest-selling daily. For reasons best known to himself, the then editor became convinced that Aids was a disease limited to drug addicts and homosexuals. On several occasions government statistics were wilfully manhandled to support this view. The most flagrant occasion was a story headlined 'Straight Sex Cannot Give You Aids —Official', which reported, among other absurdities, that the chances of getting Aids from heterosexual sex were 'statistically invisible. Anything else is homosexual propaganda.' Eventually, the volume of protests at this coverage produced an apology - which the paper ran at the bottom of page 28.

Here, and this is no isolated case, was reporting that deceived readers and possibly endangered them. Preconceived theories have no place in journalism. Newspapers should be at war with closed minds, not employing them.

This means not only money and free gifts, but also the promise of advantage or preferment. It specifically means two things. The first is hidden advertising, where journalists or their papers take money for writing public relations pieces about firms or people which then appear in the editorial columns parading as normal stories. In recent years this has become a widespread practice in countries like Russia, and the temptation to write hidden advertising in places where pay is very poor is understandable. But that does not make it journalism. It is advertising, PR, puffs, whatever you call it, dressed up to look like journalism. It is a deception, and a damaging one. First, it breaks the basic contract with readers, with stories, purporting to be a normal editorial in print only because money has changed hands.

Second, such deceptions destroy any trust that should exist between readers and papers. Third, the practice makes editors suspect their staff have taken bribes to write about a company when their story may be perfectly honest. Fourth, editors and publishers will, like hotel owners paying waiters low salaries because of tips, use hidden advertising as an excuse not to pay journalists properly. Fifth, it establishes that the journalists who do it have their pens and minds available for hire. What will they accept money for next? Writing favourable stories about criminal groups% Keeping stories about wrongdoing out of the paper: That is but a short step away from collecting information with a view to selling its destruction or suppression. In other words, blackmail.

(Lest anyone think this a good original money-making scheme, an American publisher called Robert Harrison got there first in the 1950s with a magazine called Confidential. It specialised in Hollywood scandal and, by paying large sums for tips and information, he and his investigators obtained decidedly intimate details of the stars' private lives. Each story was well-researched and Harrison's staff were not fussy about their methods, hiring prostitutes to trap victims, secretly taping and filming encounters and confessions. Sales of Confidential soared and eventually hit four million. But soon the temptation to sell the negatives, tapes and other evidence to wealthy stars proved too strong. The inevitable court case happened, a staff member killed herself, the editor shot his wife and himself in a New York taxicab, Harrison sold the magazine and both he and it went into a richly-deserved oblivion.)

Hidden advertising (which should be correctly labelled 'advertising' and typographically treated accordingly), is very rare in developed countries. Far more common is the acceptance by journalists of what they call 'freebies', that is, free trips with vacation companies, free meals from restaurants or free tickets from theatres, all given so that journalists can review them. The danger here is that the writer will feel obliged to write a favourable piece. This need not be so, and the dangers can be minimised and faith kept with the reader if it is made plain somewhere in the piece or in a footnote that the ticket/trip/meal or whatever was given free to the newspaper.

It is not unusual, especially on smaller, less profitable or local papers, for advertisers to try to use their commercial weight to bully the paper. This pressure should be resisted at all times. It normally comes from the paper's advertising department who will say to the editor that it would be helpful if this important client could have some 'good coverage'. A few years ago the Riverside Press-Enterprize, a paper in California, published a total of eleven news pieces and 22 photographs of a new department store called Nordstrom's in the six days before, during and immediately after its opening in the town. These 400 column inches appeared in the same week as 20 full pages of ads for the store. A coincidence? Unlikely.

More rarely, groups of advertisers act in concert to try to force the paper to change its coverage. When I took over as editor of a British provincial paper, one of the things I did was to stop the automatic reporting of all shop-lifting court cases because they were so common as to be boring. Within a week, all the department stores in the city approached the publisher and told him that unless reporting of all shop lifting cases was resumed they would withdraw their advertising, which was considerable. They said the coverage acted as a deterrent to would be thieves. Luckily the publisher supported me. The advertisers' threat was not carried out.

The danger of giving in to advertisers' pressure, whether individual or collective, is that your content ceases to be freely chosen. You would also find that what is granted to one advertiser would soon be demanded by many. Give in once, and you would never be free of the pressure.

A journalist has power. It should never be abused, either in the course of a story or in one's daily life. Prosecuting personal disputes with stores, neighbours, etc. by threatening exposure or reference to high-placed connections is bullying, and unsafe bullying at that. How could you ever write a future story about any person or organisation you have threatened in this way? How could you write about the connections you have used in your threat? You will be in their pocket for the favour you owe them. Neither should you use your newspaper's headed notepaper to write a letter demanding preferential treatment, compensation for some alleged negligence or faulty service. It implies to the recipient that your paper exists as a sort of private protection racket for its staff.

It sometimes happens that you are asked by someone to 'forget' a story, or part of it, in return for some favour, or even cash. It is clearly wrong to accept such an offer, for the same reasons as it is wrong to put in a story for favours. When friends are involved, refusal might be more delicately phrased, but just as swift and sure. So should it be with colleagues, as these two stories illustrate.

The first case comes from Oregon in the United States where a few years ago a local television station reported that the long-time chief of staff of the state's Republican senator had served for 25 years as director of a bank that collapsed and was bailed out at a cost to taxpayers of $100 million. It was suggested that the man's involvement with the bank may have influenced the senator's position on bank deregulation and the subsequent bailout. The story was picked up by the Associated Press and was the talk of the state, but the main newspaper in the state, the Oregonian, chose to ignore it. It also ignored allegations a week later that the chief of staff's official travel, at taxpayer's expense, had included 52 trips to New York, where he published an annual guidebook to the city that had earned him more than $1 million.

The paper's reluctance to write this story may have had something to do with the fact that the chief of staff wrote a weekly column for the paper. It eventually published parts of the story only after the Washington Post gave the revelations national exposure.

Contrast this with a paper called the Daily Item in Sudbury, Pennsylvania. Among the daily stories from the police in one issue was an uncensored account of charges filed against a town resident for driving at an unsafe speed under the influence of alcohol. The item included the man's name, age, address and occupation - editor of the Daily Item. Which paper would you trust most, the Item or the Oregonian?

Inventing information is obviously wrong and dangerous. So, too, is even a light doctoring of the facts, embellishment of the truth or temporary amnesia about certain details that inconvenience the main thrust of the story. Your report will be a cheat. This applies with equal force to photographers and the dishonest 'set-up' picture, where an event or situation is staged to imitate some alleged reality.

Some news photographers in Western Europe also have been known to carry around in their cars certain 'props' to insert into pictures. A well-known ploy used to be to have a child's shoe, or teddy bear available, so that photographers covering disasters like train or air crashes, could set this prop among the wreckage for a 'poignant' picture. Such pictures have now become a cliche. Besides, there was always the danger that the passenger list, when finally issued, would reveal that there were no children aboard. Deliberate fakes, or at least the detected ones, are very rare. Perhaps the most famous recent example was Janet Cooke's Pulitzer-winning story in the Washington Post.

It was called 'Jimmy's World' and told the story of an eight-year-old heroin addict. Jimmy, however, did not exist. The story was an invention from beginning to end. When the fiction was revealed the Post saw that, with hindsight, there were many warning signs. Some staff, for instance, had harboured doubts about the story at the time, but had either thought it best to keep quiet, or thought the story 'too good to check'. This journalistically-lethal attitude was encouraged by Cooke's warnings that her (and Jimmy's) life would be endangered if checks were made. Nor did anyone think to check Cooke's own credentials. She said she was a graduate of Vassar, had a master's degree from Toledo, studied at the Sorbonne, was an accomplished pianist and spoke four languages. No editor thought this a tall order for someone aged just 25. Among these executives, ironically, was Watergate hero Bob Woodward.

Using information you have acquired in order to make a commercial gain before the story is published is a temptation most likely to be faced by business reporters. A few years ago a reporter for the Wall Street journal called R. Foster Whinans co-wrote a column based on information from sources that traded stocks. He decided to sell information to a stock-broker friend.

He was paid $31,000 to leak the contents of the column to several stock-brokers, enabling them to buy and sell shares in companies before this information became public and thus would affect the price of the stock. The brokers made about $690,000 from the leaked information. Whinans and the brokers were eventually caught and found guilty in court of violations of the Securities Exchange Act by misappropriating confidential information. Whinans was sentenced to 18 months in prison, five years' probation, 400 hours of community service and a $ 500 fine. Many Western papers now make their financial staff declare their investments and financial dealings.

### Problems of Crucial Nature

The above issues are clear-cut. But a lot of issues in reporting are more complicated. Hard and fast rules are difficult to design and apply. Take phoney by-lines, for example. Plainly wrong if used routinely to give the impression a paper's staff is several times what it is, the practice is a good deal less harmful when sports editors use it to disguise the identity of, say, staff reporters from a daily moonlighting to cover events for a Sunday. Since the story purports to be written by someone who does not in fact exist, I would still contend phoney by-lines are a deceit. It is particularly unsafe where the story may be challenged, or even end in a law suit. Who do you produce in court', An actor taking the name of the fictitious reporter?

There have been many attempts to be dogmatic about privacy, but none can be sustained beyond the most simplistic instances. We all agree that if a President fools around with a junior employee in his office, there is a legitimate story. If someone is asking for our votes (and our taxes to pay their wages), we have a right to know about them, their lives and how they impact on their duties. On the other hand, few would suggest writing a story about a second junior employee fooling around, in their own time, with a third. The sex lives of private citizens, however fascinating, are not regarded as a legitimate target for a story, unless the law is broken. But between these two extremes, in all the less clear-cut cases, is the gaping space where we argue about privacy.

The conventional, and largely sensible, guideline is that the person should be a public figure and the invasion of their privacy must have a legitimate justification based on the public interest, not merely tickling the public's curiosity. If a man standing for public office makes a great deal of public fuss about morality and the virtues of family life, but you can prove he has a string of mistresses, then it is right to publish a story. His double standards are clearly relevant to public life.

There are two problems with this conventional wisdom. First, if a paper thinks the story is sufficiently entertaining or salacious, almost any 'public interest' pretext can be dredged up. Second, justifications tend to be applied in a partisan way: papers defend the privacy of those they admire and invade the privacy of those they seek to destroy.

Part of the answer lies in that traditionally most unjournalistic of qualities: sensitivity. Journalists must have very good reasons for invading someone's privacy and should also be aware of the consequences of such reporting. A few years ago in Britain a policeman began an affair. His wife learnt about it and persuaded him to give up his mistress. The jealous lover then told a national paper and her account was printed under the headline, 'The Love Life of a Detective'. As a result, the couple's child was teased at school, the husband had to give up his job and the family had to move. Some may think that a fitting punishment for his original sin. I do not think so, and neither would I like to justify that reporting.

An issue which comes up less frequently is where journalists get involved in wrong-doing in order to investigate it. This is not a good idea. Breaking the law in pursuit of a story is both wrong and unsafe. It removes whatever moral legitimacy their reporting may otherwise have had.

Sometimes reporters investigating drug-dealing, crime or prostitution learn information that should be passed straight to the police. I think you should do that. Otherwise you are compromising your legitimacy, and may also be putting the lives of innocent citizens at risk. Only the police - not you - can judge that. (This condition about the safety of citizens also applies to the situation where journalists are accused of merely spectating in disaster or war situations and not doing anything to help those who are in danger. Our rule should be that if you can have any influence on the outcome of a situation you should follow your normal instincts and act to help.) : Never accept a free ticket from a theatre manager, a free ride from the chamber of commerce, or a favour from a politician.

**Reorganising Process**

Regretfully, All India Radio (AIR) performance in informing, educating and entertaining its listeners has not been impressive and it has failed to come up to its promise as an instrument of mass communication. Its failure has been twofold: it has failed to provide a broadcasting service satisfactory to the community and it has failed to fulfil the purpose of the state to inform and educate the masses, to enthuse them with plans of social and economic progress and to enlist their cooperation in fulfilling them. This failure is attributable to many factors; basically they arise from organisational deficiencies and inadequate financial resources.

According to the Indian Telegraphs Act of 1885, as amended, the Government of India has the exclusive privilege of establishing, maintaining and working a broadcasting service. The Act provides that a licence may be granted to others also. This permissive provision was used when in 1926 the Indian Broadcasting Company Ltd., was granted a licence for the two stations at Calcutta and Bombay. Since 1930, when the broadcasting service was taken over by government as 'The Indian State Broadcasting Service' no licences have been issued except for small agricultural stations at Allahabad and Dehra Dun, both since defunct, and to the Madras Corporation for a restricted city service until the Madras station came on the air in 1938. AIR thus enjoys a monopoly in the field.

***Departments of Government*** : Since its inception AIR has been a department of the government. At present, its status is that of an attached office of the Ministry of Information and Broadcasting. The minister is responsible to the Cabinet and accountable to Parliament for all broadcasting activity. Except for short spells during the period 1947-65, the minister has not been a member of the Cabinet.

Since January 1966, the ministry once again is put under a minister of state. It is unfortunate that it has been so. Effective mass communication in a developing country is essential for its economic and social regeneration. The minister at the helm should have suitable authority and status for the purpose. It is equally unfortunate that the Cabinet Committee on Information and Broadcasting has been recently discontinued. This again makes the link between the minister and the Cabinet tenuous.

The Director General is responsible to the ministry for the working of AIR as its executive head. He is appointed by the government in consultation with the Union Public Service Commission. It is usual to appoint an officer of the programme cadre of AIR to be the Director General, though the post is not specifically reserved for the cadre. There have been occasions when officers of the Indian Civil Service were drafted to be Director General.

Though the pay of the Director General is the same as that allowed to a Joint Secretary, he has not been equated in status to a Joint Secretary nor does he exercise any powers of government. The heads of two other similar organisations, namely, the Director General, Posts and Telegraphs, and the Director General Tourism, both have ex-officio Secretariat status and the former is remunerated by a higher salary.

The Director General is supported by a Chief Engineer ranking next only to him and three Deputy Directors General, one each for Programmes, Inspection and Administration.

The Deputy Director General (Programmes) is in charge of the preparation of programme schedules and recruitment and utilisation of staff artists, their emoluments etc. He is assisted by eight Directors, in the rank of Station Directors, nine Chief Producers, two Deputy Chief Producers and other staff.

The Station Directors of AIR administer the various stations on behalf of the Director General. Similarly, there are Directors in charge of Units such as the Staff Training School, the TV Service, the Transcription and Programme Exchange Service, the External Services, and the News Services. They are assisted by Station Engineers/Assistant Station Engineers, Assistant Station Directors and Producers or Assistant Producers.

Like all other departments of government, the entire expenditure of AIR is met by appropriations made by Parliament. In theory, the licence fee on receivers is levied to sustain the broadcasting service. But in practice, revenue derived from licence fees, after deducting collection charges, is credited to the Consolidated Fund and both the capital and revenue budgets of AIR are debated and voted upon annually by Parliament. There is thus no direct link between licence fees collected and amounts appropriated. In many countries the entire collection of fees reduced by the cost of collection is placed at the disposal of the broadcasting organisation either directly or through a vote of Parliament without a detailed control over its activities.

**Course of Action**

We should now consider whether organised as it is today as an attached office of a ministry with concomitant financing arrangements, AIR can develop as a national organisation and provide a countrywide service of quality and excellence.

In the first place, a theme of centralisation runs through the fabric of India's administration. It is more marked in the field of financial administration. This by itself is a deterrent to the growth of departmental initiative and expeditious transaction of business. Even the ministries of government do not enjoy full financial powers over the appropriations made to them for purposes embodied in the estimates as approved by Parliament. They derive financial authority by delegations made from time to time by the Finance Ministry.

The principle that all executive levels should have administrative authority and financial power commensurate with their responsibilities and functions has yet to find acceptance. There is also a general disinclination to part with power and the Director General in his turn has been chary in delegating powers to the Station Directors.

A government department is subject to the discipline of rules and regulations both in regard to its employment policy and utilisation of resources allocated. These rules and regulations framed for administrative purposes are not wholly suitable for the commercial activities of government or for a creative medium like AIR. It is on this consideration that industrial and commercial activities of government have been entrusted to statutory corporations on companies. In the case of AIR no such dispensation has yet been made. The purpose of adopting the corporate form was to free the commercial activities of the state from inappropriate rules and regulations and to place them on a comparable footing with private enterprise.

We do not wish to overload this report with details but would refer to a few major limitations which impinge on the efficiency of AIR's administration. In the administrative field the Director General's powers for creation of posts only extend to minor posts of clerks and peons. Similarly, he can order transfers of only junior officials, not of Directors and not even of Assistant Station Directors if they hold independent charge of a station. His disciplinary powers are also extremely limited and hemmed in by archaic regulations. In this situation, it is difficult for him to administer the department efficiently nor can he command the respect of his subordinates.

His financial powers are even more limited. He cannot send out any officer on tour for more than ten days at a time and he cannot authorise air journeys where necessary. Even his powers in regard to programme planning do not allow him to make worthwhile adjustments. One might well say that he has responsibility without the authority necessary to fulfil it.

We now consider whether basic requirements of AIR would be met by enlarging the powers of the Director General.

First, he has to work within the limits of funds appropriated by Parliament In the framing of estimates AIR's proposals are first scrutinised and usually pruned down by the Ministry and the process is repeated in the Finance Ministry. Thus, it is seldom that the reductions are made in a constructive way keeping in view the main purpose for which funds were demanded. Secondly, the Director General cannot spend the amounts voted according to his requirements without adhering to detailed allocations to different activities. He has hardly any powers of reappropriation.

Thirdly, the capital grant is determined by the Planning Commission's decision regarding the rate of development and the priorities in this development. As we have mentioned earlier, broadcasting does not figure in the list of priorities drawn up by the Planning Commission. We were informed that AIR's plan has just undergone a fifth revision to accord with the Commission's proposed total allocation of resources in the Fourth Plan. This has at one stroke nullified AIR's earlier intention to provide a medium-wave network to serve 95 per cent of the people by the end of the Fourth Plan.

Fourthly, the Director General is not competent to engage the type of people he needs and offer them salaries they are worth, as all recruitment has to be made through prescribed government channels and remunerations paid according to scales laid down by government. There is thus little flexibility in the selection of staff and in determining the terms and conditions of service'. And the Director General has no authority to dispense with the services of unsuitable staff.

We say all this to pinpoint the present disabilities of AIR, but we do not for a moment suggest that the Director General should be allowed to function without control and guidance or that he should be given all the resources he demands. He should, however, be brought into closer collaboration in the shaping of policy and programmes and given greater flexibility in their fulfilment.

Before we discuss what would be the most suitable organisation for AIR, we should make one point of substance and that is that the stations and other units of AIR must be given greater autonomy than they enjoy at present. It is the stations which are actually concerned with broadcasts and the test of a broadcasting organisation is the quality of its programmes. The need for speedy decisions and initiative at the stations is indisputable but cannot be met if their Directors have to obtain the Director General's approval for every little thing that they need or propose to do. Their status in the organisation has been progressively whittled down over the years.

For reasons we have developed earlier, it is not possible in the Indian context for a creative medium like broadcasting to flourish under a regiment of departmental rules and regulations. It is only by an *institutional chance* that AIR can be liberated from the present rigid financial and administrative procedures of government.

We first explored the possibility of adopting the form of one or other governmental agency which has greater freedom in movement than departments of government. The Railway Board, the Atomic Energy Commission, the Council of Scientific and Industrial Research, were suggested by some as a possible model for AIR.

Anxious as we were to limit structural changes to the minimum, we studied these organisations but came to the conclusion that none of the patterns would meet the needs of AIR. The reasons for our conclusions are as follows: There is a clear division of functions in Railway operations and it is not so in broadcasting. Secondly, the Railway Board is not engaged in creative activity. And thirdly, as a ministry of government, the Board has to work within the limitation of rules and regulations framed for recruitment, promotion, etc. On all these counts, the Railway Board pattern would not meet the needs of AIR.

Similarly, both the Atomic Energy Commission and the Council of Scientific and Industrial Research are engaged in specialised activities which do not make it necessary for them to be in constant touch with political, cultural and social developments with which Radio is intimately involved.

We, therefore, proceed to consider whether it would not be best to give AIR the corporate form which has been successfully adopted by broadcasting organisations in countries with a democratic constitution. In this consideration it would be relevant to examine the policy resolution which led to the acceptance of the corporate form for state industrial enterprises.

It was acknowledged that subject to the observance of certain general principles, the organisation of management suitable for each undertaking must necessarily be determined with reference to its particular requirements. The method of recruitment, the regulation of scales of pay, conditions of service and discipline of employees, the procedure for financial control, the system of accounting applicable to the normal activities of government could not obviously be adopted for the efficient administration of industrial enterprises. We feel that the same considerations apply with equal force in the case of AIR.

Experience has shown that the corporate form by itself has not brought about a psychological transformation nor given flexibility in operation because the Boards as constituted do not ensure independence implicit in the form. It is necessary to safeguard this position by making AIR a *national authority* in which major national interests would be represented to give it balance, quality, poise and purpose. Secondly, even with such a constitution the autonomy of the corporation would not be real unless it is financially independent and viable.

We have carefully studied in detail the major types of broadcasting organisations in different parts of the world. Major broadcasting systems are either in private hands largely exploited for profit, or they are owned by the state but entrusted to autonomous corporations subject to specified control over policies and programmes.

It is necessary at the outset to make the point that all radio and television organisations are subject to control and regulations by the state. First there is the international obligation in the use of wave lengths and frequencies. This requires the issue of a licence to operate as prescribed by the International Telecommunication Union. The grant of licence is subject to certain legal formalities and regulations framed by each government. Apart from legal requirements, no state can allow unrestricted authority to a broadcasting organisation to embark on programmes which offend against social and moral values.

These media have a tremendous potential in moulding public opinion; they can equally enslave or liberate the human mind. The state has to safeguard the public interest through its regulatory power. It is largely on this consideration that the Supreme Court of the United States of America had declared: 'Unlike other modes of expression, radio inherently is not available to all. That is its unique characteristic. That is why unlike other modes of expression it is subject to government regulations.'

The outstanding example of private ownership and management is provided by the United States of America where licences to operate Radio and Television Stations are issued by the Federal Communication Commission subject to certain laws and regulations. This system also operates in many other countries, notably, Japan, Canada and Australia. All the three countries have each a public corporation owned wholly by the state, but they have also licensed private stations which operate in competition.

There is a variation of this form which provides for joint state and private collaboration. The best examples of blending of public and private ownership are provided by the Italian and Swedish organisation. RAI, the Italian organisation, is a private limited company which has been granted a monopoly of Radio and Television and wire distribution. The majority of its shares are held by the Institute of Industrial Reconstruction which is a government agency. Although RAI enjoys a considerable measure of independence, it is subject to obligations and inspections by the state. The Board of Management and the Board of Auditors have government members.

In Sweden, programming rights are vested since 1925 solely in a company known as Sveriges Radio. The state owns the transmitting network and is responsible for its maintenance and operation. The programme company is privately owned; the state has no financial interest in it. Two-fifths of the shares are held by the Press, another two-fifths by large national organisations and popular movements and one-fifth by business and industrial interests. The government, however, reserves the right to appoint the Chairman and one half of the members of the Board of Governors; the other half being elected by the shareholders.

In the other category are public corporations constituted by Royal Charter of Statute. They are run independently by a body specifically set up for the purpose and are largely independent of government financially. All governments, however, retain overriding control by prescribing regulations under which the corporations must operate and also have discretion to alter the regulations from time to time. Theoretically the supervisory powers vested in the governments are extensive but in practice they are invoked only if the corporations tend to behave in an irresponsible manner or offend against the public interest.

Unlike privately owned corporations, they are not actuated by the profit motive. They are under an obligation to utilise their income to promote denned objectives. The best known examples of this type of broadcasting organisation are the corporations and commissions in the United Kingdom, Canada, Japan, Australia, France and West Germany.

We reproduce below an extract from the Beveridge Report on Broadcasting in the United Kingdom as an example to show how autonomy has been reconciled with control:

The formal power of the government over the British Broadcasting Corporation is absolute. The Governors who constitute the Corporation can be removed at any time by order in Council and can be replaced by others. The licence can be revoked by the Postmaster General, if at any time the Corporation in his opinion is failing in its duties. The Postmaster General can veto any proposed broadcast or class of broadcast, and in doing so can require the Corporation to refrain from announcing that a veto has been imposed. Any government department can require the Corporation to broadcast any announcement or other matter desired by it.

In practice it has become the agreed policy of successive governments, accepted by Parliament, that the Corporation should be independent of the government in the day-to-day conduct of its business, including both the making of programmes for broadcasting and general administration.

We now discuss the suitability or otherwise of the two forms we have outlined. On many consideration we are not attracted to the idea of entrusting radio and television to commercial interests. First, there is the consideration that no commercial interest would be able to undertake the enormous capital outlay involved in setting up a radio and television organisation, unless it were given unfettered discretion to earn revenue from advertisements. They might not also provide requisite time and resources for programmes of educative value, and indulge in sensationalism, sacrificing objectivity and integrity in presenting news. We must, therefore, turn our face against this form of organisation.

The most important consideration on which we have rejected this form, however, is that radio and television have a purposeful role to fulfil in our developing economy. They have to mobilise public opinion to support the plans of development, they have to educate and inform the people and strive to better their social and economic life. That should be the major role and purpose of radio and television in India.

Several witnesses including some Union and state ministers and officials were in favour of allowing private stations to operate side by side with the national network. They felt that the national network should be supplemented by private endeavour to meet the requirements of the local communities. They also felt that independent private stations would be able to provide programmes which would give greater satisfaction to the listening public. This in our view is a danger. It may lead to a lowering of standards. We, therefore, are unable to subscribe to this view and would retain for the national network a monopoly in the field of broadcasting.

We are also averse to the system in which these two media are used primarily for purposes of propagating a particular ideology and regimentation of its citizens. We are thus left with the only alternative of entrusting the broadcasting services to an autonomous corporation set up by statute which would clearly define the authority and control which government would exercise over its activities. We found overwhelming support for this idea from the officials of AIR, distinguished witnesses whose advice we sought and from others who either sent in written memoranda or gave evidence in addition. The Press also largely supported the transformation of AIR into a Corporation.

There are other valid considerations which influence us in making this recommendation. AIR must not be considered by the people as an instrument of the government of the day as it is widely regarded today. If its organisation were to be made autonomous and its programmes based on the concept of social responsibility, its value and effectiveness would be considerably enhanced. It would create public confidence and lead to the acceptance of its programmes as objective and unbiased and consequently their impact would be far greater.

**Political Angle**

There is also a political consideration which cannot be lightly dismissed, more so in a federal state. If some of the states come to be controlled by parties other than the one in power at the Centre, AIR would be exposed to stresses and strains which are best avoided.

We now turn to the nature of the Corporation we recommend. The Corporation should be set up by an Act of Parliament in which its objectives should also be clearly defined and be free of ambiguity. The right to require the Corporation to broadcast certain programmes as also the right to veto broadcasts in certain subjects may be reserved to government. It must be understood that such powers must be sparingly used and only when the national interest so demands. These reservations would automatically define the accountability of the minister to Parliament. We also consider that the Act itself should lay down the authority and powers of the Governors to prevent possible encroachment.

The constitution and composition of the governing body are all-important. The Chairman of the Corporation should be a *public figure* with a national reputation for his integrity, ability and independence. The members, the number of whom we consider should not exceed seven, should similarly be drawn from diverse fields of national life, each enjoying a reputation in his particular field.

One of the complaints in the functioning of autonomous corporations, here as elsewhere, had been that the ministers are able to influence their policies without issuing directives, thus escaping parliamentary accountability. This position can be safeguarded only when the composition of the Board is such that it will not be amenable to undue and unreasonable pressure.

The people who constitute the Board must understand fully the purposes of broadcasting and see that they are fulfilled. They must also take note of public opinion and ensure that the programmes respond to it.

Various suggestions for ensuring independence have been made. One is that appointments should be made by the President, the other that they should be made by him on the recommendation of the Chief Justice, a third is that public organisations and associations with related activities should each submit a panel and selections should be confined to the names included.

We do not favour any of these suggestions. A responsible government is expected to function in a responsible way and we would much rather leave selections to government indicating only the broad principles to be observed. Secondly, experience has shown that once selected to such autonomous bodies people act independently and do not sacrifice the interest of the organisation to outside pressure.

It now remains to consider whether members of Parliament and service personnel should be categories specifically excluded as suggested by some. We are against such a blanket ban and would not demur if, by reason of eminence and specialisation, one or two were drawn from these sources.

The term of office of the Chairman and Governors should, we feel, be six years and it should be provided mat for the sake of continuity two members should retire every other year in rotation.

The Director-General: The selection of the Director General requires equally careful consideration. As Chief Executive, on him will devolve the responsibility for maintaining objectivity, ensuring efficiency and economy and building up an attractive image of the organisation. He has undoubtedly to be a person with a dynamic personality endowed with drive, imagination and initiative, capable of creating a well knit team of devoted workers and giving it resolute leadership. It is difficult anywhere to find one with all these attributes.

It will be more so in India, particularly if according to present practice the selection is confined to government servants. The net will have to be cast much wider. It may even become necessary to persuade an outstanding personality in the fields of journalism, advertising, the film industry and the academic world to accept this assignment in a spirit of dedication and service. If a civil servant is selected by the Board of Governors, there should be a stipulation, as in the case of the Reserve Bank, that he should resign from service.

The question of the status of the Director General was also mooted by some, it being suggested that in a protocol-ridden society it is important that the Director General should be accorded a high rank commensurate with his responsibilities. We, however, do not attach importance to his suggestion. The status of the Board and its Chief Executive would automatically come to be determined by the place the organisation comes to occupy in our national life and the public esteem it is able to command by its independence, integrity and excellence.

Though the details of the organisation and the rules or business should be drawn up by the Board, we should suggest certain broad principles so mat in inheriting the organisation it does not inherit the deficiencies.

Even at the risk of being repetitive, we should stress once again the need for decentralisation of authority and functions. This is necessary in the interests of efficiency in any organisation, it is more so in a broadcasting organisation. For example, in a country so vast as ours with a multiplicity of languages and cultural patterns and with, regions in different stages of development, central control of programme planning and the imposition of uniformity in their contents and presentation would not only be inappropriate but would defeat the basic purposes of the broadcasting system. We would, therefore, give the Station Directors complete freedom in the matter and subject them only to policy directions as to the types of broadcasts which should be discouraged.

We do not suggest that this decentralisation should be absolute. It should be obligatory to relay the national news bulletins and other national programmes of interest. It is necessary though that determination of themes of broadcasts as national should be made with circumspection and discretion.

Another way to achieve decentralisation is to have several channels of broadcasting, one of which would provide the national programme, the other regional programmes and the third a local service on local transmitters which we have recommended earlier. The only practical way as we have stressed, is through such local stations.

The establishment of competitive channel of broadcasting was advocated by several witnesses. They argued that a monopolist enterprise tends to become complacent, stale and ineffective. It needs the stimulus of competition to make its staff more alert and enterprising and the programmes more lively. It was said that the establishment of the Independent Television Authority in Britain had a tonic effect on the BBC's TV Services.

We have considered this question carefully. We have come to the conclusion that having regard to the availability of resources both in manpower and in funds, and the role we envisage for broadcasting, we should not at this stage bring in considerations which might well come in the way of the development of radio.

We should, however, encourage universities to instal closed circuit radio and television services, or the state governments and major municipal corporations to set up local transmitters for agricultural, social and educational purposes to meet the needs of local communities which cannot be effectively served by the national network.

It is necessary to consider how the Corporation we have proposed should be financed. The question falls into two parts: capital expenditure to add to the network by installing additional transmitters, studios and other equipment; revenue expenditure for sustaining and improving the service.

We now turn to the question how future capital expenditure should be financed and how best the revenue of AIR should be augmented. In the case of state enterprises, government have provided both equity capital and loans to maintain a proper ratio between the two. While interest is chargeable on the loan (there has been a period of moratorium in many cases), the return on equity investment depends on the profits, if any earned. This is the policy adopted in the case of commercial activities. Similarly, government meet the capital expenditure on welfare measures, on education, health and activities necessary to increase agricultural production.

Broadcasting is not a commercial activity, though a monopoly, it cannot, unlike other monopolies, adjust prices, rates and fees to meet interest liability on capital expended. On all considerations and having regard to its primary role as a medium of education and information, we consider that capital expenditure is a legitimate charge on public revenues.

We propose, therefore, that the assets of AIR should be transferred to the Corporation without any interest or any other financial liability. Similarly, the allocation in the Fourth Plan should be made available to the Corporation free of charge. We consider that thereafter the proposals we make on revenue account, would make the Corporation fully viable, able to expand with its own resources taking resource to borrowing, if necessary, on its own financial standing.

We have one important observation to make in regard to capital expenditure. We find that organisationally AIR is geared to an expenditure of about Rs 2 crores a year. To enlarge its spending capacity efficiently, it would be necessary to bring about a reorganisation and the sooner it is undertaken the better it would be. The allocation in the Fourth Plan is bound to be larger and we have recommended certain priorities for providing local transmitters and the reorientation of the external services.

To fulfil this plan, AIR needs organisation and effort which should be preplanned.

There has been a suggestion that licence fees should be discontinued. We do not accept this suggestion. It would be unfair to burden the community at large to support a service when the beneficiaries are small in number. The fee should continue to be recovered from users of the service. (Licence fee has since been abolished).

We consider that considerable improvement in the recovery of licence fees is possible. It is common knowledge that a number of sets in the country are unlicensed; some suggest that it is as high as sixty per cent.

The steps we have recommended would give elbow room to AIR but would not make it fully viable nor enable it to finance.

By far the most fruitful source of additional revenue would be the acceptance of advertisement in programmes. In dealing with Television we have marshalled the arguments in favour of its acceptance with certain safeguards and restrictions. We do not feel that there are any special considerations which would justify making a distinction on this question between television and sound broadcasting. Consistent with our thinking on this subject, we would limit advertisements to the Vividh Bharati channel alone. By timing the spot advertisements suitably there need be no interference with a programme or its continuity. Vividh Bharati is a light programme predominantly of film music and the inclusion of advertisements is not likely to infringe on its quality or appeal.

Television is a comparatively new medium far more sophisticated than radio. There are basic differences between radio and television in important matters of technique and financing of operators and planning and execution of programmes. Television also presents other problems infinitely more complicated.

Even so, many countries with well-established broadcasting systems found it convenient to entrust the development of television to their existing organisations. This arrangement soon proved to be little more than a marriage of convenience. The rapid growth of television, the remarkable advances in its technology and programme planning, and its versatility in use, brought new responsibilities which could be hardly fulfilled within the resources of existing organisations. This difficulty has been sought to be met by investing the television wing with virtual autonomy. In the United Kingdom, the Union of Soviet Socialist Republics and in Italy, the television centre has now become a distinct, separate and powerful entity with tenuous links with the parent organisation.

In the light of these developments, it has to be considered whether it will be possible or wise to place television under the aegis of AIR. This possibility has to be ruled out as AIR is not organisationally and financially equipped to shoulder this responsibility. It would also be unfair to tag on television to AIR and expose it at its birth to prejudices which exist against AIR. On all these considerations, we would strongly advise against the development and management of this new medium, requiring a dynamic and imaginative approach and ample resources, being linked as an ancillary to an organisation which itself needs a major overhaul and refurbishing.

The question still remains whether the new organisation should follow the pattern of AIR and become an attached office of a ministry or whether it should be made an autonomous corporation, created by a special statute of Parliament. Having carefully considered the question in all its aspects, we have come to the conclusion that to develop on correct lines television must not be hampered by the limitations of a department; it should have a broader outlook, greater flexibility and freedom of action which the corporate form alone can give.

While discussing the future organisation of AIR we have already stated in detail the reasons for our recommendation that an autonomous statutory corporation would be the best form of organisation for providing a broadcasting service. These consideration apply with equal, if not greater force, in case of television.

We consider that to give shape to our recommendations immediate steps should be taken to invite a competent agency to prepare the project report. An officer of the status of a Chief

Engineer, should be associated with their team in its preparatory work, who could later be selected to head the technical wing.

To ensure that the two processes of project study and operation planning go hand in hand, it would be necessary to form the Television Corporation with the nucleus of staff necessary to access the ultimate requirements of staff, organise training, draw up the programme policy and prepare an estimate of the finances required. It should also initiate negotiations with potential collaborators but keep government closely informed of developments. The agreements reached should naturally be subject to government approval.

We have already given our views on the staffing of AIR and suggested reorganisation. The staffing pattern and employment policy of the Television Corporation we propose will have to be differently conceived and designed.

As mentioned earlier, television is basically a different medium from radio and cannot be given the same treatment. Being, however, a part of AIR, the Delhi Television Centre has unfortunately the same organisation as a radio unit and has developed unsuitable trends and nuances. For one thing, it has tended to become a top-heavy organisation in which the more expensive technical staff was until recently being incorrectly employed; for another, its programmes being produced on the basis of radio techniques and experience, are indifferent and even colourless. It is essential that the two activities should be separated at the large scale inception of television, to give it a fair wind.

We are in agreement with our Consultant mat 'television needs a lively, decisive, imaginative, adventurous yet responsible staff. This implies that its control and operations should be in the hands of those who have these attributes.

Taking a look at the Delhi Centre, the first point that struck us was the strength of the staff deployed for its limited output. It appeared that there had not been a proper assessment of the staff required in different categories and that as problems arose they were sought to be met by hurriedly transferring whoever was conveniently available in the radio wing. As a consequence of this haphazard and irrational staffing, the sanctioned strength has been raised to 271 to allow for the recent extension of the service.

The Centre provides a one-hour evening programme of news and entertainment of which only about a third is produced at the Centre itself, the rest being films or recorded material obtained locally or from abroad. It also provides three twenty-minute school lessons a day for six days a week for each of the two shifts in the schools, giving a total broadcast time of about 120 minutes a day. But of these lessons one or two a week are repetitions of old lessons already recorded and telecast, thus reducing the output of the studio to about eight hours a week.

In the opinion of our Consultant, the Centre is grossly overstaffed. Our Sub-Committee concurs in this assessment on the basis of its study abroad. 'Telescuola' in Italy, running school and adult literacy programmes, is on the air for 41½ hours a week but it employs a total of 128 people only including 27 technicians and 16 teachers, e.g. Admittedly, its telecasts do not require certain categories of staff which an inclusive service of information, education and entertainment would need, but even so the contrast is striking.

Our Consultant also informed us that a firm International Television Consultants had recommended a total staff of approximately 50 for certain African countries embarking on television with a daily programme output of four hours. Similarly, a UNESCO Mission, which advised Israel on the introduction of television, recommended a total staff of 226 distributed between the three organisations of the Central Administration (the equivalent of the directorate general of AIR), the Jerusalem and the Tel Aviv Studio Centres. This requirement was based on a suggested output of 23 hours of programmes a week of which over 12 hours were to originate in the two Studio Centres.

The second point that struck us was that at its inception the Television Centre was manned largely if not entirely by people drawn from sound broadcasting without a mature consideration whether this arrangement was suitable either for the installation or the development of this medium.

Training is essential for the success of all human endeavour. The more difficult the objective, the greater is the need for training for its attainment. Yet the necessity of advance training of the required number of people in the difficult and varied techniques of television had been ignored before the Delhi pilot project was launched in 1959.

It was only after six years, in 1965, that a producer was obtained on loan from the BBC to give a course of training to a small number of selected production staff. We consider that this is totally inadequate even to sustain the extended programmes of the Centre and to improve their quality, leave alone to handle the expansion we recommend.

We have earlier mentioned that the installation of a television network needs massive financial outlay, a large part of it in foreign exchange. On both these counts, some acceptable form of foreign collaboration will have to be considered. Financing of the television service is another matter; it needs a different treatment.

Because of the low priority given to broadcasting, the allocation of Plan resources has so far been minuscule. We have already adduced many considerations why television should receive equal priority with industrial and agricultural schemes of development. Even so, the competing demands of other nation-building activities might make it difficult to allocate to television all the money it needs for developing a countrywide network by the end of the Fifth Plan. We have perforce to consider alternatives which would ensure adequate financial support.

We have made as detailed a study as is possible, in the absence of complete documentation, of developments elsewhere and the manner in which countries similarly situated have set about to bring the benefits of television to their people.

Foreign collaboration in two different forms has been adopted to cover fully the foreign exchange component of the project for the supply of capital goods such as transmitters, studio equipment, installation of links and other ancillary facilities. It has either taken the shape of participation in the equity issue of the corporation or it has been a straight loan with a period of moratorium before repayment commences. Some countries have adopted the former method in which a consortium of industrialists has a minority financial interest, the controlling interest being retained by government. Some others have preferred the latter method but have not encountered any lack of response because of this choice. We also consider that we must not have any foreign equity participation in the proposed Television Corporation. It is needles to add that the provision of a loan must not give any voice to the donors in deciding the policy of the Corporation.

In addition, it has been arranged either separately or as a part of the same scheme that the foreign exchange requirements of manufacturing television sets and the essential equipment would be provided by the foreign associates, the inducement being that they would themselves supply the television sets until, manufacture has been established but without an appreciable outflow of foreign exchange.

It is found impractical for a single county to provide the required financial support, the formation of a consortium might become necessary. The idea of forming a consortium has caught on even in the matter of international aid to developing countries. It should not, therefore, be difficult to bring about the formation of a consortium to assist our project should this become necessary. We contemplate a package deal in which the collaborator would also accept responsibility for the manufacture of television sets and other equipment. It may be necessary to set up a separate manufacturing unit.

The willingness to collaborate with technical assistance and a loan will naturally depend on the viability of the project and its ability to generate enough resources to be able to repay the loan in agreed installments. Under the plan we later discuss, we have no doubts that the revenues of the Corporation will be ample to meet all its commitments. We are confident that foreign collaborator would feel equally reassured.

The question will still remain how the rupee finance of the project can best be found. The allocation of a high priority for television together with the realisation that the acceptance of the plan we later unfold would make television a viable and even a productive venture should make it possible for the Planning Commission to release necessary resources. The expectation that television would become self-financing within a short time, if not at its inception, and that it would not, therefore, make annual demands for its running expenses should be a weighty consideration in the allocation of resources. It would imply that the initial investment needed would be little more than a capitalisation of a few years recurring expenses, provision for which would have to be made otherwise, being inherent in the acceptance of a television scheme, however, unambitious it may be.

There is another aspect developed earlier, that is the extensive use of television for educational, agriculture, health and other socioeconomic purposes. On a long term view, it may be found more economical, yet more effective to invest in television than, for example, to build schools for which teacher cannot be found, or equipment provided, or build health centres which can only be manned by indifferent and unimaginative people. Similarly, recurring expenditure on publicity to give an impetus to programmes for self-sufficiency in the production of foodgrains and other expenditure now incurred for popularising the introduction of improved strains of seeds, the use of fertilisers and pesticides, the rotation of crops, etc., could be considerably minimised by visual presentation which television alone can provide.

These savings would be a recurring annual feature and should give welcome relief to the budgets of these departments. Once his important aspect of television is realised, there should be no difficulty in either increasing the allocation for television by corresponding reduction in the capital budgets of the ministries concerned; alternatively, they should invest a part, albeit a small part, of their capital grants in building up a countrywide television network. A small advisory body of the participants in programme planning should ensure the allocation of adequate time to each.

The cost of operating the network depends on its output, the standard of the producers and artists it employs, the level of remuneration it pays, and the type and quality of programmes it provides. It must obviously be the aim to give the optimum out-put within the capability of the network and to plan and produce programmes of the highest quality employing first class artists. This implies that there must be resources available for establishing and sustaining a high professional standard comparable to other television services.

The method evolved by the British Broadcasting Corporation, and followed by some other broadcasting systems, is to levy a licence fee from the owners of receiving sets and to allocate the proceeds, after deducting the cost of collection, to broadcasting. The yield is thus directly related to the number of receiving sets held and licensed. The limitation of this arrangement is that the rate of levy cannot be easily adjusted to accord with the needs of the service. There are many factors including public resistance which have to be taken into account in a revision of the fee.

When the British Broadcasting Corporation entered the field of television, a separate and higher scale of levy was designed to finance its programmes and other operating costs. This levy has been adjusted upwards from time to time to sustain an expansion of programmes, to improve their quality and to neutralise rising costs. The public had gone along with these increases. More recently an Independent Television Authority was created by statute and was given freedom to run its services with advertising revenues without sharing with the British Broadcasting Corroboration the licence fees collected. This brought a new concept of financing television in tradition-bound and conventional Britain.

The programmes controlled by the Independent Television Authority not only proved attractive but were made available without any payment by the viewing audiences. We shall refer to the ITA later in the narration but mention it at this stage because of its indirect impact on the recent demand of the British Broadcasting Corporation for a substantial increase in licence fees both for existing services and for opening up a fourth channel which has become available. Government considered the increase demanded unreasonable and also unfair to licence-holders and conceded a smaller increase. This has left the British Broadcasting Corporation in a quandary.

It has to be appreciated that in a country like India the licence fees have to be kept reasonably low to accord with the people's capacity to pay. On the one hand, the number of sets in private hands in the initial stages will be small and the yield of licence fees negligible, on the other, there will be the need for a wide network to bring the social programmes within the reach of the community which needs them most. It will thus become necessary to accept commercial advertisements to supplement the revenue derived from licence fees.

We are aware of the opinion which still persists against the acceptance of commercial broadcasts. There is the apprehension that were commercial advertisements to be accepted television would become largely dependent on revenues derived from commercial interests and this might well lead to the political, economic and social policies of the organisation being influenced and even indirectly controlled by these interests. There is also the apprehension that the advertisements to have a popular appeal, might tend to become somewhat vulgar and demoralising.

Experience elsewhere has shown that the acceptance of advertisements to accord with the programme policy of a television organisation does not bring it even remotely under the control of commercial interests nor does it lead to the presentation of material which is in questionable taste.

It is necessary to review in a brief compass, the policy adopted by different organisations, discussing later their merits and demerits. In the United States of America and Latin American countries as also in Iran, Lebanon, Thailand and the Philippines, television is in the hands of private interests who finance their operations, including the setting up and expansion of their existing networks, from revenues derived entirely from the sale of time to advertisers. In the United States of America and most of these countries, the advertisers not only buy time but also provide programmes of their choice which go with the advertisements.

In Australia, Japan and Canada this system has been adopted by a number of comparatively small television stations which operate in competition with the national organisations which are maintained out of licence revenues. The acceptance of commercial programmes, known as 'sponsored programme' has resulted in the largest and most prosperous television network in the world being built up in the United States of America and it has also given impetus to the growth of television in the countries mentioned and in Latin America and some countries of Asia. The major undesirable feature of this system is that the television organisation has very little control over the programmes put on the air with the result that they are often in questionable taste and have a demoralising effect on impressionable and immature minds. It has been suggested that the increase in the rate of child delinquency in the United States of America is attributable to these programmes.

Benefiting by the experience of the United States of America, countries which entered the television field later, more particularly the European countries, evolved a new system.

While accepting commercial advertisements as inescapable for supporting the growth of a sound television system and also the U.S. practice of selling time, they safeguarded the quality and standard to the programmes by refusing to allow the advertisers to produce them or even to have a say in the programmes which would include their advertisement material. By this method commonly known as 'spot advertising' or 'spot announcements', the organisations retained full control over their programme policy.

An additional safeguard was also introduced, by stature where necessary, but mainly by a code of conduct voluntarily agreed upon by the organisations and the advertisers, to control the make-up of the advertisements. Italy went a step further and set up a corporation to handle and produce all advertisement shots.

Television stations in West Germany, Ireland, Italy, Spain, the United Arab Republic, Iraq, Pakistan, to mention a few countries, have adopted this system of spot advertising to raise resources to supplement revenues from licence fees. Some countries such as Italy and West Germany have introduced the practice of presenting in a single special programme all advertisements within an allocated period of time, usually 20 to 30 minutes, at an excellent viewing hour, between eight and nine o'clock in the evening. Other countries intersperse the spots, not exceeding five or six minutes in an hour, in their daily programmes.

It is necessary to discuss the two practices, their merits and demerits and their revenue potential. The practice of concentrating all advertisements in one programme has two attractive features: First, it enables the viewers who are not interested in commercials to switch off at the hour when they are on the air; secondly, by not breaking into a programme, it preserves the continuity and entertainment value of the programme and also the atmosphere it creates. The advertisers, however, do not consider this method as attractive as spots in regular programmes. They also consider that a spot should be repeated in a number of programmes in any one day to have worthwhile advertisement value.

The latter practice has undoubtedly greater advertisement value, as it provides a captive audience and a repeated presentation of the same spots in different programmes at different viewing hours. The irritation caused by the spots breaking into a programme has been sought to be removed by putting the advertisements at the beginning, the intermission and the end of the programmes. This is an improvement from the viewers point and meets the advertisers' demands to a certain extent. The revenue potential of this practice is undoubtedly greater.

We have very carefully considered which of the two systems, the U.S. one of sponsored programmes or the European one of spot advertisement to recommend, or whether a combination of the two would be more suitable. We do not feel that one need be squeamish about sponsored programmes as such so long as they have an educative and cultural value and do not include any advertisement material except to mention at their commencement or conclusion that they were presented by the courtesy of so and so (naming the sponsors). Such programmes do not have the connotation or implications of sponsored programmes in the United States of America and should even be welcome as being useful and valuable additions to the repertoire of the television organisation.

Such programmes are not uncommon elsewhere and have been viewed and appreciated by some of us abroad. These 'prestige' programmes are presented by sponsors who are inspired to contribute to the growth of the television system and incidentally bring their names and contributions to the notice of the viewing public. However, the revenues from this type of sponsored programmes will not be substantial but that should be no reason for excluding them.

The acceptance of advertisements should be considered

only if it brings significant financial support to the growth of television. There is nothing non-ethical in accepting advertisements prepared in good taste provided that they do not affect the quality of the telecasts or make excessive demands. If the educational, social and children's programmes do not carry spots and they are confined to the entertainment programmes, there should not be any objection in adopting a practice which has now become more or less universal.

A 12-Member Working Group headed by B.G. Verghese was set up on August 17, 1977, to go into the working of AIR and Doordarshan and suggest changes. The following were the other members of his Group: V.G. Rajadhyaksha, Dr. Malcolm S. Adiseshiah, Chanchal Sarkar, P.L. Deshpande, Umashankar Joshi, A.G. Noorani, G.R. Subramanian, Mrs. Nayantara Sehgal and Dr. Ishwar Das (Member Secretary).

The group made wide-ranging recommendations to transform All-India Radio and Television into a more responsive organisation from a mere government department.

The two-volume report running into 405 pages was presented to Parliament on March 9, 1978. In its unanimous report, the working group suggested that the national broadcasting services should be vested exclusively in an independent impartial and autonomous organization established by law to act as a trustee for the national interest.

The legal framework of the autonomous national trust, as envisaged by the working group, was that the establishment of the corporation should not await a constitutional amendment. The law establishing the corporation could be enacted and the organisation brought into being to be followed subsequently by an amendment of the Constitution.

The autonomy of the corporation and its independence from government control should be entrenched in the Constitution itself and the idea of a trust woven into it.

In making recommendations, the working group was

guided by a factor that mass media, radio and television must fit into a wider perspective of national communication policy or philosophy.

It rejected a proposal to create two separate corporations for All-India Radio and Television. However, it conceded the need to recognize the distinctive identity of radio and television within the ambit of a new integrated structure.

The group also did not favour the creation of autonomous regional corporations or even a federation of State Government corporations.

While rejecting the proposal to create two separate corporations or set up autonomous regional corporations, the working group argued that there would be a large measure of power delegated to the regional and local level.

This was kept to the fore so that the organisation enjoyed the advantages of quick decision making, sensitivity to local problems and tasks, and close linkages with various governments and institutions.

In recommending the new set-up, the working group did not apparently follow any model operating in any other country.

At the apex of NBT, the working group suggested a board of trustees consisting of 12 persons, and not exceeding 21 persons. The trustees would be guardians of the charter given to the NBT by statute.

The Controller-General of Broadcasting (CGB), heading the central executive board, was conceived by the working group as a link between the trustees and the entire broadcasting organisation. He would be ex-officio secretary to the board of trustees so as to provide an organic link between these two tiers.

Apart from the Chairman, the board of trustees would have three other full-time members to devote themselves to the fields of current affairs, extension and culture. They will operate through the CGB.

In addition to the Chairman and the three full-time trustees, the board would have two part-time trustees—one highly experienced in the field of finance and management and the other an eminent scientist or engineer familiar with the technology of broadcasting.

For the first time in the history of over half-a-century of broadcasting in India, there would be a complaints board comprising persons selected by the Chief Justice of India.

The recommendation of the working group for constituting a complaint board assumed significance in the light of the experience gained during the Emergency when the broadcasting system was blatantly used by the previous regime to further partisan ends.

According to the report, the board of trustees would be responsible to Parliament through its budget and an annual report. Together with accounts and auditor's comments, reports of the complaints board, among other things, would also figure in the annual report.

The complaints board would deal with complaints from the public relating to charges of unjust or unfair treatment including unwarranted invasion of privacy and misrepresentation, provided the right of resources to court was waived. The findings should be published by NBT in the programme 'Journal' and broadcast in special programmes.

In order to ensure the independence of the proposed NBT, the report recommended that the trustees, with six-year terms of office, would be appointed by the President on the recommendation of the Prime Minister from a list of names forwarded to him by a nominating panel.

The nominating panel for trustees would consist of the Chief Justice of India, the Lokpal and the Chairman of the UPSC. It would be a healthy convention if the Prime Minister consulted the leader of the Opposition before submitting the list of names to the President.

The trustees would enjoy the status of Supreme Court judges.

In regard to financial autonomy, the report recommended several measures. Initially, the government should make up the revenue deficit for a period of five years, after transferring the existing assets of All-India Radio and TV.

Later, NBT should be expected to stand on its own feet or raise additional resources by charging for broadcast time, made available by it to various users, including the Central and state governments.

It also felt that the Trust should undertake a comprehensive review of commercial broadcasting rates and procedures. The group also recommended an increase in broadcast receiver licences for certain categories of radio and TV sets.

The report comprehensively surveyed the entire scene of broadcasting and television network since the Chanda Committee submitted its report on radio more than 12 years ago. The Chanda Committee had a.so recommended an autonomous set-up for AIR.

According to the report, there were now some 20 million radio receivers and 600,000 TV sets. 'With population rising to say, 950 million by 2000 A.D. and 'an end to destitution' and fuller employment, at least 80 to 90 per cent of all households should possess radios,' the report added.

In a perspective study for 2000 A.D. there would be 160 to 180 million radio sets and between 12 to 15 million TV sets by the turn of the century.

In the opinion of the working group, AIR and TV combined in themselves the characteristics of the marketplace, newspaper, university, national extension agency and cultural academy. As such a unique institution must enjoy a unique autonomy.

The report called upon the National Broadcast Trust to bridge the urban-rural divide and combine modernity with relevant tradition.

It recommended the establishment of a strong audience research division. It noted that the audience research unit had a very limited staff and budget. It was, therefore, impossible to conduct any regular audience surveys or to operate on more than very small samples.

The audience research reports should be made available simultaneously and directly to the board of trustees, since these reports would constitute one of the most important antenna of the broadcasting organisation.

***Prasar Bharati Bill :*** The Prasar Bharati Bill was introduced in the Lok Sabha on December 30, 1989, by the National Front Government led by V.P. Singh. The purpose of this Bill was to grant autonomy to the electronic media, that is AIR and Doordarshan.

The Lok Sabha passed the Bill on August 30, 1990 and the Rajya Sabha approved it on September 6, 1990. The President accorded assent to the Bill soon after.

The changes in the original Bill ran as follows:

> The autonomous Prasar Bharati or Broadcasting Corporation of India will be directly answerable to three authorities—a Parliamentary Committee, the Central Government and the proposed Broadcasting Council.

The original draft of the Prasar Bharati Bill introduced in the Lok Sabha did not contain any provision for the Parliamentary Committee. The government inserted this provision on August 29,1990, as one of the 65 amendments proposed by an all-party consensus. Members of the committee will be elected by proportional representation and will ensure that the Corporation functions in the manner set out in the Bill.

There was no opposition in Parliament to this particular provision as it was only intended to make the autonomous body accountable. Besides being answerable to the Committee, the corporation has to submit annual reports of its activities to Parliament.

The powers envisaged for the Central government, however, have given rise to immense misgivings. The initial draft said the Central government could give directions to make or not to make a certain broadcast only when 'the security of the state or preservation of public order' was at stake. But the August 29 changes widened the ambit by saying that the Central government can also issue directions 'in the interest of sovereignty, unity and integrity of India'. These concepts are very subjective and have been left undefined, tremendously increasing the scope for abuse of power.

Further, the Central government has been empowered to demand any information from the corporation. This means, for instance, that it can order Doordarshan to divulge the source of a news report. If the corporation 'persistently' refuses to comply with any direction, the Central government has been empowered to recommend to Parliament any action, including supersession of the Prasar Bharati Board. The government's recommendation has been given such weight that a ratification by a simple majority will be enough to supersede the board.

The only constraint is that the President, before issuing the notification of supersession, will have to give 'a reasonable opportunity to the board to show cause as to why it should not be superseded'.

The maximum permissible period of supersession is six months. The powers and functions of the board during that period will be discharged by 'such person or persons as the President may direct.'

The third authority which will be vested with some power over the corporation is the Broadcasting Council, which corresponds to the Press Council. The original draft of the Bill, envisaged as a watchdog to protect the interests of the citizens, empowered the Broadcasting Council to decide complaints against the corporation and recommend appropriate remedial action to it. What happens when the corporation rejects the Broadcasting Council's recommendation? An amendment provides for such a contingency: The Broadcasting Council will have the authority to force the corporation to broadcast the recommendation. This, in fact, is the only form of vindication the Bill offers to a citizen aggrieved by the corporation.

If Doordarshan or Akashvani, after they are unfettered, broadcast a programme or news report defamatory to somebody, he cannot sue or initiate criminal proceedings against the corporation or anybody in it. This is due to a clause granting immunity against all legal action to the corporation and its employees.

Thus, on the one hand, the proposed corporation is sought to be given the freedom enjoyed by newspapers, on the other, the producers and reporters in the broadcasting field will not be liable for their mistakes as their counterparts in the print media.

The relevant section (24) in the initial draft grants the legal immunity 'for anything which is in good faith done or intended to be done in pursuance of this act or of any rules or regulations made thereunder.' The language is general enough to enable anybody in the corporation to take refuge under this clause for any error committed by him. Yet this section has surprisingly managed to survive the radical amendments made in the Lok Sabha to the original draft.

The Prasar Bharati Board which forms the core of the legislation has also undergone many changes. In the first place, its name was 'Board of Governors'. But the high sounding 'governor' has been replaced by the simple 'member'. The strength of the board has been increased by the inclusion of two ex-officio members—the Director-General of Akashvani and Doordarshan and two elected members from among the employees of the Corporation. The whole-time chairman has been made a part-time one.

All the whole-time members of the board have been made employees of the Corporation.

Among other amendments are: the inclusion of four MPs (two from each House) in the Broadcasting Council, the stipulation on the Broadcasting Council present an annual report to Parliament, deletion of the power to dismiss an employee without being given an opportunity to defend himself and the bar on the Corporation from ceiling its assets.

The Verghese Committee which also advocated autonomy to the electronic media wanted the Ministry of Information and Broadcasting to shed its control over Broadcasting. But the Prasar Bharati Bill puts a representative of the Ministry on the Board of the Corporation.

The most controversial clause as stated earlier is Parliament's power to supersede the Prasar Bharati Board.

In the original version of the bill, this power was sought to be vested in the government.

The present dispensation is an improvement but the effect is the same to ensure that the Prasar Bharati behaves. BJP leader, L.K. Advani sought to soften the blow by suggesting during the discussion of the Bill, an amendment that would have required any resolution on supersession to be passed by two-thirds majority instead of a simple majority. But surprisingly except for one member, nobody supported his suggestion. Strangely, the CPI(M) appeared particularly averse to Mr. Advani's plea.

Voting in Parliament is on strictly party lines and it is unimaginable that if an official resolution is moved for supersession of board of governors, the ruling party members would vote against the resolution.

The official justification for such sweeping Parliamentary control is that if the Prasar Bharati were to be left completely to its devices there was a danger of its being taken over by big business. According to P. Upendra, all autonomous corporations are accountable to Parliament and their functioning is supervised by the Committee on Public Undertakings. This according to him, has not led to interference in their day-to-day affairs, so why should there be fears about such interference in the case of Prasar Bharati.

The fact is that no political party, especially the Left and the Congress wanted an absolutely free Prasar Bharati. They wanted to avoid a situation when the corporation could go 'amuck' in the name of autonomy.

The Congress party also opposed the decision to transfer the assets of AIR and Doordarshan to Prasar Bharati. It is on the insistence of the Congress party that the Bill was amended to say that the new corporation would use the assets in accordance with the terms and conditions prescribed by the government.

Commenting on the question of how autonomous would be the electronic media under the new set up, B.G. Verghese said that the concept is to de-governmentalise broadcasting, both radio as well as television, by placing it under an autonomous corporation—as against where it is now as a subordinate department of the government. Its autonomy would be safeguarded by two or three things.

One is that, according to the Bill, the corporation's accountability is not to the Information & Broadcasting Ministry, but to Parliament. Secondly, the appointment of its top board will be done by a selection committee consisting of the Chairman of Rajya Sabha, the Chairman of the Press Council and a third member to be selected by the President and their decision will be final. This prevents the body from being packed by government favourites.

The third safeguard is that if these people are to be removed it will have to be by a special procedure which is applicable to the members and chairman of the UPSC. They cannot be sacked. And now, they have also added the clause that if the board collectively misbehaves by persistently defying the government directives, then the ministry can make a report to Parliament in which it could recommend supersession, and following a decision of Parliament, supersession can take place. According to Mr. Verghese, Parliamentary control is unnecessary and he feels that the contingencies in which these powers would be used are extreme. They are theoretically possible but in practical terms, they are unlikely to be used.

According to Mr. Khushwant Singh, the well-known journalist, freeing the electronic media from government control deserves to be applauded as the National Front government's biggest achievement of its nine-month rule. All our past Prime Ministers and Ministers of Information and Broadcasting paid lip-services to the principle of freedom of expression for Press, Radio and Television, but everyone of them meddled with their free functioning when they found themselves at the receiving end of criticism.

Jawaharlal Nehru was no exception. He was riled by what Durga Das (father of Inderjit, Member of the Lok Sabha) wrote about him and did his best to damage his career. His Minister of Information and Broadcasting, Keskar, had Nirad Chaudhuri dismissed from AIR and then blacklisted for eulogising the British in the dedication of his autobiography of an unknown Indian. Keskar had not bothered to read the book.

Mrs. Gandhi had scant respect for Press freedom and blatantly misused Radio and Television to propagate herself and denigrate rivals like Jayaprakash Narayan. She pressurised proprietors of newspapers to remove editors she did not like. Her sycophantic ministers like N.K.P. Salve and H.K.L. Bhagat (Vasant Sathe was one exception) went a step ahead to cancel programmes like 'The World of Nature' which had nothing whatsoever to do with politics for the sole reason that it was written by someone who Mrs. Gandhi regarded as her critic.

It was the same during the short regimes of Morarji Desai and Charan Singh: editors were fired, broadcasters, they did not approve, removed. Blacklists continued to be maintained by AIR and Doordarshan throughout Rajiv Gandhi's tenure as Prime Minister. Who is the Congress (I) to talk about freedom of speech and expression? For Messrs Salve, Bhagat and their likes to extol them is like harlots extolling the virtues of chastity.

It is still not clear how free from political meddling will be the board that will control Radio and Doordarshan. However, a very bold and significant step has been taken. Full credit for this must go to P. Upendra and V.P. Singh.

This is what Mr. Nikhil Chakarvarty, a columnist, said about the electronic media's autonomy. He said there was little consultation even with the media circles before the Bill was drafted, but the criticism was more than negated by two things. First, the speech made by Information and Broadcasting Minister, P. Upendra, while introducing the Bill had a ring of sincerity that reassured many that the present government was earnest about autonomy for the government owned media.

Second, the Minister, on his own, announced that there would be free and wide-ranging national debate on the proposed legislation and the criticisms, suggestions and comments to be made in such discussions would be taken into consideration in amending the bill before it was taken up by Parliament. Not only that, his ministry promoted such discussions all over the country. But after the much publicised computerisation of proposals and suggestions, the amendments which the government announced came as a big shock. These were largely retrogressive.

Meanwhile, the government has been remiss on another count. Upendra had promised that there would be a non-official committee to oversee the functioning of the Akashvani and Doordarshan in the interim period until the proposed Prasar Bharati Corporation took over. It was stated that within a couple of weeks this interim set-up would start functioning. Nothing of this kind happened.

Looking at the amendments so far tabled in the Lok Sabha, I for one cannot be optimistic about our setting up a genuinely autonomous corporation. For instance, there is an amendment seeking to establish a Parliamentary Committee to control the set-up. This sounds very impressive as evidence of democratic control but in practice it would have meant not the autonomy of the media but its domination by the party bosses in Parliament.

Vasant Sathe, one of the more competent among the long line of Information Ministers, has been harping on behalf of the Congress, on the need for functional autonomy instead of a new autonomous set-up as envisaged in the Bill. Functional autonomy would mean that the functionaries of the Radio and Television set-up would be ensured autonomy irrespective of ownership-government or a corporation.

In fact, such functional autonomy would be needed even if and when the Prasar Bharati is set up.

The Prasar Bharati Bill was supported by the Congress under Rajiv Gandhi and received the President's assent on September 12, 1990. The election manifesto of the Congress party issued in April, 1991, contained a pledge to implement the Act. But the Congress government has now developed cold feet towards its implementation.

In March 1992, the Information and Broadcasting Ministry, in a note to Prime Minister P.V. Narasimha Rao, observed that the 'circumstances have changed' since the time when the idea of autonomy to the electronic media was mooted.

The note cites some of the fruits of the government's recent liberalisation policy on media, including the advent of satellite broadcasting, video news cassettes and cable TV networks as evidence of the fact that the government no longer holds a monopoly over the electronic media.

The ministry wanted the Prime Minister to consider whether the notification on Prasar Bharati should be deferred.

The note also sought the Prime Minister's opinion on whether second Doordarshan channels in the four metropolitan cities should be simultaneously leased out to one or more entities who may share time among themselves.

With regard to cable television, the I&B Ministry note solicited the Prime Minister's opinion on whether permission should be given for the cables to operate with or without dish antennae. It has asked whether such permission, if given, should be through a system of licensing, or a mere registration with a local authority would suffice.

The government constituted an interdepartmental committee on September 3, 1991, under the Chairmanship of K.A. Varadan, Additional Secretary, Ministry of Information and Broadcasting, to suggest options available for implementation of the scheme for offering broadcasting rights to public corporations. The committee submitted its report in October 1991.

A major recommendation of the Varadan Committee relates to leasing out the second channel of Doordarshan in the four metropolitan cities to suitable licencees. At the same time, additional radio channels including FM stations wherever available, could also be leased out.

The government proposed to set up a Broadcasting Council of India. The Council could, among other things, serve as the agency for redressal of complaints emanating from individuals or institutions in regard to any programme broadcast by a new channel.

The Varadan Committee's Report on leasing out broadcasting rights of Doordarshan and Radio channels has offered a way out to the Congress government dilemma of liberalising the media without upsetting the existing power structure or losing its propaganda advantage.

It has achieved this by watering down and moderating many of the radical reforms that the government had earlier proposed.

The government has refused to give broadcasting rights to individuals and private firms. Instead, it has recommended that the government would lease out parts of Doordarshan's second channel and extra channel of AIR to potential licenees.

In addition, the Varadan panel has recommended that the so-called 'public limited companies' to which such broadcasting rights are to be granted are to be decided by a single statutory or autonomous body known as the Broadcasting Council of India.

By adopting a more cautious approach towards privatisation, the Committee has done well to ensure that the autonomy does not mean replacement of state control with market ownership.

In a developing society like India, privatisation would only succeed in promoting elitism and consumerism which could be socially disastrous. It would help prevent perpetuation of monopoly by industrial houses running the newspapers.

Unfortunately, the Varadan Committee does not effectively tackle the two most important questions before it—the threat of foreign TV networks' invasion and the related issue of improving Doordarshans' fallen credibility.

While cognisant of and cautioning against the evil design of media Multinational Corporations (MNCs) which subject newly freed countries to cultural imperialism, the Committee pleads that nothing can be done to stop these transmissions or ban their receptions. The government must establish some kind of regulatory mechanism to monitor the programmes being beamed into the country from outside.,

At the same time the government must implement the Prasar Bharati Act at the earliest. It is only by injecting professionalism and credibility into Doordarshan that the government can hope to wean away Indian audiences who are getting hooked to alien broadcasting networks.

# Bibliography

Ahuja, B.N. : *Theory and Practice of Journalism,* Surjeet Publications, Delhi, 1979.

Alfred, John : *Mass Communication in the New Millennium,* Prime Publication, New Jersey, 2003.

Apter, Michel : *The New Technology of Education,* MacMillan, London, 1968.

Aronson, James : *The Press and the Cold War,* Beacon Press, Boston, 1970.

Awasthy, G.C. : *Broadcasting in India,* Allied Publishers Private Ltd., Bombay, 1965.

Bard, F. Eraser : *An Introduction to Journalism,* The MacMillan Co., New York, 1958.

Bernard, H. W. : *Principles of Journalism: A Basic Text,* Allied Publishers Private Ltd., New Delhi, 1998.

Bhatia, A. : *Journalism in Modern India,* Asia Publishing House, Bombay, 1964.

Brank, S.M. : *Journalism Characteristics and School Learning,* Harper, New York, 1976.

Carrol, L. : *Occupational Information,* Prentice Hall, New York, 1961.

Cattell, B.B. : *Media Structure, Growth and Action,* Houghton Mifflin Co., Boston, 1999.

Chatterjee, R.K. : *Mass Communication,* National Book Trust, New Delhi, 2002.

Chauhan, S.S. : *A Textbook of Mass Communication*, Sterling Publishers, New Delhi, 2001.

Cottle, W.C. : *Interest and Personality Inventories*, Houghton Miffling Co., New York, 1968.

Cream, David : *Explaining Teaching Machines and Programmes*, Featon, San Fracisco, 1961.

Critchfield, Richard : *The Indian Reporter's Guide*, Allied Pacific Pvt. Ltd., Bombay, 1962.

Curfis, D. : *Interpretotive Reporting*, MacMillan Co., New York, 1957.

Dale, Edgare : *Audio-Visual Method in Teaching*, Dryden Rinehart and Winston, New York, 1969.

Das, R.C. : *Educational Technology*, Sterling Publishers, New Delhi, 2000.

Donald, H. : *Developmental Counselling*, The Ronald Press, New York, 1966.

Donald, Mc. : *The Art of Radio*, Faber & Faber, London, 1961.

Emery, Edwin : *The Press and America*, Prentice Hall, New Jersey, 1999.

Eve, A. A. : *Micro-teaching Theory into Practice*, Oxford, New York, 1969.

Frank, H. Krouse : *Media Technique with Youth*, Charles and Mervil, Ohio, 1990.

Gagne, R.M. : *The Conditions of Learning*, Holt Binsort and Winston, New York, 1965.

Gaur, J.S. and Saraswat, R.K. : *Mass Media*, NCERT, New Delhi, 1998.

Ghiselli, Edwin E. : *Personnel and Industrial Media*, McGraw Hill Book Co., New York, 1955.

Gunning, Robert : *The Technique of Clear Writing*, McGraw Hill Book Co., New York.

Haban, F. : *Movies that Teach*, Dryden Press, New York, 1945.

Hancock, Alan : *Planning for Educational Mass Media*, Longmans, London, 1977.

Hercleread, A.V. : *Instruction: Materials and Methods,* Mc Graw Hill Book Co., New York, 1964.

Hoppock, Rebert : *Occupational Information,* McGraw Hill Book Co., New York, 1997.

Hudson, Kenneth : *The Dictionary of Diseased English,* The MacMillan Co., Bombay, 1977.

James, S. : *Audio-Visual Materials and Techniques,* American Book Company, New York, 1959.

John, A. : *The Asian Newspaper's Reluctant Revolution,* The Iowa State University Press, Iowa, 1977.

John, Hohenberg : *The Professional Journalist,* Rinehort and Winston, New York, 1969.

Johnson, Stanley and Julian Harriss : *The Complete Reporter,* The MacMillan Co., New York, 1942.

Joseph and Jospeth : *Idyels Past and Present: An Editor's Wet Copy,* Orient Longman, Bombay, 1979.

Kaul, B.N. : *Studies in Mass Media,* Har Anand, New Delhi, 1998.

Knight, R. : *Intelligence and Intelligence Tests,* Methuen and Co. Ltd. London, 1943.

Kothari, O.S. : *Report of the Indian Education Commission, 1964-66,* Publication Divison, New Delhi, 1966.

Krug, R.E. : *Ability Testing in Developing Countries: A Handbook of Principles and Techniques,* Praeger, New York, 1972.

Laxman, N.J. : *Introduction to Media Technology,* Oxford Publishing Company, New Delhi, 2003.

Lowman, J. : *Mastering Techniques of Media,* Prentice Hall, New York, 1999.

Luhan, Mc : *Understanding Media,* Routludge, London, 1964.

Mahler, C.A. : *Media Counselling in the Schools,* Houghton Mifflin, Boston, 1969.

Matheson, Alastair : *The Communication Materials and Methods,* McGraw Hill Book Company, New Delhi, 1964.

McCully, C.H. : *The Media—Instrument of Change*, National College Record, Bombay, 2001.

Mehta, D.S. : *Mass Communication and Journalism in India*, Allied Publishers Pvt. Ltd., Bombay, 1979.

Menon, Narayan : *The Communication Revolution*, National Book Trust, New Delhi, 1976.

Miller, Care G. : *Modern Journalism*, Rinehart and Winston, New York, 1962.

Miller, Carroll, H. : *Foundations of Guidance*, Harper and Brothers, New York, 1961.

Mitchell, V. : *Reporting*, Rinehart and Winston, New York, 1960.

Mohanty, J. : *Educational Broadcasting: Radio & Television in Education*, Sterling Publishers, New Delhi, 1984.

Mojar, N.F. : *Current Trends in Mass Communication*, Deep & Deep Publications, New Delhi, 2001.

Mokam, K.B. : *Dynamics of Mass Media in India*, Deep & Deep Publications, New Delhi, 2000.

Mosan, N.N. : *Indian Education in the Emerging Society*, Sterling Publishers, New Delhi, 1982.

Moven, Kiran : *Studies in Educational Broadcasting*, Deep & Deep Publications, New Delhi, 1996.

Mujuni, J.P. : *Studies in Media Education*, Deep & Deep Publications, New Delhi, 1995.

Muni, K.W. : *Media Technology*, Deep & Deep Publications, New Delhi, 2003.

Murthy, Nadig Krishna : *Indian Journalism*, University of Mysore, Prasaranga, 1966.

Natrajan, J. : *History of Indian Journalism*, Publications Division, New Delhi, 1999.

Natrajan, S. : *A History of the Press in India*, Asia Publishing House, Bombay, 1962.

Oscar, Krisen : *Encyclopaedia of Mass Media and Journalism*, Oxford, New York, 1998.

Ottaway, A.K.C. : *Press and Society*, Routldge and Kegan Paul, London, 1962.

Oxtoby, J.S. : *Media and Cultural Environment*, Methuen, London, 1969

Page, C.M. : *Society and Media*, MacMillan, London, 1950.

Panda, K.C. : *Role of Mass Media in School Learning*, RCE, Bhubaneswar, 1978.

Parikh, R.D. : *The Press and Society*, Popular Prakashan, Bombay, 1965.

Quirk, A. : *Editor and Editorial Writer*, Rinehart & Co., New York, 1955.

Reston, James : *The Artillery of the Press: Its Influence on American Foreign Policy*, Harper & Row, New York, 1967.

Rewntreu, Desk : *Media Technology in Curriculum Development*, Harper and Row Publishers, London, 2001.

Richder L. : *Handbook of Broadcasting*, McGraw- Hill Book Co., New York, 1957.

Roland, E. : *Exploring Journalism*, Prentice Hall, New Jersey, 1958.

Sadanand, K.R. : *New Media: Memo to Educational Planners*, John, Wiley, London, 2002.

Sahni, J.N. : *Truth About the Indian Press*, Allied Publishers, Bombay, 1974.

Schramm, Wilbur : *Big Media, Little Media*, Edward Arnold, London, 2000.

Sethi, Patanjali : *Professional Journalism*, Orient Longman, Bombay, 1974.

Shaw, David : *Journalism Today*, Harper's College Press, London, 1977.

Shelly, C. : *Fundamentals of Mass Media*, Houghton Miffin Co., Boston, 1976.

Thedore, M. : *Headlines and Deadlines*, Columbia University Press, New York, 1961.

Thorndike, R.L. : *Media Psychology and Education*, Wiley Eastern Pvt. Ltd., New Delhi, 2001.

Ullan, J. : *Technical Reporting,* Rinehart and Winston, New York, 1963.

Vedanayagam, G. : *Media Teaching Technology for College Teachers,* Sterling Publishers, New Delhi, 1989.

Viner, B. : *The Practice of Journalism,* Heinemann London, 1963.

Warich, D. : *Modular Circula: International Encyclopaedia,* Pergamone Publications, London, 1994.

Whinnie, Donald : *The Art of Broadcasting,* Faber & Faber, London, 1961.

Willian, Charvat : *Handbook for Writers,* Prentice Hall, New Jersey, 1962.

Wolseley, E. : *How to Report and Write the News?*, Prentice Hall, New Jersey, 1961.

Zanda, B. : *Journalism as Guidance,* MacMillan Co., New York, 1998.

Zohar, B. : *Principles and Techniques of Journalism,* Vikas Publishing House, New Delhi, 1982.

# Index


**A**

Advertisements, 274.
All India Radio, 6, 20, 170, 316.
America, 78, 143, 178, 180, 195, 197, 200, 324, 342, 344.
Australia, 74, 75, 94, 178, 324, 325, 342.

**B**

Broadcast Corporation, 180.
Broadcasting Service, 180, 317, 318, 327, 334, 345.

**C**

China, 40, 177, 237.
Chinese Revolution, 237.
Communication, 1, 2, 3, 4, 5, 6, 7, 8, 9, 10, 11, 12, 13, 14, 15, 16, 17, 18, 19, 20, 21, 22, 23, 24, 27, 31, 34, 35, 38, 41, 51, 113, 120, 128, 132, 133, 149, 151, 152, 153, 154, 155, 156, 161, 162, 163, 164, 165, 166, 167, 168, 169, 171, 174, 175, 176, 190, 192, 194, 195, 198, 204, 213, 214, 215, 217, 220, 222, 223, 226, 236, 285, 291, 316, 317, 324, 346.
Community, 12, 27, 28, 44, 48, 66, 100, 120, 128, 143, 145, 152, 175, 186, 201, 245, 314, 317, 332, 341.
Copy Readers, 218.
Crime Comics, 30.

**D**

Department of Culture, 58, 172.
Doordarshan, 14, 15, 57, 58, 130, 151, 155, 170, 345, 349, 350, 351, 353, 354, 355, 356, 357, 358.

## E

Editors, 33, 60, 61, 63, 64, 65, 67, 70, 81, 84, 95, 96, 98, 110, 111, 135, 136, 137, 139, 141, 146, 158, 160, 161, 163, 172, 176, 185, 186, 187, 188, 189, 198, 204, 212, 216, 218, 221, 222, 224, 228, 235, 240, 242, 247, 249, 256, 257, 264, 266, 270, 273, 275, 278, 279, 280, 281, 282, 283, 284, 285, 286, 287, 290, 291, 292, 295, 296, 305, 310, 315, 354.

Editorial Desk, 266.

Employment Policy, 319, 335.

England, 74, 90, 91, 92, 197, 233, 293.

## G

Germany, 77, 112, 177, 233, 291, 325, 343.

Global Agencies, 176.

## I

India, 5, 6, 10, 11, 12, 13, 14, 15, 16, 19, 20, 21, 22, 23, 40, 41, 42, 43, 44, 45, 46, 48, 49, 50, 51, 53, 55, 57, 59, 60, 61, 62, 64, 65, 67, 70, 72, 73, 74, 75, 76, 96, 100, 101, 102, 105, 106, 109, 113, 114, 115, 117, 118, 120, 122, 123, 124, 125, 126, 127, 128, 129, 130, 132, 133, 134, 135, 138, 140, 141, 142, 143, 144, 145, 146, 151, 152, 153, 154, 155, 156, 158, 160, 161, 163, 170, 171, 172, 173, 176, 193, 194, 195, 197, 211, 223, 233, 234, 241, 274, 278, 279, 280, 284, 288, 291, 292, 296, 316, 317, 326, 329, 341, 345, 346, 347, 348, 349, 357, 358.

Information Agency, 168, 179, 180.

International Broadcasting, 179, 180.

Iranian Revolution, 179.

## J

Japan, 112, 154, 177, 233, 324, 325, 342.

Journalists, 50, 59, 64, 69, 70, 71, 72, 81, 83, 86, 96, 102, 106, 110, 111, 112, 114, 120, 121, 129, 142, 143, 144, 157, 159, 160, 161, 162, 172, 173, 178, 179, 181, 186, 187, 188, 189, 198, 200, 201, 203, 204, 213, 216, 226, 227, 228, 235, 236, 284, 297, 305, 306, 307, 308, 309, 310, 311, 316.

## M

Magazines, 21, 30, 62, 67, 99, 100, 102, 109, 112, 113, 114, 115, 116, 122, 124, 170, 183, 185, 186, 189, 191, 192, 193, 198, 228, 269, 274.

Media, 2, 4, 5, 6, 7, 10, 11, 12, 13, 14, 15, 16, 17, 19, 20, 21, 22, 23, 24, 25, 26, 27, 29, 30, 31, 33, 34, 35, 36, 37, 38, 39, 52, 53, 56, 57, 58, 59, 62, 68, 71, 73, 79, 83, 99, 100, 101, 103, 109, 111, 118, 127, 129, 130, 131, 132, 149, 150, 151, 152, 154, 155, 157, 158, 161, 162, 164, 166, 167, 168, 169, 170, 171, 173, 174, 176, 177, 180, 181, 182, 183, 184, 185, 186, 187, 188, 189, 190, 191, 192, 193, 194, 195, 196, 197, 198, 199, 200, 201, 202, 203, 204, 205, 206, 207, 208, 210, 212, 213, 215, 217, 218, 219, 220, 221, 222, 223, 226, 227, 228, 229, 230, 231, 232, 233, 234, 237, 291, 294, 324, 327, 346, 349, 351, 352, 353, 354, 355, 356, 357, 358.

Ministry of Human Resources Development, 172.

## N

National Broadcasting, 345.

National Trust, 345.

Nature, 1, 4, 6, 18, 31, 39, 81, 97, 101, 110, 153, 179, 180, 183, 212, 216, 222, 226, 238, 239, 285, 292, 295, 314, 328.

News, 14, 96, 97, 98, 114, 130, 131, 132, 160, 162, 164, 167, 171, 174, 176, 178, 191, 209, 212, 220, 226, 228, 233, 245, 247, 249, 251, 252, 259, 264, 276, 286, 293, 296, 318.

News Agencies, 14, 50, 71, 76, 129, 130, 131, 132, 133, 137, 138, 159, 161, 162, 164, 167, 170, 172, 173, 174, 175, 176, 177, 178, 231, 232, 237, 248, 251, 297, 300, 303, 306.

News Selection, 209, 220, 222, 229, 232, 234.

Newspapers, 6, 20, 21, 24, 25, 32, 37, 49, 50, 52, 62, 64, 67, 71, 74, 76, 77, 81, 84, 86, 88, 89, 92, 95, 96, 97, 98, 99, 100, 101, 102, 103, 104, 105, 106, 108, 109, 110, 111, 112, 113, 114, 117, 118, 119, 121, 122, 123, 124, 125, 127, 128, 129, 130, 131, 134, 135, 136, 137, 138, 139, 140, 141, 142, 146, 147, 151, 156, 159, 160,

161, 163, 170, 172, 173, 174, 177, 178, 183, 191, 193, 198, 199, 208, 209, 211, 212, 213, 219, 220, 222, 223, 224, 226, 227, 228, 229, 230, 232, 233, 234, 235, 236, 237, 238, 240, 241, 242, 244, 245, 247, 249, 250, 251, 253, 254, 255, 256, 258, 260, 263, 264, 265, 266, 267, 269, 270, 271, 273, 274, 275, 276, 277, 280, 281, 284, 287, 290, 291, 292, 296, 297, 298, 299, 300, 301, 302, 303, 307, 308, 309, 311, 312, 348, 351, 354, 358.

## P

Pakistan, 44, 146, 147, 233, 236, 343.

Photographs, 60, 78, 81, 85, 107, 108, 130, 131, 171, 269, 273, 276, 297, 303, 311.

Pictures, 30, 77, 84, 86, 98, 217, 221, 222, 227, 228, 269, 270, 274, 306, 313.

Police Complaints Authority, 98.

Political Development, 7, 234.

Population, 5, 6, 11, 21, 48, 101, 104, 105, 113, 114, 115, 128, 149, 150, 151, 156, 192, 348.

Prasar Bharati, 349, 350, 351, 352, 353, 355, 356, 358.

Press, 13, 14, 15, 19, 20, 47, 48, 49, 50, 51, 52, 59, 60, 61, 63, 65, 67, 68, 70, 71, 72, 73, 74, 75, 76, 78, 82, 83, 85, 86, 87, 89, 90, 91, 92, 93, 94, 100, 101, 103, 104, 105, 106, 107, 108, 109, 110, 111, 112, 115, 116, 117, 118, 119, 120, 121, 123, 124, 126, 127, 128, 129, 130, 131, 133, 134, 135, 136, 137, 138, 139, 140, 141, 143, 144, 145, 146, 147, 148, 150, 151, 153, 155, 156, 157, 158, 159, 160, 161, 168, 171, 172, 173, 176, 177, 178, 179, 180, 181, 186, 190, 191, 192, 195, 196, 197, 198, 199, 202, 203, 207, 208, 210, 211, 212, 216, 219, 220, 221, 222, 223, 230, 231, 236, 237, 238, 240, 241, 244, 248, 249, 261, 266, 271, 278, 279, 280, 284, 292, 293, 294, 295, 311, 312, 325, 327, 350, 353, 354.

Press Complaints Commission, 90, 92, 93, 94, 95, 96, 97, 98.

Print Media, 4, 5, 6, 7, 151, 227, 351.

Publications, 20, 80, 81, 171.

## R

Reporters, 62, 84, 110, 111, 118, 140, 218, 221, 222, 224, 241, 242, 243, 244, 245, 248, 251, 291, 297, 299, 300, 302, 303, 306, 307, 308, 314, 315, 316, 351.
Revolution, 13, 19, 62, 104, 236, 237.
Russia, 179, 309.

## T

Television, 5, 6, 7, 14, 20, 25, 30, 33, 34, 36, 38, 39, 71, 155, 161, 176, 177, 179, 180, 192, 193, 195, 198, 199, 214, 219, 224, 227, 312, 323, 324, 26, 331, 333, 334, 335, 336, 337, 338, 339, 340, 341, 342, 343, 344, 345, 346, 348, 353, 354, 356, 357.
TV Service, 318.

## V

Vietnam, 218, 219, 233, 236.

## W

World, 5, 15, 17, 18, 22, 25, 43, 45, 46, 51, 54, 57, 94, 96, 98, 106, 109, 115, 116, 120, 125, 131, 132, 133, 143, 144, 154, 155, 157, 159, 160, 161, 163, 164, 165, 167, 168, 169, 170, 174, 176, 177, 179, 190, 194, 199, 210, 211, 212, 220, 221, 228, 230, 231, 232, 233, 234, 237, 284, 288, 289, 290, 293, 297, 302, 313, 323, 329, 342, 354.

□□□